Smart Connected World

Sarika Jain • San Murugesan

Editors

Smart Connected World

Technologies and Applications Shaping
the Future

 Springer

Editors
Sarika Jain
National Institute of Technology
Kurukshetra, India

San Murugesan
BRITE Professional Services
Sydney, Australia

ISBN 978-3-030-76389-3   ISBN 978-3-030-76387-9   (eBook)
https://doi.org/10.1007/978-3-030-76387-9

This Springer imprint is published by the registered company Springer Nature Switzerland AG.
The registered company address is: Gewerbestrasse 11, 6330 Cham, Switzerland

Foreword

I am very glad to write a foreword for this book edited by Sarika Jain and San Murugesan. I got to know both of them during the organization of the International Semantic Intelligence Conference (ISIC 2021). Anyone who has organized a big international conference knows about the large efforts and the unlimited energy needed, especially for attracting new and high-profile contributors. With their attitude of hard work, ISIC 2021 as a conference in its first year included four workshops, three keynotes, eight invited talks of well-known and top-ranked international researchers, and 13 special sessions contributed to the main conference. Conferences already running for several decades often do not reach this size. Hence, I am not surprised that for this edited book Sarika and San again attracted contributors with indisputable reputations, who are true experts in the domains of their chapters.

As chair of the Very Large Internet of Things (VLIoT) workshop series (so far from 2017 to 2021) in conjunction with the top-ranked Very Large Database (VLDB) conferences, I have been watching the enormous development of the Internet of Things in research and industry from toy examples to stable large installations with applications that are increasingly beneficial for daily life in the long term.

Hence I have no doubt that we will soon be living in a largely interconnected world that will blur the distinction between reality and digital realms, known as "virtual reality."

This book, *Smart Connected World: Technologies and Applications Shaping the Future*, discusses several key aspects of the emerging interconnected world. Though the concept of a connected world is not entirely new, there is now renewed and growing interest in creating a smart and connected world. This welcomed trend is fuelled by the timely confluence of pervasive computing, reliable and affordable networking, miniaturized and low-cost sensors, processing of massive volumes of different types of data, and significant advances in artificial intelligence and machine learning algorithms and their adoption in practice. In the 1950s, Alan Turing, the famous English computer scientist, addressed the question: "Can machines think?"

Now, progress over the last few decades in addressing this question has made machines not only think but also learn, recommend, act autonomously, and even explain their reasoning to humans. Thus, the connectivity that links real-world objects and processes, people and cyber systems, and the intelligence exhibited by machines makes the new smart connected world that the book editors envisage a current reality.

This book is a timely and a valuable addition to a small set of books in the area. It covers a variety of topics at the forefront of the two computing paradigms, namely, semantic computing and cognitive computing, as applied to the Internet of Things. I am delighted to see that the semantic technologies are transitioning to practical applications and the research community is facilitating their further advances and adoption in practice. In addition to introducing readers to promising tools and technologies, this book presents a number of insightful case studies discussing practical applications and real-world experiences to provide a balanced research and practice nexus.

The editors, drawing on their individual complementary expertise and experience, have brought out a unique book by choosing appropriate topics to deliberate and have invited established experts from academia and industry across the globe to write a chapter on each of the topics. The presentation is nice and of tutorial nature and is suitable for a wider audience, including graduate students and novice researchers.

I enjoyed reading the book and found it informative and inspiring for my own research. I am happy to introduce it to a wider audience for their benefits. I believe the readers will also find the book informative and insightful. Enjoy reading the book!

Institute of Information Systems (IFIS)   Sven Groppe
University of Lübeck, Lübeck, Germany

Preface

Emerging trends center around artificial intelligence, machine learning, cloud computing, the Internet of Things, Semantic Web technologies, data analytics, and improved user interactivity and experience. These trends are shaping our world in numerous ways and further transforming our work and our personal lives. The future world is going to be different than it is today. This book presents a brief look at the envisioned new world that would be smarter and well connected.

The smart devices in the Internet of Things (IoT) communicate and share data-enabling tasks to be performed without the need for human intervention. A smart world is context-aware and knows what the user wants and his preferences and intentions, for example the information the user needs and how he prefers it to be presented. The smart devices in an application can create, represent, store, and share data. These devices can also make smart decisions. Furthermore, it would be a huge advantage if the smart connected devices were to communicate using the standard web protocols, instead of relying on incompatible networking protocols.

The current and future connected digital world poses a few key challenges: interoperability with open data, open formats, and APIs; portability of identities, profiles, and content; information overload; modeling of context and intent; understanding complex interactions; incompleteness or missing data; uncertainty (veracity) and dynamism (velocity) of data; machine understanding of data; ability to scale beyond human-only usage; and ubiquitous personalization and individualization. To address these challenges, the underlying system has to be smart to dynamically adapt to its environment and tasks and also be self-configuring, self-describing and self-explaining, self-healing, self-protecting, self-organizing, context-aware, and both reactive and proactive. Furthermore, these systems should also be capable of assessing the relevance, quality, and reliability of the data and recognize the context of their use and the user's preference. This calls for a shift from simple raw data processing to more intelligent processing of data (Data-Information-Knowledge-Wisdom (DIKW) pyramid)—for instance, the need to not only deal with data but make sense of the data to identify patterns in information to gain knowledge.

Web 3.0 is smarter than Web 2.0 and Web 1.0 as it incorporates semantics and artificial intelligence. Semantic computing technologies have been under development for about two decades. Semantic data models play important roles in facilitating interoperable data stores, and sensor data need to be represented in the form of ontologies. Despite their benefits, semantic computing technologies are not being utilized and exploited to their full potential. They have remained solely a research fantasy by a small number of people interested in this area. There are two reasons for this. First, standards did not exist for a long time. Second, even after the emergence of web standards that were open, free, robust, and easy to adopt, until the 1990s there was no technological consensus on their usage. These limitations were subsequently addressed. Here is a brief outline of the technological advancements in the domain of semantic computing.

- Development of major semantic web standards RDF and OWL (1994–2004).
- Major industry players entered the game. SPARQL was developed and a new initiative, Linked Open Data, came up (2006 to 2014).
- Google announced Knowledge Vault, and people turned to what we can call the Knowledge Graph era.
- A paradigm shift from RDBMS to NoSQL databases to today's Triple Stores.

This book provides readers an overview of the emerging smart connected world and discusses the roles of semantic computing technologies and IoT in this new world. It also discusses how developers can use the established semantic technologies and gain the required skills in this field. The book will interest researchers, data scientists, and the industry and help them embrace the technology. The book also helps readers understand how the hybrid of the syntactic and the symbolic approaches to computing benefit the connected ecosystem.

Key Features

- This book discusses trends toward a smart connected world and presents them as a digestible narrative.
- The structure and contents of the book have been reviewed by a panel of accomplished international experts in the respective areas.
- Each chapter is self-contained and can be read independently; taken together, readers get a bigger picture of the technological and application landscape of the smart connected world.
- The contributors of the book are geographically diverse, with editors and authors from the UK, Turkey, Yemen, India, Australia, Serbia, and Malaysia, and are drawn from both academia and industry.
- The book will serve as a reference book for instructors and students taking courses in hybrid computing getting abreast of cutting-edge and future directions of a connected ecosystem, hence providing a synergy between web technologies and applications.

- It will be helpful for researchers and scholars who are pursuing research in Semantic Web and IoT and allied fields. It will also benefit industry professionals, software engineers, and academicians, and will enable them to embrace the potential of the Semantic Web.

Chapter Preview

Across the connected ecosystem, the amount of data being generated is multiplying in an unprecedented manner. The smart connected world is focused on collecting, storing, analyzing, as well as processing relevant data for real-time decisions. Sharing and using cross-domain knowledge is a challenge in this agile world of today. The tendency is toward embedding semantics in every aspect of the connected ecosystem to better understand the ambient environment. The book comprises 10 chapters grouped into two parts. Part I consist of seven chapters and provides a holistic overview of the smart connected world and the supporting tools and technologies. Part II consists of three chapters that describe applications and case studies of the smart connected world.

Part I: Smart Connected World: Overview and Technologies

This part provides an overview of the smart connected world from its evolution to predicting the future.

Chapter 1, authored by the editors of the book Sarika Jain and San Murugesan, provides a broader perspective on the smart connected world. After discussing the interplay of the Internet of Things (IoT) and Artificial Intelligence (AI), it examines the potential barriers to a smart and connected ecosystem. The chapter moves forward by providing the reader with an overview of the strengths and benefits of semantic computing and cognitive computing. The chapter aims to provide developers an overview of how they can use the technologies and enhance their knowledge in realizing and maintaining such systems.

In recent years, devices and systems have been transformed into smart connected devices or systems, giving rise to the Internet of Things (IoT) and Cyber Physical Social Systems (CPSSs). Chapter 2 by Regina Reine (Twigx Research), Filbert H. Juwono (Curtin University Malaysia), Zee Ang Sim (Heriot-Watt University Malaysia), and W.K. Wong (Curtin University Malaysia) discusses the concept of the CPSSs and their supporting technologies such as the 5G networks, wireless sensor networks, big data, artificial intelligence, virtual reality (VR), and augmented reality (AR). The chapter also discusses the implementation and challenges of CPSSs.

In Chap. 3, Anindita Saha, Mayurakshi Jana, Chandreyee Chowdhury, and Suparna Biswas from India, and Diptanshu Pandit from the UK speak about the importance and benefits of utilizing web technologies as the application layer of IoT resulting in the so-called Web of Things (WoT) framework. Without WoT, IoT applications would have to rely on the networking protocol stack where the application layer of the stack is differently implemented by different applications.

Having set the pace of the connected ecosystem in Chaps. 2 and 3, in Chap. 4 we demystify the semantic intelligence that leverages semantic computing to handle large data at scale and address challenges (such as heterogeneity, interoperability, explainability) in the context of different industrial applications. Authored by Valentina Janev from the University of Belgrade, Serbia, this chapter introduces semantic intelligence in distributed, enterprise, and web-based information systems. Semantic intelligence technologies are the most important ingredient in building artificially intelligent knowledge-based systems as they aid machines in integrating and processing resources contextually and intelligently.

To achieve a fully functional smart connected world, organizations face critical challenges related to user privacy, system availability, and resilience to cyber-attacks, among others. Chapter 5 by Yang Lu from the University of Kent, UK, identifies the challenges in ensuring privacy, security, and trust of the Internet of Things (IoT) paradigm and reviews existing solutions adopted to protect the smart connected world from malicious attacks, unauthorized access, and privacy breaches. The chapter proposes semantic-enabled solutions to protect sensitive data access and sharing in the clinical collaboration scenario, e.g., record linkage. As semantic reasoning allows effective management of user privileges and anonymity schemes, data privacy and utility can be ensured in the release of record linkage.

Data analytics is used in many different areas, such as increasing market shares of a firm, customer behavior analysis, predicting the life of an electronic device, detection of the anomaly on a network, social network analysis, healthcare systems, chemical component interactions, and bank operations. Ontologies can be used for facilitating data collection, improving the quality of the data used, analyzing data, visualizing the obtained results, and ensuring the reusability of the designed system. Chapter 6 by Fatmana Senturk from Turkey introduces an overview of data analytics and seeks to answer the question of how to enrich and improve a data analytic system by using ontologies.

Chapter 7 by Abhisek Sharma and Sarika Jain of NIT Kurukshetra India outlines the importance of multilingual and multimodal ontologies today. Our world is multilingual with an array of different languages in use and encompasses a wide variety of cultures and ethnic and racial groups. Understanding and accounting for cultural variations is crucial for effective natural language communication because it affects how the language is formed and used in practice. The Artificial Intelligence of Things (AIoT) systems are required to recognize a sentence from the user, interpreting what it means, and performing tasks accordingly. The sentence may be biased because of the effect of different languages, cultural variations, and ethnic and racial groups on the user's input. This chapter covers just that, from the use and working of AIoT to how the computer can store and understand language-specific information and work with it.

Part II: Applications and Case Studies

This part focuses on the potential implications of a smart connected world in manufacturing, cities, health, and more.

The first chapter in this part, Chap. 8, authored by Paul D Clough and Jon Stammers from the University of Sheffield, UK, discusses the elevation of manufacturing to new levels of smartness as a result of the ability to collectively embrace a range of technologies, such as sensors, Internet of (Industrial) Things, cloud computing, Big Data analytics, AI, mobile devices, and Augmented/Virtual Reality. Together they present new opportunities to transform, automate, and bring smartness and learning to manufacturing processes and drive manufacturing to the next generation. This chapter describes the manufacturing context, emerging concepts, such as Industry 4.0, and technologies that are driving change and innovation within the manufacturing industry.

Smart cities are cities that provide smart solutions for different life issues, either for citizens or for the environment itself, by collecting and analyzing information based on conceptualized contexts. In Chap. 9, Neama Abdulaziz and Fadl Ba-Alwi from Sana'a University, Yemen, advocate that smart city information should be gathered considering the semantics of both the statuses and the related devices.

Finally, Chap. 10 authored by Tameem Ahmad, Sayyed Usman Ahmed, and Nesar Ahmad from Aligarh Muslim University, India, examines the social webs and ways to analyze users' interaction patterns to depict the personality and hence the depression state of the user. Semantic Web technologies are better suited for this kind of analysis and ideally overcome the limitations of traditional approaches. An early indication of depression can help to initiate a recovery action to avoid devastating results.

We believe this book, covering technologies and applications shaping the connected world which is smarter and agile, will be helpful to a wide range of readers in gaining an informed understanding of the emerging new world.

Kurukshetra, India Sarika Jain
Sydney, Australia San Murugesan
April 2021

Acknowledgments

Publication of this book would not have been possible without the contribution, support, and cooperation of several people, whom we acknowledge here.

We would to thank each one of the chapter authors for enthusiastically contributing to the book, and thereby sharing their expertise, experiences, and insights with the readers. We gratefully acknowledge their support and cooperation. We also extend our gratitude to the reviewers who have provided valuable comments on the book chapters.

We profusely thank Sven Groppe from the University of Lübeck, Germany, for writing a foreword to this book.

The editorial team at Springer deserves our commendation for their key roles in publishing this volume and in ensuring its quality. In particular, I would like to thank Ralf Gerstner for his enthusiasm, support, and cooperation. We would also like to thank Ramya Prakash, Nancey Biswas and the whole production team for their excellent work on this book. We highly commend their professionalism and commitment.

Finally, we would like to thank our respective family members for their encouragement, support, and cooperation, which enabled us to make this venture a reality.

Contents

Editors and Contributors

About the Editors

Sarika Jain graduated from Jawaharlal Nehru University (India) in 2001. Her doctorate, awarded in 2011, is in the field of knowledge representation in Artificial Intelligence. She has served in the field of education for over 19 years and is currently in service at the National Institute of Technology Kurukshetra (Institute of National Importance), India. Dr. Jain has authored or co-authored over 100 publications including books. Her current research interests are knowledge management and analytics, the Semantic Web, ontological engineering, and intelligent systems. Dr. Jain serves as a reviewer for journals published by the Institute of Electrical and Electronics Engineers (IEEE), Elsevier, and Springer. She has been involved as a program and steering committee member at many flagship conferences in India and abroad. She has completed two funded research projects: one funded by CSIR TEQIP-III and worth Rs 2.58 lakhs, and the other funded by the Defence Research and Development Organisation, India, and worth Rs 40 lakhs. She has held various administrative positions at the department and institute level in her career, such as head of department, hostel warden, faculty in charge of technical and cultural fests, member of research degree committee, and Center Incharge Examinations.Dr. Jain has visited the United Kingdom and Singapore to present her research work. She has continuously supervised German Academic Exchange Service (DAAD) interns from different universities of Germany and many interns from

India every summer. She works in collaboration with various researchers across the globe, including in Germany, Austria, Australia, Malaysia, the USA, and Romania. She has organized various challenges, conferences, and workshops and is a senior member of the IEEE, member of ACM, and a Life Member of the CSI. Dr. Jain is highly interested in worldwide collaborations and is seeking scholars and interns for her research group. For more up-to-date information, see https://sites.google.com/view/nitkkrsarikajain/.

San Murugesan is Director of BRITE Professional Services, an adjunct professor at the School of Computing at Western Sydney University, Honorary Professor at Amity University, and former Editor-in-Chief of the IEEE Computer Society's *IT Professional* magazine. He has vast experience in both academia and industry. He has successfully led development of innovative IT projects; provided leadership in research and development; conceived and led several academic programs; and offered consultancy services. His expertise and interests span a range of areas: smart systems, artificial intelligence, autonomous systems, quantum computing, green computing, cloud computing, digital transformation, Internet of Things (IoT), sustainability, and emerging trends in IT. He is editor or co-editor of 12 books and author of 17 book chapters and 17 reports on contemporary topics in IT. His books include *Encyclopedia of Cloud Computing* (Wiley and IEEE Press, July 2016) and *Harnessing Green IT: Principles and Practices* (Wiley 2012 and IEEE Press), both translated into Chinese. He has guest edited 40 special issues of IEEE CS magazines and international journals on a range of topics. He has organized several symposia, workshops, and conferences. He has presented keynotes, invited tutorials, and seminars at conferences, professional meetings, and universities. He is a distinguished speaker of the ACM and Distinguished Visitor of the IEEE Computer Society. Murugesan has worked as a senior research fellow at the NASA Ames Research Center in California and served as Professor of Computer Science at Southern Cross University in Australia. Prior to this, he worked at the Indian Space Agency in Bangalore in senior roles and led development of onboard microcomputer systems for attitude control of several Indian satellites. Murugesan is a fellow of the Australian Computer Society, Institution of Electronics and Tele-communication Engineers, and IICA. He is a Golden Core member of IEEE CS and a Life Senior Member of IEEE. In recognition of his "wide-ranging significant contributions," he was awarded the IEEE Computer Society's highest service award, the "T. Michael Elliott Distinguished Service Certificate." He holds a PhD from the Indian Institute of Science, an MTech from the Indian Institute of Technology Madras, and a BE (Honours) from PSG College of Technology in India. For further details, see his webpage (http://tinyurl.com/san1bio).

Contributors

Neama Abdulaziz Sana'a University, Sana'a, Yemen

Nesar Ahmad Aligarh Muslim University, Aligarh, India

Tameem Ahmad Aligarh Muslim University, Aligarh, India

Sayyed Usman Ahmed Aligarh Muslim University, Aligarh, India

Fadl Ba-Alwi Sana'a University, Sana'a, Yemen

Suparna Biswas Jadavpur University, Kolkata, India

Chandreyee Chowdhury Jadavpur University, Kolkata, India

Paul D. Clough The University of Sheffield, Sheffield, UK

Sarika Jain NIT Kurukshetra, Kurukshetra, Haryana, India

Mayurakshi Jana Bijay Krishna Girls' College, Howrah, India

Valentina Janev Institute Mihajlo Pupin, University of Belgrade, Belgrade, Serbia

Filbert H. Juwono Curtin University, Miri, Malaysia

Yang Lu School of Science, Technology and Health, York St John University, York, UK

San Murugesan BRITE Professional Services, Sydney, NSW, Australia

Diptangshu Pandit Teesside University, Middlesbrough, UK

Regina Reine Twigx Research, London, UK

Anindita Saha Techno Main Salt Lake, Kolkata, West Bengal, India

Fatmana Şentürk Pamukkale University, Denizli, Turkey

Abhisek Sharma NIT Kurukshetra, Kurukshetra, Haryana, India

Zee Ang Sim Heriot-Watt University Malaysia, Putrajaya, Malaysia

Jon Stammers The University of Sheffield, Sheffield, UK

W. K. Wong Curtin University, Miri, Malaysia

Abbreviations and Acronyms

6LoWPAN	IPv6 over Low-Power Wireless Personal Area Networks
ABAC	Attribute-based Access Control
ACID	Atomicity, Consistency, Isolation, and Durability
ACS	Autonomous Control Systems
AE	Acoustic emission
AES	Advanced Encryption Standard
AGV	Automated guided vehicle
AI	Artificial Intelligence
AIoT	Artificial Intelligence of Things
AM	Additive manufacturing
AMA	Artificial moral agents
AmI	Ambient Intelligence
AML	Agreement Maker Light
AMRC	University of Sheffield Advanced Manufacturing Research Centre
AOI	Automatic optical inspection
API	Application Programming Interface
AR	Augmented reality
CHE	Computing for human experience
CMfg	Cloud manufacturing
CMM	Coordinate measuring machine
CNC	Computer numerical control
CNN	Convolutional Neural Network
CoAP	Constrained Application Protocol
CPSS	Cyber-physical-social system
DAQ	Data acquisition
DCAT	Data Catalog Vocabulary
DES	Discrete-event simulation
DNS	Domain Name System
DoS	Denial of Service
DQL	Data Quality Vocabulary

DRON	The drug ontology
DTLS	Data Transport Layer Security Protocol
EHCPR	Extended Hierarchical Censored Production Rules
EHR	Electronic Health Records
EIoTG	Edge IoT Gateways
EO	Emotion Ontology
EPC	Electronic Product Code
ERD	Entity Relationship Diagram
ERP	Enterprise resource planning
FMA	Foundational Model of Anatomy
FMEA	Failure modes and effect analysis
FOAF	Friend of a Friend
GOFAI	Good Old Fashioned AI
GPS	Global Positioning System
HCI	Human-computer interaction
HTTP	Hypertext Transfer Protocol
HUD	Heads-up display
HVAC	Heating, ventilation, and air conditioning
IC	Integrated Circuit
IDC	International Data Corporation
IDII	Interaction Design Institute Ivrea
IIoT	Industrial IoT
INPDR	International Niemann-Pick Disease Registry
IoT	Internet of Things
IR	Industrial revolution
IT	Information Technology
JSON	JavaScript Object Notation
KDD	Knowledge Discovery in Databases
KGs	Knowledge Graphs
lemon	Lexicon Model for Ontologies
LIR	Linguistic Information Repository
LLOD	Linguistic Linked Open Data
LOD	Linked Open Data
LPWA	Low-power wide area
M2M	Machine-to-Machine
MDD	Major Depressive Disorder
MDO	Metal Disease Ontology
MES	Manufacturing execution system
MITM	Man-in-the-middle attack
ML	Machine Learning
MLLOD	Multilingual Lexical Linked Open Data
MOOC	Massive Open Online Course
MTC	Machine-type communications
NCI	National Cancer Institute

NFC	Near-field communication
NLP	Natural Language Processing
NoSQL	Not only SQL
OAuth	Open Authorization
OEE	Overall equipment effectiveness
OGC	Open Geospatial Consortium
OLiA	Ontologies of Linguistic Annotation
OWL	Web Ontology Language
P2P	Peer-to-peer
PCB	Printed circuit board
PdM	Predictive maintenance
PLC	Programmable logic controller
PPDQ	Privacy-Preserving Database Query
P-WoT	Plain Web of Things
RBAC	Role-based Access Control
RDBs	Relational Databases
RDF	Resource Description Framework
RDS	Resource Description Schema
REST	Representational State Transfer
RFID	Radio Frequency Identification
RML	RDF Mapping Language
RPC	Remote Procedure Call
RSA	Rivest–Shamir–Adleman
RSS	Received Signal Strength
RUL	Remaining useful life
SAWSDL	Semantic Annotations for WSDL and XML Schema
SCADA	Supervisory control and data acquisition
SHA	Secure Hashing Algorithm
SHACL	Shapes Constraint Language
SIOC	Semantically Interlinked Online Communities
SLKA	Semantic Linkage k-Anonymity Linkage
SME	Small-to-medium enterprise
SMOB	Semantic MicrOBlogging
SMS	Smart manufacturing system
SNS	Social Networking Service
SOA	Service-oriented Architecture
SOAP	Simple Object Access Protocol
SPARQL	Protocol and RDF Query Language
SPARQL	SPARQL Protocol and RDF Query Language
SQL	Structured Query Language
SVM	Support Vector Machine
SW	Semantic Web
SWE	Sensor Web Enablement
SWeTI	Semantic Web of Things for Industry

SWoT	Semantic Web of Things
UAV	Unmanned Aerial Vehicle
UDDI	Universal Description, Discovery, and Integration
URI	Uniform Resource Identifiers
VODG	Voluntary Organisations Disability Group
VR	Virtual reality
W3C	World Wide Web Consortium
WoT	Web of Things
WSDL	Web Services Description Language
WSN	Wireless sensor network
XACML	eXtensible Access Control Markup Language
XMap	eXtensible Mapping
XML	eXstensible Markup Language
XR	eXtended reality
ZB	Zettabytes

Part I
Smart Connected World: Overview and Technologies

Chapter 1
Smart Connected World: A Broader Perspective

Sarika Jain and San Murugesan

Abstract The most important aspect of a smart and connected ecosystem is the integration of varied and heterogeneous data as well as devices to provide value. The existing data communications for all forms of computing often rely on syntactic data models that lack in providing machine-interpretable meanings, reasoning power, and device and data interoperability. The semantic standards for sensors provide a uniform way of representing and reasoning over heterogeneous data streams to facilitate situation awareness along with creating actionable information. The machines will be able to better understand their environment and act contextually. This chapter presents a broader perspective on the smart connected world by providing the reader with an overview of the strengths and benefits of semantic computing and cognitive computing, so that researchers, data scientists, and the industry can embrace the technology.

Keywords Smart connected world · Cognitive computing · Semantic computing · Artificial Intelligence of Things · Ontology

Key Points
- Briefly looks into the pre IoT-inception and the post IoT-inception technologies.
- Discusses the interplay of the Internet of Things (IoT) and artificial intelligence (AI) and states the same as the AIoT knot.
- Examines the potential barriers to a smart and connected ecosystem.
- Provides an overview of the strengths and benefits of semantic computing and cognitive computing.

S. Jain (✉)
National Institute of Technology Kurukshetra, Kurukshetra, India
e-mail: jasarika@nitkkr.ac.in

S. Murugesan
BRITE Professional Services, Sydney, NSW, Australia
e-mail: san1@internode.net

- Presents Resource Description Framework (RDF) as the semantic data model for the symbolic representation of the smart connected world.
- Depicts a high-level abstraction of the data flow in intelligent applications.

1.1 Introduction

In a mere 40 years, computers have evolved significantly, becoming much smaller in size and more powerful, along with a tremendous increase in memory and storage capacity. The prediction made by Intel Co-founder and CEO Gordon Moore in 1975 that the number of transistors in an integrated circuit (IC) will double every 2 years, known as Moore's law, has now come to pass. The transistor count in 2019 microchips is around 50 billion (Wikipedia), but further increase in density is facing barriers. Nvidia CEO Jensen Huang declared that "Moore's Law is dead, as now it's more expensive and more technically difficult to double the number of transistors driving the processing power." Recent studies show that designing gates for nano-scale transistors is getting more difficult, limiting further advances in our traditional computers. To address this, new computing paradigms such as quantum computing and molecular computing and advanced architectures are being explored with some promise.

The introduction of the Internet, the Web, advances in wireless communications, and rapid adoption of cloud computing have driven widespread application of computers and handheld mobile devices. And advances in low-cost sensors, the Internet of Things (IoT), artificial intelligence and machine learning have led to the emergence of a smart digital world where computers, people, and almost every other object or thing are connected, sharing information and collaborating with each other as required. Fiber optic cables have been laid around the world, where a single fiber can transmit as much as 100 billion bits per second. These advancements have been one of the major motivations behind the growth of the Internet. Today, almost 70% of the world's youth are using the Internet and mobile apps. The growth of the Internet has significantly enhanced the connectivity among various entities facilitating information exchange never seen before.

Internet of Things (IoT) is being seen as the major driver of real-time data. More things are being connected today, such as devices and appliances used in daily life, healthcare devices, and business devices. The things are connected with other things and to people in a connected and heterogeneous network of resources. Sensor devices are becoming widely available. The proliferation of IoT could drive down costs and drive the growth of consumer- and enterprise-wide IoT-based platforms and applications, evolving into a vibrant IoT ecosystem. The consumer IoT is also known as "The Internet of Me" and aims to enrich human life. The enterprise application is known as "The Internet of IT" and consists of large-scale smarter systems. All these advancements and applications present a lot of promise and presents opportunities as well as problems and challenges.

It is remarkable that vast quantities of data are being created on the Internet every minute. Data collected by sensory devices and other crowd-sensing heterogeneous sources is, however, in different formats. Integrating this data and making sense (value) out of them is a major challenge facing us in the era of the smart connected world. Another problem is the privacy and security of the data gathered. Still another problem relates to the nature of data—the data originating from the physical smart connected world is real-time, heterogeneous, noisy, vast, and dynamic. We also need to work on the power management of devices and more data-centric networking.

The existing data communications for all forms of computing often rely on syntactic data models or, in some cases, XML-based data that lack in providing machine-interpretable meanings to the data; their focus is just on processing and interpreting the data in whatever way possible. There is no consensus on annotating the data between the involved entities. These syntactic data models provide limited or no reasoning that is based on the content and context and have a limited device and data interoperability.

The semantic web provides, on the other hand, a well-defined meaning to information so that people and machines can work cooperatively. The semantic standards for sensors provide a uniform way of representing and reasoning over heterogeneous data streams. The goal is to create actionable information utilizing the knowledge derived from smart data. This type of web where information carries meaning and devices and people can interact autonomously is termed the semantic sensor web. Applying semantic technologies to the Internet of Things will provide the necessary device and data interoperability, facilitating situation awareness. Machines will be able to better understand their environment and act contextually.

This chapter presents a brief overview of semantic technologies supporting the smart connected world. After providing a historical timeline of the connectedness in Sect. 1.2 and a brief background of the artificial intelligence and IoT knot (the AIoT knot) in Sect. 1.3, it discusses the various potential barriers to a smart and connected ecosystem in Sect. 1.4. Further, Sects. 1.5 and 1.6 are specifically devoted to exploitation of semantic technologies in achieving the smart connected world.

1.2 IoT: The Trajectory of Technological Progress

In 1999, while working on a presentation on RFID in supply chains for Procter & Gamble, the then executive director of the Auto-ID Center, Kevin Ashton, coined the term "Internet of Things." The world came to realize the vast prospects of IoT following the awareness of its niche applications such as smart egg trays, connected pacifier, smartwatch, smart pet feeder, smart toothbrush, and many more consumer-usable products. In 2003, the world population was around 6.3 billion, and the number of connected devices was around 500 million. The number of smart devices and web-enabled apps/services started crossing the number of people in the mid-2000s. By 2025, the world population will be around 7.6 billion, and International Data Corporation (IDC) predicts that the number of connected devices will be around 41.6 billion. Also by 2025, 75% of the world population will be connected. Let us have a brief look at early technologies that gave rise to IoT and subsequent advances.

- *Electric telegraphs*: The thought of connectedness started in the 1830s with electric telegraphs. Samuel Morse sent the first Morse code public telegraph message from Washington, D.C., to Baltimore. Way back in 1966, German computer science pioneer Karl Steinbuch said, "In a few decades, computers will be interwoven into almost every industrial product."
- *Connecting through the Internet*: Following the launch of ARPANET in 1969 and the introduction of TCP/IP in 1974, Carnegie Mellon University developed the first connected smart appliance in 1982, a modified Coke machine. Using the local network of the university, students could find out the stock of drinks and whether they were cold. Subsequently, Domain Name System (DNS) was developed in 1984, and in 1989, Tim Berners-Lee proposed the now widely used World Wide Web.
- *IoT devices*: Since 1990, several IoT devices were developed. The following are a few examples:

  - John Romkey created a toaster that could be turned on and off over the Internet (1990).
  - The Trojan Room Coffee Pot was created by Quentin Stafford-Fraser and Paul Jardetzky of the University of Cambridge (1993). Every 3 min, an image of the coffee pot was sent to the server to monitor the pot levels.
  - WearCam came as another experiment in connectivity in 1994.
  - RFID-based solutions emerged in 1994. It was in 1999 when the term "Internet of Things" was coined. From then, more equipment got connected to the Internet than people by a factor of 8 to 1.
  - In 1998, three professors at MIT came with a project inTouch to create a "tangible telephone" for long-distance haptic communication.
  - In 1998, a water fountain was constructed by Mark Weiser outside his office. This water fountain could speak the price trends of the stock market through its water flow and height.
  - Since its inception in 1999, IoT has led to the smart connected world.

- *EPC*: In 1999, an Electronic Product Code (EPC) was developed by Auto-ID Labs, a successor to the MIT Auto-ID Center, as a global RFID-based item identification system. LG announced its first Internet refrigerator plans in the year 2000.
- *Arduino*: In 2005, a team of faculty members at the Interaction Design Institute Ivrea (IDII) in Italy developed Arduino, an open-source electronic prototyping platform enabling users to create interactive electronic objects. It and other such platforms that followed made a huge impact on the development and deployment of IoT applications and contributed to the emergence of a cyber-physical-system.
- *Mobile phones*: With the increase in the use of smartphones and tablet PCs around 2008, more things were connected to the Internet than people.

- *Web of Things (WoT)*: Following continued interest and realization of prospects of IoT and the need for standards, several IoT standards (like MQTT for data transmission, 6LoWPAN for connectivity infrastructure, and WiFi and Bluetooth for communications, to cite a few) and software were developed. However, there was no application layer protocol to date. Hence, the architectures and initial implementations of IoT tend to be siloed. Standards existed at the physical layer, but higher layers are highly burdened with insufficient interoperability. There was a need to converge the data coming from different IoT devices. To address these, in 2007, the web was considered as the application layer of IoT, giving rise to the Web of Things (WoT). WoT provides a higher-level interoperability layer above IoT and complements it.
- *IPv6*: IPv6 Internet Protocol was launched in 2011 allowing for huge address space, 2^{128} addresses. This number is just sufficient for many such planets as earth taken together.
- *Further developments*: Advances continued in multiple directions, protocols, platforms, and hardware. For example, Constrained Application Protocol (CoAP) is a specialized Internet Application Protocol for constrained devices, and Paraimpu is a platform for the social Web of Things. Progress then spread into new areas such as cyber-physical-social systems, linked data, semantics, and machine-to-machine (M2M) communications.

These and other related developments led to the widespread adoption of IoT in business, industry, and consumer domains.

1.3 Artificial Intelligence and IoT

Internet of Things (IoT) is a disruptive technology, where "things" such as digital assistants, wearable devices, sensors, refrigerators, and other equipment are networked together to exchange data over the Internet. Figure 1.1a depicts some niche applications of IoT. During the inception stage, i.e., around 2011, several barriers had the potential to slow the development of IoT. The major barriers to IoT included:

- *Bigger address space.* The connected ecosystem ran short of IPv4 addresses, and in February 2010, IPv6 was deployed.
- *Self-sustaining sensors.* Changing the batteries of billions of devices is not possible.
- *Agreement on standards.* At that time, only IEEE standardization existed.

Once these major barriers/challenges are overcome, what next? The connected ecosystem should demonstrate tangible value to people' lives.

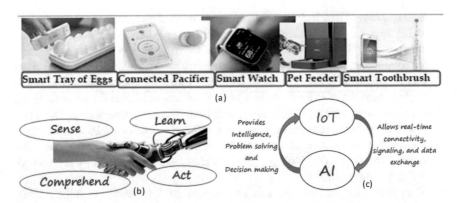

Fig. 1.1 Artificial intelligence and IoT. (**a**) Niche applications of IoT. (**b**) Artificial intelligence. (**c**) Artificial Intelligence of Things (AIoT)

1.3.1 Artificial Intelligence of Things

Artificial intelligence (AI) exhibited by software or machines (Fig. 1.1b) can sense, comprehend, act, and learn. Artificial Intelligence of Things (AIoT), as depicted in Fig. 1.1c, provides AI-powered IoT, i.e., embedding AI technology into IoT components. AI provides intelligence, problem-solving, and decision-making; and IoT allows real-time connectivity, signaling, and data exchange to the connected ecosystem. In this way, the AIoT knot gears the already smart things of IoT to become intelligent. AI can make IoT more intelligent by transforming IoT data into valuable and usable information for improved decision-making, both remotely and on-site. IoT is the digital nervous system, and AI is the brain (Jain, 2020b, Video).

Potential Applications of AIoT
Here are few examples of AIoT applications where AIoT knot is applied to the connected ecosystem:

- *Automated vacuum cleaners, like iRobot Roomba*
  AI aids in mapping and in remembering the home layout when executing various tasks such as room cleaning. Subsequently, AI devices automatically dock themselves to recharge their batteries. In doing so, it can also adapt to different surfaces or new items, if encountered.
- *Smart thermostat, like Nest Labs thermostat*
  Nest's device, trained with the regular temperature preferences of the owner, can adapt to the various work schedules of its owner. In doing so, it can turn down its energy usage whenever required.
- *Self-driving vehicles, such as Tesla Motors*
  Tesla CEO Elon Musk mentioned in an article in Fortune: "The whole Tesla fleet operates as a network. When one car learns something, they all learn it."

These examples depict "collective intelligence." The connected environments and smart devices can learn from the network of data sources (including each other) and create collective intelligence, like vehicle-to-vehicle communication and situational awareness. For example, the logistics companies can monitor and gather various parameters of a cargo container such as temperature and humidity to maintain the right condition of a cargo. AIoT can also be embraced in digital twins. Digital twins are replicas or virtual simulations of real-world objects used to run simulations before deploying the actual devices. The data engineers can virtually analyze the real equipment while reducing the cost and ensuring safety. Drones can interpret or localize unknown surroundings in addition to mapping the environment. It helps in hazardous areas like mines. The autonomous robotic platforms detect and avoid obstacles, or even reroute if required, and can drive autonomously through large warehouses, picking up articles and delivering them to the right place. In the domain of agriculture, IoT helps in collecting and monitoring data about temperature, soil moisture, humidity, rainfall, wind speed, and other parameters. AI helps in automating farming and taking informed decisions. The results are improved quality and quantity of the produce, minimized waste, lowered risk, and reduced effort required to manage crops. In production, AIoT helps in detecting anomalies in the production process and predicting when equipment requires maintenance before it starts to cost the manufacturer heavily.

1.3.2 Ambient Intelligence (AmI)

AI started to be implemented on hardware, such as Walter's robot Turtle and the SNARC by Marvin Minsky and Dean Edmonds. Neural nets were one of the technologies implemented on such systems. In the second phase, AI centered on computers, with the MYCIN expert system as a good example of Good Old-Fashioned AI (GOFAI). Then knowledge-based systems emerged. In the 1990s, several search engines and recommender systems started using intelligent agents and, more recently, semantic technologies like ontologies and knowledge graphs. The current trend is to embed intelligence into our environments. Ambient intelligence (AmI) is the way to achieve this.

"Ambient intelligence allows devices to work in concert to support people in carrying out their everyday life activities, tasks and rituals in an intuitive way using information and intelligence that is hidden in the network connecting these devices" (Wikipedia). IoT brings in information in the connecting network, while AI brings in intelligence in the connecting network. So the AIoT knot has come as a boon for the expansion of AmI.

An *Autonomous Control System (ACS)* performs control functions on the physical systems and also compensates the system failures without external intervention. For example, a smart thermostat is trained to control the central heating systems autonomously based on the users' routine and their presence.

When AmI is combined with ACS, the IoT devices can automatically sense the current state of the environment (e.g., sensing home temperature) and perform the desired actions (e.g., turn HVAC on or off). The machine learning (ML) algorithms may find it hard to train an IoT device to provide an autonomous and ambient environment to human beings. The reinforcement learning approach can allow these IoT devices to learn through maximizing accumulated rewards they receive in the long term.

1.3.3   AIoT on the Edge/Fog/Cloud

AIoT intelligence can be offered at three levels: on the edge (IoT devices), the fog (network edge) nodes, or the cloud.

- The edge (exact device)—real-time and local data processing (at the source)
- The fog (network edge)—on processors/gateways that are connected to the LAN hardware
- The cloud—big data processing and data warehousing

In some applications, the complexity of data analytics is more important, while in others, the uptime and speed are crucial over the other factors. Edge computing is the preferred solution:

(a) When we require faster results and less bandwidth (because of low latency; latency is the time lag between the action taken and the result).
(b) For devices that monitor, diagnose, and take action directly on equipment, like home automation systems and remote-controlled autonomous driving. In such cases, it makes sense to perform the analysis as close to the device as possible. What is the use if by the time the decision comes back from the cloud, equipment already failed?
(c) To avoid the costly network traffic for the data to be sent to the cloud, the draining of battery-operated devices, and the delaying of decisions.
(d) To provide better security practices by filtering sensitive data at the source and avoiding the transfer of these data to the centralized location.

The use of edge computing is a better option in these applications:

- *Autonomous delivery robots/self-driving cars*: Object detection, deciding own path, taking turns, and unexpected traffic changes are done at the edge.
- *City traffic surveillance*: Vehicle recognition and traffic flow assessment are done at the edge, while redirecting traffic, altering speed limits, and adjusting traffic lights are done at the cloud.

Edge computing will not replace the cloud services but will complement them. Though it will remain as the primary location for the creation of data, more data will be stored in the cloud in the long run by 2025.

1.4 Potential Barriers to a Smart and Connected Ecosystem

The vision of a smart, empowered, and interconnected world brings both challenges and benefits. IoT technologies provided new opportunities for businesses. The challenge is, however, to understand the business model and the value chain for the type of connectedness required—like for consumers (smart cars, watches, phones), for commercial use (device tracker, medical devices), or industrial use (manufacturing robots, electric meters).

1.4.1 Data Explosion and Actionable Insights

International Data Corporation (IDC), a premier global provider of market intelligence and advisory services, predicted that more than 59 zettabytes (ZB) of data will be created and consumed in the world in 2020 (Völske et al., 2021). According to the Global DataSphere, which quantifies and analyzes the amount of data created, captured, and replicated in any given year across the world, data generated in a year will grow from 59 zettabytes in 2020 to 175 zettabytes by 2025 with a huge rise in real-time data (Völske et al., 2021). Because of an abrupt increase in the number of work-from-home employees this year due to the COVID-19 pandemic, there is a migration from more unique data to more replicated data. The same data is being continually re-processed, exponentially increasing the recursion rate and decreasing the "unique" DataSphere to 10% of the total DataSphere by 2024.

$$\text{Today,} \ \frac{\text{Unique data (created and captured)}}{\text{Replicated data (copied and consumed)}} = 1:9$$

$$\text{By 2024,} \ \frac{\text{Unique data (created and captured)}}{\text{Replicated data (copied and consumed)}} = 1:10$$

From 2020 onward, real-time data has started becoming the major driver of the total Global DataSphere. Moreover, IDC predicts there will be around 40 billion IoT devices by 2025 and all this real-time data will be generated from IoT devices. Owing to these growing numbers, the smart connected world of today features billions of things, quintillion bytes of data per day, and billions of devices resulting in the following issues:

- Data volume and velocity are generated from millions of sensory devices and crowd-sensing sources.
- Dynamic and unreliable data because of continuous streaming data.
- Data is noisy and incomplete and time and location dependent.
- Data is multimodal, distributed, and heterogeneous.
- Trust, privacy, and security are the major issues.
- Complexity and diversity of IoT datasets.

The huge and increasing influx of data poses challenges for enterprises to drive operational insights. There is a gap between the potential and the delivered value and between the data and the actionable insights and value. AI could help in deriving insights from IoT data. However, enterprises are not yet well prepared in making better use of AI. A recent study by Forrester for HP Enterprise surveyed around 5000 + machine learning (ML) practitioners and found only 14% of the respondents had a defined, repeatable, and scalable process to operationalize ML models that had delivered a range of demonstrable projects; and about 86% of companies have yet to formalize the process or are struggling to operationalize ML models. It also includes those that are still at the proof-of-concept stage. This reveals a significant gap between what is feasible and what is a reality. Despite advances in big data management and analytics, all the relevant data is not analyzed; this creates the so-called insight gap—the gap between the relevant data and the analyzed data. Further, derived insights are not fully exploited or used, resulting in an "execution gap"—the gap between the analyzed data and the data that has actually been fully exploited.

1.4.2   Challenges and Opportunities

In the smart connected world, the integration of devices into our environments induces unique privacy issues that go beyond data privacy and get worsened when the scope of activities crosses the social and cultural boundaries. There are challenges from the customers' perspective like changing customers' requirements, new devices, and gaining customers' confidence. Guidelines and regulatory standards are also required on the retention, use, and security of data as well as the metadata. Besides these business, societal, social, legal, and privacy challenges, several technological challenges arise due to a large number of connected devices and huge volumes of data they generate. These challenges need to be addressed for the new connected ecosystem to thrive and be successful.

We envision four major challenges:

1.1. *Scalability*: The number of devices, users, and interactions is ever increasing in the real world. We need to design for a large scale.
1.2. *Device/data interoperability* (heterogeneity of the enabling devices and platforms): Manufacturers of IoT devices use many different mechanisms for communication (APIs, socket communication, messaging protocols). Things, devices, resources, APIs, services, and people all have to be treated homogeneously. Annotation using metadata will support their integration and will provide a direction to deal with interoperability.
1.3. *Reusability of models and applications*: Though a better model can always be devised, the focus should be on facilitating the reusability of models and applications across multiple domains and contexts (e.g., smart homes/offices/

cities) irrespective of the device infrastructure in use. The semantic descriptions and the data should be linked to other existing data sets on the web.

1.4. *Semantic gap*: The data captured by IoT is low level in nature. There exists a semantic gap between the data as captured by IoT devices and the user understanding of that data. An associated challenge is that semantic descriptions can be highly static. The IoT data is highly dynamic and constrained, and its intended meaning and also annotations may change over time and space.

1.5   Semantic Technologies as the Enabler of Smart Connected World

To address the challenges outlined earlier, systems need to be intelligent enough to dynamically adapt to their environment and tasks; self-configuring, self-describing/explaining, self-healing, self-protecting, and self-organizing; context-aware; and reactive and proactive. The complete solution calls for sifting data to identify the quality and relevant data, understand why only this identified data (context and personalization), and finally generating actionable insights from the data, i.e., make sense of this data. To derive real benefits from the connected world, we need to decrease the insight gap as well as the execution gap.

1.5.1   Cognitive Computing

Different varieties and types of data coexist in the smart connected world. There is a deluge of sensor data from the physical world (which is mostly unstructured); a deluge of structured, semi-structured, and unstructured data from the digital world; social data; web data; and more. To deal with data and also make sense of it, we need to move from Data (D) to Information (I) to Knowledge (K) to Wisdom (W) in the DIKW pyramid. Wisdom is the highest level of intelligence. Only humans are said to have wisdom as it encompasses many said and even unsaid things. Figure 1.2 presents the DIKW pyramid as the pipeline to wisdom.

Traditional representation approaches fail to capture the nuances in semantic meanings of essential vocabulary and thus fail to reflect different contextual dimensions. The knowledge-infused learning approach will help overcome obstacles like lack of surplus, quality, and diversified training data; poor interpretability; inherent bias in the dataset; and non-explainability of models. This hybrid of the syntactical and the symbolic (semantic) approaches paves the way to cognitive computing and the neuro-symbolic intelligent systems. The idea is to infuse the necessary conceptual information into machine/deep learning architectures to make systems learn, interact, and reason.

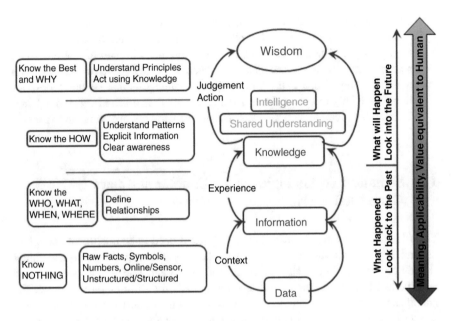

Fig. 1.2 The DIKW pyramid as the pipeline to wisdom

1.5.2 The Semantic Data Model

In data, syntax describes the correct format, and semantics describes the required comprehension and correct interpretation. In other words,

$$\text{Semantics} = \text{Words (Symbols)} + \text{Accumulated Knowledge} + \text{Context}$$

Users may have different interpretations for the same vocabulary, causing a semantic gap (Jain & Groppe, 2021). Closing the semantic gap means translating the high-level contextual knowledge into reproducible low-level machine representation. The semantic technologies are to be utilized as kernel technologies to overcome the challenges listed in Sect. 1.4.2. Starting from simple web technologies (such as Unicode, HTTP, and HTML) as the foundation technologies, we have various serialization formats such as XML, JSON, RDFa, microformats, Turtle, and more. For metadata, we have the Resource Description Framework (RDF) data model and more expressive RDFS and OWL. RDF is a W3C standard for data exchange on the web. RDF consists of triples in the form of <subject, predicate, object> and provides metadata about resources. In 1997, we had the first working draft of RDF/XML. The year 1999 brought the first W3C recommendation for the RDF model and syntax. Around 2004, RDF was revised for concepts and abstract syntax. SPARQL, Turtle, and Linked Data emerged then. In 2017, we had SHACL/ ShEx for RDF validation. RDFS extends RDF by describing a group of related resources and provides basic elements like *class*, *property*, *type*, *subClassOf*, *domain*, and *range* for the description of ontologies (vocabularies). OWL provides still more possibilities for complex applications such as *similarity, differences, construct classes*, and *reason about terms*. SPARQL is a semantic query language to retrieve and manipulate the RDF data.

The cognitive computing approach combines machine intelligence with human intelligence to reach conclusions faster than possible by humans alone along with the explanations needed for trust in the decisions and results while requiring far fewer data samples for training and conversing in natural language. This hybrid model can generalize and is excellent at perceiving, learning, and reasoning with minimal supervision. We need to train computers as to what taxonomies (terminology) to use to explain their recommendations, decisions, or results. For computers to be able to reason, the words describing the object of interest, its properties, and its values, as well as the relationships between them, all have to be accurately defined in a system commonly known as a knowledge organization system (ontology). Knowledge organization systems are systematized knowledge of domains (conceptual models) and make search more robust. Many different forms of conceptual models are arguably interpreted as ontologies. They vary in appearance, scope, and degree of formality. The simplest form of an ontology is a controlled vocabulary, which is also termed glossary; others are taxonomy, thesauri, and folksonomy. The study of ontologies is based on the works of Plato and Aristotle. An ontology acts as a schema and describes a set of concepts and their relationships in a domain. A knowledge base is a set of individual instances of classes and their relationships.

For data exchange, the Resource Description Framework (RDF) is preferable over the Extensible Markup Language (XML). XML representation lacks a semantic model. For data stores, we recommend RDF over relational data stores. The human mind does not think in terms of a relational database. It is much easier to pass information between our heads and a graph than creating weird database models. Understanding an entity relationship diagram (ERD) is much easier than understanding tables. Tables are made for machine understanding. What if machines can understand the ERD directly? That is why RDF graphs came. Relational databases (RDBs) store highly structured data in tables with predetermined schema; the RDF graphs are not rigid in structure and organization. RDBs are for the discrete data problems; the RDF graphs are for the connected data. The IoT data is highly unstructured, real-time, massive, high velocity, and coming from different locations with multiple formats. For example, being real-time, an attribute in RDB changes from single-valued to multi-valued. The solution with existing RDBs will be to delete all the data for that attribute and create an entirely new table holding all the multiple values for that attribute along with a foreign key reference. This is time-consuming and also all indices with the original table get invalidated. Even all the previous SQL queries get invalidated. In contrast, the RDF graph model is incremental in nature. They connect to the data lake and create a graph (i.e., analytics-ready datasets) automatically! The RDF graphs provide a platform to reveal complex relationships between unrelated datasets. Data scientists can focus on solving problems than ending with just dealing with and cleaning data.

1.5.3 Semantic Standards

Most of the ontologies developed after 2012 are based on the Open Geospatial Consortium (OGC) standard (Botts et al., 2006). The OGC Sensor Web Enablement (SWE) is an important work for sharing and exchanging sensor observation data. "In much the same way that the HTML and HTTP enabled the establishment of the WWW, OGC SWE will allow Sensor Webs to become a reality" (Mike Botts, OGC, 2001). Many large organizations such as NOAA, NASA, NRC, AAFC, and ESA have adopted this standard. This standard has defined a conceptual data model/ontology (O&M, ISO 19156). OGC SensorThings API (http://ogc-iot.github.io/ogc-iot-api/) is an IoT cloud API standard based on the OGC SWE. It is a lightweight protocol of the SWE family and designed specifically for IoT. Some early research work has been done to use JSON-LD to annotate SensorThings. OGC SWE fulfills all the basic requirements for the sensor web like all sensors are connected to the web and are metadata registered, they can report their position, and they are readable and controllable remotely.

For growth, we need to go horizontal and build an ecosystem where every application can access all the services. We need data from several data services all supporting the same open standard but organized differently. Adapting the "p" applications and "q" services will require writing "pq" pieces of code. Hypercat is a standard for representing and exposing the IoT data hub catalogs over web technologies to improve data discoverability and interoperability. The data in the Hypercat Data Hub is stored in relational databases. Tachmazidis et al. (2017) devised Hypercat Ontology to capture the semantics of Hypercat and also provided a SPARQL-SQL endpoint to query the data. Ontop (http://ontop.inf.unibz.it/) was used as an external library for the SPARQL-SQL endpoint. Other options could be to convert the data in the Hypercat Data Hub from RDBs to RDF triple stores or JSON-LD. Georgiou et al. (2019) chose JSON-LD. The authors developed a JSON-LD equivalent for the Hypercat specification. They developed a parser translating Hypercat JSON-based catalog to semantic Hypercat JSON-LD-based catalog. The authors utilized the same ontology developed by Tachmazidis et al. (2017). The Hypercat JSON-LD catalog is stored in MongoDB. They also designed and proposed a semantic search mechanism.

1.6 Intelligent Applications in a Connected World

Figure 1.3 depicts a high-level abstraction of the data flow in intelligent applications utilizing a semantic data model. Data from the smart connected world in any available format (CSV, RDF tuples, JSON, XML, etc.) enters into the system and transformed and integrated as a knowledge graph (Jain, 2020a; Jain et al., 2020). The RDF graph is providing a 360-degree view of an entity, its surrounding entities, and all relationships. In addition to providing answers, it is capable of explaining them.

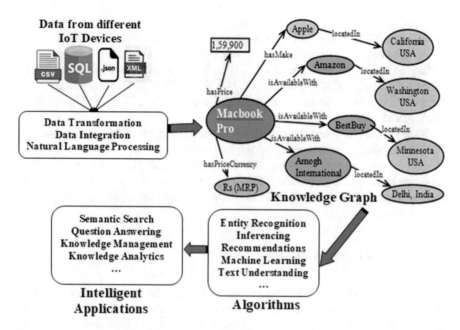

Fig. 1.3 Data flow utilizing a semantic data model

Now different algorithms ranging from recognizing an entity to machine learning and recommendation may be applied over it to perform some end-user applications. Effective methods, APIs, and open-source tools have to be created (many are already in place) to design, handle, use, and process the semantics while considering the dynamicity of the IoT data.

1.6.1 Ontologies for Sensor Network

The Semantic Sensor (& Actuator) Web by Sheth et al. (2008) proposed an extension of the current Web/Internet to enable the devices to interact and communicate. The objects and people could now work in cooperation as now the information is well defined. The sensor data is semantically annotated with situational knowledge to make it contextual and enhance interoperability. Various application-specific ontologies, as well as general ontologies, have been developed for sensor networks, including SWAMO (Witt et al., 2008), CESN (Matheus et al., 2006), MMI (Rueda et al., 2010), ISTAR (Gomez et al., 2008), A3ME (Herzog & Buchmann, 2008), OOSTethys (Bridger et al., 2009), Avancha (Avancha et al., 2004), and WISNO (Hu et al., 2007). The Semantic Sensor Network Incubator Group from W3C has come up with an SSN ontology2 (mainly for sensors and sensor networks, platforms, and systems) as an upgradation of the existing ontologies. This incubator group also recommended methods to use the SSN ontology following the available standards such as the Open Geospatial Consortium's (OGC™) Sensor Web Enablement (SWE) standards. Since its inception, SSN ontology has found its application in many projects, viz., Semantic Perception (Henson et al., 2012), IoT.est project (Wang et al., 2013; Barnaghi et al., 2012), SemSorGrid4Env (Calbimonte et al., 2010; Gray et al., 2011; Page et al., 2011), SPITFIRE project (Pfisterer et al., 2011; Leggieri et al., 2011), Swiss Experiment (Calbimonte et al., 2011), SECURE (Desai et al., 2011), etc.

Various extensions and specializations to particular projects have been developed for SSN ontology. All the sensor ontologies have been created in different flavors of Web Ontology Language (OWL). IoT-Lite is a lightweight instantiation of the SSN ontology by Bermudez-Edo et al. (2016). The IoT-Lite ontology enables device and data interoperability and advanced knowledge analytics for intelligent applications.

1.6.2   Data Integration

According to an IET technical report, after collecting the context-sensitive data, its format and source have to be validated and checked for accuracy and integrity. The data then has to be analyzed on various parameters and correlated with benchmarks for computation or compliance. The data is thus ready for sharing or to be brought to action. Several models, ontologies, and semantic annotation frameworks are already available to bring this data cycle to practice. The challenge, however, lies in integrating this data and querying it in the end-user applications. The vertical technology transfer is also an important issue, i.e., the end user adopting it and transforming these discoveries into innovations. The available software systems are designed vertically and are not integrated at a horizontal level. They are not able to perform data sharing or even exploit the data collected from other sources. The sensor ontology provides a shared vocabulary, and the stream data (an infinite sequence of time-stamped tuples) is to be mapped with this ontology to realize the queries and perform reasoning. Various representation syntax (serializations like Turtle and XML), mapping languages (D2RQ, R2RML, Ontop, RML, S$_2$O), and mapping processors are available to date. The most notable and general mapping language is RML (the RDF Mapping Language), which can take data in any possible syntax. The S$_2$O mapping language has been specially designed for the sensor stream data.

1.6.3   Intelligent Applications

Once the stream data is mapped to the semantic data model, it is queried using some query language. SPARQL (SPARQL Protocol and RDF Query Language) is the default standard for querying the RDF data. But it is not able to handle the continuous and time-stamped sensor stream data. Various extensions of SPARQL have already been proposed including T-SPARQL (Grandi, 2010), TA-SPARQL (Rodrıguez et al., 2009; Analyti & Pachoulakis, 2008), stSPARQL (Koubarakis & Kyzirakos, 2010; Kyzirakos et al., 2010), EP-SPARQL (Anicic et al., 2011), C-SPARQL (Barbieri et al., 2010), and SPARQLstream (Calbimonte et al., 2012). Next, let us consider two examples.

1. Smart City Projects
As urbanization has brought pressure on major important resources, the realization of smart cities is gaining interest but with a little care for unified models, architectures, and services. Many independent projects have been undertaken in recent years like OpenIoT in 2012 (Soldatos et al., 2015). The OpenIoT (openiot.eu) architecture formulates and deploys IoT services on the cloud, hence enabling Sensing as a Service. All the data streams are annotated based on the W3C SSN ontology. The VITAL platform (Petrolo et al., 2014) presents a Cloud-of-Things architecture that enables data integration to bridge IoT silos by designing VITAL ontologies. The CityPulse project (Barnaghi et al., 2014) proposes a model for processing the IoT data streams with semantic annotations in smart cities. It virtualizes the IoT resources and annotates the data and streams semantically. It adopts SSN and other semantic technologies to create advanced smart cities. For a comparison of semantic-based projects for smart cities, see http://sensormeasurement.appspot.com/?p=stateOfTheArt.

2. Smart Homes
Smart homes are capable of sensing parameters of interest, communicating sensed information, and also initiating appropriate actions to facilitate the users. One of the tasks could be to minimize or optimize overall energy consumption. The OntoSmart system (Ismail et al., 2016) provides Sensing as a Service. The semantic rules and the SPARQL service provide intelligent decision-making. The SMART Appliances Reference (SAREF) (Daniele et al., 2015) is one of the top recommended ontologies for the smart home use case. The SESAME-S project (SEmantic SmArt Metering— Services for Energy Efficient Houses) (Fensel et al., 2013) provides efficient and sustainable energy usage in smart homes. SESAME-S uses semantically linked data in making well-informed decisions and controlling their energy consumption. The POSTECH U-Health Smart Home project (Kim & Park, 2015) provides a semantic model to make accurate and intelligent decisions. The open standard CIM version 2.22 has been used by this project as ontology.

1.7   Conclusion

AI (specifically semantic technologies) and IoT together present a powerful mixture that offers smart connectedness, intelligence, and autonomy among objects, entities, processes, and humans in the emerging smart connected world that has the potential to transform again many facets of our world. This chapter has provided a broad perspective on the emerging smart connected world and traced and highlighted developments in IoT and semantic technologies—the foundations for the new world we envisage. Semantic technologies provide a promising direction for achieving interoperability and bridging the information silos in data gathered from the IoT. Ontologies enrich the data with contextualized information leading to linked (open) data-based systems.

The rest of the chapters in this book discuss technologies, applications and challenges and the potential solutions in detail.

We hope and look forward to the smart connected world of the future which will be open and accessible to everyone with full control over their data.

Review Questions
1. What are the major challenges brought by ever-increasing data on the web and the number of connected devices?
2. What do you consider as major developments that drove IoT?
3. What is AIoT? Compare and contrast the features of IoT and AIoT. List some illustrative examples where AI is supplementing IoT to obtain better value.
4. Differentiate between cloud computing and edge computing.
5. Highlight the major challenges toward the realization of the vision of a truly smart connected world and the tangible values derived from it.
6. What do you understand by cognitive computing? Write a short note on the cognitive paradigm of computing and its significance.
7. What do you mean by the semantic data models? What other phrases could be used for the same concept? Summarize some data models that are semantic in nature.

Discussion Questions
8. Discuss potential impacts of the smart connected world on our lives, infrastructure, and the healthcare sector.
9. Highlight the major challenges toward the realization of the vision of a truly smart connected world. List and discuss the problems brought forward by these challenges in the context of (a) transportation, (b) healthcare, and (c) other domains.
10. Defend upon some of the real-world use cases where you feel that the semantic approaches could complement the statistical approaches by filling certain gaps.
11. Discuss and evaluate statistical approaches and semantic approaches to computing when they are used in isolation.

Problem Statements for Researchers
12. In this chapter, we briefly mentioned the Hypercat ontology and the SPARQL-SQL endpoint. Consider this use case. One has stored the Hypercat Data Hub data into a relational database. Another has developed a JSON-LD equivalent for the Hypercat specification and stored the catalog in MongoDB. Think of more extensions in these works toward the attainment of the smart connected world as envisioned in this chapter.

13. We highlighted a few ontologies for a sensor network. Carry out a comprehensive review of available ontologies in this domain and provide a comparative study on various parameters. Prepare a detailed report. Also, summarize the projects that have utilized these ontologies to enable device and data interoperability and advanced knowledge analytics for intelligent applications.

References

Analyti, A., & Pachoulakis, I. (2008). A survey on models and query languages for temporally annotated RDF. *International Journal of Advanced Computer Science and Applications, 3,* 28–35.

Anicic, D., Fodor, P., Rudolph, S., & Stojanovic, N. (2011). EP-SPARQL: A unified language for event processing and stream reasoning. In *Proceedings of the 20th International Conference on World wide web.*

Avancha, Patel, C., & Joshi, A. (2004). Ontology-driven adaptive sensor networks. In *MobiQuitous* (pp. 194–202).

Barbieri, D. F., Braga, D., Ceri, S., VALLE, E. D., & Grossniklaus, M. (2010). C-sparql: A continuous query language for rdf data streams. *International Journal of Semantic Computing, 4,* 3–25.

Barnaghi, P., Wang, W., Henson, C., & Taylor, K. (2012). Semantics for the Internet of Things: Early progress and back to the future. *International Journal on Semantic Web and Information Systems (IJSWIS), 8,* 1–21.

Barnaghi, P., Tönjes, R., Höller, J., Hauswirth, M., Sheth, A., & Anantharam, P. (2014, October). Citypulse: Real-time iot stream processing and large-scale data analytics for smart city applications. In *European Semantic Web Conference (ESWC)* (Vol. 2014). sn.

Bermudez-Edo, M., Elsaleh, T., Barnaghi, P., & Taylor, K. (2016, July). IoT-Lite: A lightweight semantic model for the Internet of Things. In *2016 Intl IEEE Conferences on Ubiquitous Intelligence & Computing, Advanced and Trusted Computing, Scalable Computing and Communications, Cloud and Big Data Computing, Internet of People, and Smart World Congress (UIC/ATC/ScalCom/CBDCom/IoP/SmartWorld)* (pp. 90–97). IEEE.

Botts, M., Percivall, G., Reed, C., & Davidson, J. (2006, October). OGC® sensor web enablement: Overview and high level architecture. In *International Conference on GeoSensor Networks* (pp. 175–190). Berlin: Springer.

Bridger, E., Bermudez, L., Maskey, M., Rueda, C., Babin, B., & Blair, R. (2009). OOSTethys-open source software for the global earth observing systems of systems. In *AGU Fall Meeting Abstracts* (pp. 1065).

Calbimonte, J.-P., Corcho, O., & Gray, A. J. (2010). Enabling ontology-based access to streaming data sources. In *The semantic web–ISWC 2010* (pp. 96–111). Springer.

Calbimonte, J.-P., Jeung, H., Corcho, O., & Aberer, K. (2011). *Semantic sensor data search in a large-scale federated sensor network.*

Calbimonte, J. P., Jeung, H., Corcho, Ó., & Aberer, K. (2012). Enabling query technologies for the semantic sensor web. *International Journal on Semantic Web and Information Systems, 8,* 43–63.

Daniele, L., den Hartog, F., & Roes, J. (2015, August). Created in close interaction with the industry: The smart appliances reference (SAREF) ontology. In *International Workshop Formal Ontologies Meet Industries* (pp. 100–112). Cham: Springer.

Desai, P., Henson, C., Anatharam, P., & Sheth, A. (2011). SECURE: Semantics empowered resCUe environment (Demonstration Paper). In *4th International Workshop on Semantic Sensor Networks 2011 (SSN 2011)* (pp. 115–118).

Fensel, A., Tomic, S., Kumar, V., Stefanovic, M., Aleshin, S. V., & Novikov, D. O. (2013). SESAME-S: Semantic smart home system for energy efficiency. *Inform. Spektrum, 36*, 46–57.

Georgiou, M., Tachmazidis, I., & Antoniou, G. (2019, June). Hypercat JSON-LD: A semantically enriched catalogue format for IoT. In *Proceedings of the 9th International Conference on Web Intelligence, Mining and Semantics* (pp. 1–12).

Gomez, M., Preece, A., Johnson, M. P., De Mel, G., Vasconcelos, W., Gibson, C., et al. (2008). An ontology-centric approach to sensor-mission assignment. In *Knowledge engineering: Practice and patterns* (pp. 347–363). Springer.

Grandi, F. (2010). T-SPARQL: A TSQL2-like temporal query language for RDF. In *ADBIS (Local Proceedings)* (pp. 21–30).

Gray, J., García-Castro, R., Kyzirakos, K., Karpathiotakis, M., Calbimonte, J.-P., Page, K., et al. (2011). A semantically enabled service architecture for mashups over streaming and stored data. In *The semantic web: Research and applications* (pp. 300–314). Springer.

Henson, C., Sheth, A., & Thirunarayan, K. (2012). Semantic perception: Converting sensory observations to abstractions. *Internet Computing, IEEE, 16*, 26–34.

Herzog, D. J., & Buchmann, A. (2008). A3ME-an Agent-Based middleware approach for mixed mode environments. In *The Second International Conference on Mobile Ubiquitous Computing, Systems, Services and Technologies, UBICOMM'08* (pp. 191–196).

Hu, Y., Wu, Z., & Guo, M. (2007). Ontology driven adaptive data processing in wireless sensor networks. In *Proceedings of the 2nd International Conference on Scalable Information Systems* (pp. 46).

Ismail, L. N., Girod-Genet, M., & El Hassan, B. (2016). Semantic techniques for IoT data and service management: ONTOSMART system. *International Journal of Wireless & Mobile Networks (IJWMN), 8*(4), 43–63.

Jain, S. (2020a). Exploiting knowledge graphs for facilitating product/service discovery. arXiv preprint arXiv:2010.05213.

Jain, S. (2020b). Semantic Intelligence, "Artificial Intelligence of Things AIOT", Faculty Development Programme sponsored by AICTE ATAL Academy, organized by SRM Modinagar [Video]. Retrieved from https://youtu.be/Z_tbR02wsB4

Jain, S., & Groppe, S. (2021, March). ISIC 2021 front matter. In *International Semantic Intelligence Conference ISIC 2021* (Vol. 2786, pp. 1–13). CEUR-WS.

Jain, S., Jain, V., & Balas, V. E. (Eds.). (2020). *Web semantics – Cutting edge and future directions in health care*. Elsevier. ISBN: 9780128224687.

Kim, J., & Park, S. O. (2015). U-health smart system architecture and ontology model. *The Journal of Supercomputing, 71*(6), 2121–2137.

Koubarakis, M., & Kyzirakos, K. (2010). Modeling and querying metadata in the semantic sensor web: The model stRDF and the query language stSPARQL. In *The semantic web: Research and applications* (Vol. 6088, pp. 425–439). Berlin: Springer.

Kyzirakos, K., Karpathiotakis, M., & Koubarakis, M. (2010). Developing registries for the semantic sensor web using stRDF and stSPARQL. In *International Workshop on Semantic Sensor Networks*.

Leggieri, M., Passant, A., & Hauswirth, M. (2011). In context-sensing: LOD augmented sensor data. In *Proceedings of the 10th International Semantic Web Conference (ISWC 2011)*.

Matheus, C. J., Tribble, D., Kokar, M. M., Ceruti, M. G., & McGirr, S. C. (2006). *Towards a formal pedigree ontology for level-one sensor fusion*. DTIC Document.

Page, K. R., Frazer, A. J., Nagel, B. J., De Roure, D. C., & Martinez, K. (2011). Semantic access to sensor observations through web APIs. In *2011 Fifth IEEE International Conference on Semantic Computing (ICSC)* (pp. 336–343).

Petrolo, R., Loscri, V., & Mitton, N. (2014). Towards a cloud of things smart city. *IEEE COMSOC MMTC E-Letter, 9*(5).

Tachmazidis, I., Batsakis, S., Davies, J., Duke, A., Vallati, M., Antoniou, G., & Clarke, S. S. (2017, May). A Hypercat-enabled semantic Internet of Things data hub. In *European Semantic Web Conference* (pp. 125–137). Cham: Springer.

Soldatos, J., Kefalakis, N., Hauswirth, M., Serrano, M., Calbimonte, J. P., Riahi, M., Aberer, K., Jayaraman, P. P., Zaslavsky, A., Žarko, I. P., et al. (2015). *OpenIoT: Open source Internet-of-Things in the cloud* (pp. 13–25). Cham: Springer International Publishing.

Sheth, A., Henson, C., & Sahoo, S. S. (2008). Semantic sensor web. *IEEE Internet Computing, 12* (4), 78–83.

Witt, K. J., Stanley, J., Smithbauer, D., Mandl, D., Ly, V., Underbrink, A., et al. (2008). Enabling sensor webs by utilizing SWAMO for autonomous operations. In *NASA Earth Science Technology Conference (ESTC2008)*.

Rueda, C., Galbraith, N., Morris, R. A., Bermudez, L. E., Arko, R. A., & Graybeal, J. (2010). The MMI device ontology: Enabling sensor integration. In *AGU Fall Meeting Abstracts* (pp. 08).

Völske, M., Bevendorff, J., Kiesel, J., Stein, B., Fröbe, M., Hagen, M., & Potthast, M. (2021). Web archive analytics. *INFORMATIK 2020*.

Wang, W., De, S., Cassar, G., & Moessner, K. (2013). Knowledge representation in the internet of things: Semantic modelling and its applications. *Automatika–Journal for Control, Measurement, Electronics, Computing and Communications, 54*.

Pfisterer, D., Romer, K., Bimschas, D., Kleine, O., Mietz, R., Truong, C., et al. (2011). SPITFIRE: Toward a semantic web of things. *Communications Magazine, IEEE, 49*, 40–48.

Rodrıguez, A., McGrath, R., Liu, Y., Myers, J., & Urbana-Champaign, I. (2009). Semantic management of streaming data. *Proceedings of Semantic Sensor Networks, 80*, 80–95.

Sarika Jain   graduated from Jawaharlal Nehru University (India) in 2001. Her doctorate, awarded in 2011, is in the field of knowledge representation in Artificial Intelligence. She has served in the field of education for over 19 years and is currently in service at the National Institute of Technology, Kurukshetra (Institute of National Importance), India. Dr. Jain has authored or co-authored over 150 publications including books. Her current research interests are knowledge management and analytics, the semantic web, ontological engineering, and intelligent systems. She is a senior member of the IEEE, member of ACM, and a Life Member of the CSI.

San Murugesan   is Director of BRITE Professional Services, an Adjunct Professor in the School of Computing at Western Sydney University, Honorary Professor at Amity University, and former Editor-in-Chief of the IEEE Computer Society's *IT Professional* magazine. He has vast experience in both academia and industry. He successfully led development of innovative IT projects; provided leadership in research and development; conceived and led several academic programs; and offered consultancy services. His expertise and interests span a range of areas: smart systems, artificial intelligence, autonomous systems, quantum computing, green computing, cloud computing, digital transformation, Internet of Things (IoT), sustainability, and emerging trends in IT.

Chapter 2
Cyber-Physical-Social Systems: An Overview

Regina Reine, Filbert H. Juwono, Zee Ang Sim, and W. K. Wong

Abstract For the past few years, devices or systems have been transformed into smart connected devices or systems, which are widely named as Internet of Things (IoT) and cyber-physical systems (CPSs). Integrating social networks to CPSs results in a new paradigm called cyber-physical-social systems (CPSSs). CPSSs include the human-to-device communications and device-to-device communications and create continuous interaction of human-device relationships. The fifth-generation (5G) wireless communication networks, wireless sensor networks, big data, artificial intelligence (AI), virtual reality (VR), and augmented reality (AR) are the supporting technologies of CPSSs. This chapter discusses the concept of the CPSSs, their supporting technologies, and the implementation of CPSSs in different domains. It also observes current challenges such as privacy concerns, ethical issues, safety, security, interdependence, and compatibility.

Keywords 5G communication network · Artificial intelligence (AI) · Assistive technology · Augmented reality (AR) · Big data · Compromised-key attack · Cyber layer · Cyber-physical-social system (CPSS) · Denial-of-service attack · E-hailing · Industrial revolution · Internet of Things (IoT) · Man-in-the-middle attack · Massive open online courses (MOOCs) · Physical layer · Prosumer · Smart city · Social layer · Telecare · Telehealth · Virtual reality (VR) · Wireless sensor network (WSN)

R. Reine
Twigx Research, London, UK
e-mail: reginareine@twigxresearch.com

F. H. Juwono (✉) · W. K. Wong
Curtin University Malaysia, Miri, Sarawak, Malaysia
e-mail: filbert.hilman@curtin.edu.my; weikitt.w@curtin.edu.my

Z. A. Sim
Heriot-Watt University Malaysia, Putrajaya, Malaysia
e-mail: z.sim@hw.ac.uk

Key Points
- Presents an overview on the concept of a cyber-physical-social system (CPSS) and its supporting technologies
- Provides an in-depth discussion on the different layers of the CPSS architecture
- Briefly looks into the applications of CPSSs in eight different domains
- Depicts the challenges faced in the implementation of CPSSs

2.1   Introduction

In the beginning, the Internet was used to connect computers and created freedom from geographical constraint. For the past decades, the communication protocol standards have been developed, the telecommunication infrastructure in cities and rural areas has been rapidly built, and the quality of services has been continuously improved. These create continuous evolution in the Internet standard. The emerging innovations in electronics, semiconductors, and signal processing technologies shifted the world from the analog technology era to the digital technology era. This is also known as the *Third Industrial Revolution* (IR 3.0) era. IR 3.0 has been reflected by the rapid increase in the number of Internet connections and users in the past decade. It is estimated that there were 250 million Internet connections in 2015 and the number of Internet users had exponentially increased to 650 million in 2020. The connected urban population had nearly doubled from 80 million users (in 2015) to 150 million users (in 2020).

As the number of Internet connections increases, every *thing* can be connected. This leads to the *Fourth Industrial Revolution* (IR 4.0) era, and the technology underpinning IR 4.0 is cyber-physical systems (CPSs). CPSs and Internet of Things (IoT) may be used interchangeably. However, it should be noted that there is a distinct difference between the two. CPS focuses on the interconnection between the physical world and the cyber world, while IoT focuses on the interconnection between devices. IoT in a small scale can be considered as machine-type communications (MTC) (Atzori et al., 2010). Digitalization has transformed lives in terms of access to information, workflow and process automation, and the way people interact with the machines and devices. The human-machine relationship has increasingly become more fluid and more personalized. Using artificial intelligence (AI), CPSs interconnect diverse sensors and devices to assist human daily activities and interactions, such as smart houses, smart cities, and smart vehicles (Yakub & Reine, 2018; Aksu et al., 2018; Memos et al., 2018).

The integration of these technologies enhances the capabilities to capture and apply the knowledge, characteristics, or intelligence of humans on machines to improve the quality of life. The development of human-machine integration enables us to collect, observe, and analyze the information in a large scale ubiquitously, and it is often named as computing for human experience (CHE) or human-computer interaction (HCI). The CHE is designed to emulate human experience in anticipating certain situations where relevant knowledge and intelligence that are related to the physical and abstract concept (e.g., emotions and sentiments) will be used (Weiser, 1999). To achieve the seamless interactions between the human-computer world, CPSs with the supporting technologies introduce a new paradigm, called the cyber--physical-social systems (CPSSs), where the systems consider human factors as part of the system operation and the management of CPSs. CPSSs will be the foundation of the next *Fifth Industrial Revolution* (IR 5.0) era, where a fully connected world can be realized.

The concept of a connected world aims to create a converged (or integrated) network, and it refers not only to devices and people but also to other systems, such as electricity and energy supplies. The term "connected" cannot be separated with the terms "automated" and "smart" as a whole as the concept intends to build reliable systems. To design the connected world, CPSSs must be supported by the emerging technologies such as wireless sensor networks (WSNs), fifth-generation (5G) communication networks, artificial intelligence (AI), big data, virtual reality (VR), and augmented reality (AR).

Wireless Sensor Networks (WSNs)
WSNs commonly consist of a massive number of sensors that are interconnected and able to communicate with each other to perform certain tasks without human intervention. The sensors in a WSN measure ambient conditions in the surrounding environment to obtain certain characteristics in the environment. A WSN may have hundreds or thousands of sensors where the sensors communicate with each other directly or via an external base station (Al-Karaki & Kamal, 2004). The current challenges in WSN include routing protocols, energy efficiency, and security issues.

Fifth-Generation (5G) Communication Networks
In 5G communication, achieving high-speed data transfer is not the sole objective. A 5G communication network is envisioned to accommodate the connectivity of a massive number of devices (up to 100 times compared with the existing 4G LTE) at low latency, 100% coverage, and low energy consumption. Some of the key enablers for the 5G communication are ultra-densification, mmWave, and massive multiple-input multiple-output (massive MIMO) (Andrews et al., 2014).

Big Data
Along with the massive number of devices which are connected to the Internet, the amount of processed data each day is enormous, reaching up to 2.5 quintillion bytes (Wu et al., 2014). The data can be collected either from a large number of sensors or from various social media platforms in the forms of photos, videos, feeds from news updates, etc. These data can be analyzed to obtain useful information regarding the behavior of a certain surrounding or how social media react to certain situations. However, processing a large amount of data to extract the essence of the information can be complex and time-consuming. The generally accepted contemporary solution is to apply artificial intelligence (AI).

Artificial Intelligence (AI)
AI is a set of algorithms or computational techniques that enables machines to perform actions intelligently like how humans behave. Several factors have contributed to the maturing of the AI revolution. The key factor is the development of

machine learning, supported by emerging cloud computing technologies and ubiquitous web-based data mining. Deep learning is the "deeper" technique of machine learning, a form of adaptive artificial neural networks trained where the backpropagation method is utilized. Using machine learning, information retrieved from big data can be processed and analyzed efficiently (Chen & Lin, 2014). Many well-known applications such as weather reports, search engines, or voice assistants process large complex data in various forms (i.e., numbers, text, voice) using big data and AI technologies. It can be seen that big data and AI have been some of the important foundations in developing intelligent applications.

Virtual Reality (VR) and Augmented Reality (AR)
The VR technology allows us to be immersed into a virtual world and brings us to interact with objects or beings in that virtual world (Bowman & McMahan, 2007). Sensors in the VR technology collect movement data while providing visual, sound, and sensory feedback. Meanwhile, the AR technology allows us to see virtual objects that overlay in the real-world surrounding via visual devices such as phone cameras and head-worn displays (Azuma et al., 2001). Location tracking and updated information of the surrounding area are often required to display virtual objects accurately.

2.2 Cyber-Physical-Social Systems (CPSSs)

As described in the previous section, CPSs refer to smart systems where sensors, actuators, and controllers are used for interactions between the physical world and the cyber world (Sheth et al., 2013). Generally, a CPS consists of three layers: the perception layer (to capture the information and apply the feedback decisions), the transport layer (to transfer the information), and the application layer (to observe, control, and analyze the results of the received information) (Aksu et al., 2018). The physical systems enable the close human-machine interaction within the networks. This type of interaction leads to the emergence of the CPSS concept where humans and the environment are interactively and ubiquitously connected. The CPSS includes how data, information, and knowledge are processed from the CPSS networks, followed by integration and interpretation to produce meaningful context interpretation for humans.

A CPSS is viewed as the future industrial system where it integrates the computing, physical, and human resources to connect interactions among the cyber, physical, and social worlds. A CPSS has three main tasks. It incorporates interdependence and relationships between sensors and devices at physical layers, it performs social interactions using various technologies, and it collects a large amount of data to be processed. A cyber-network is used to perform all of these tasks. A cyber-network can be seen as the fundamental structure where it includes Internet connection with the computing technologies as its processing power.

Figure 2.1 illustrates the architecture of a CPSS which can be realized by using the existing communication protocols commonly used for CPS such as IEEE

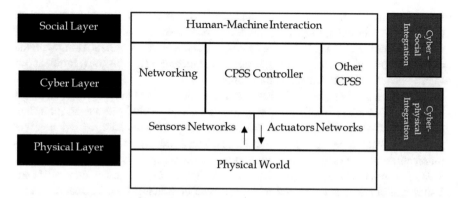

Fig. 2.1 The layered architecture of CPSS

802.15.4 (Zigbee), LoRa, and Wi-Fi. In the cyber layer, which is the brain layer of CPSS, the data is processed and intelligent decision-making is executed. Above the cyber layer is the social layer representing human societies or networks. Below the cyber layer is the physical layer where it represents the physical components such as sensors and actuators. Sensors and actuators are part of the network that connects the physical and the cyber layer, acting as the interface. Humans in the social layer contribute their part in CPSS through social-like applications.

CPSS computing can be used for different domains or sectors, but the implementation may differ considerably within sectors. This chapter will focus on eight different applications: transportation, home service, robot services, healthcare, education, entertainment, social network, and digital commerce. Apart from its advantages, there are technical challenges faced by the CPSS, which include the compatibility of different protocols, networks and communication systems, ubiquitous access, and the massive numbers of connected users. These eight applications will be discussed separately in Sect. 2.3. Technical challenges in a CPSS will be discussed subsequently.

2.2.1   Physical Layer and Communications

The physical system represents the physical environment including sensors and actuators. A sensor is a device that converts physical quantities to electrical signals. On the contrary, an actuator is a device that converts electrical signals to physical quantities. There are many types of sensors available in the market: temperature sensors, smoke sensors, rain sensors, particle sensors, ultrasonic sensors, gyroscope, touch sensors, capacitive sensors, and many more. In general, sensors are classified into active and passive sensors. Active sensors require external power to operate (e.g., infrared sensors), while passive sensors do not need external power (e.g., capacitive sensors). Sensors can also be categorized into analog and digital depending on the nature of the input signal. The characteristics of a sensor can be analyzed from several parameters such as sensitivity, resolution, accuracy, precision, etc. On the other hand, in general, there are four types of actuators: manual (gears, wheels), pneumatic (gas), hydraulic (pressure), and electric (motors). Along with the advancement of microtechnology and nanotechnology, the development of microsensors and nanosensors is inevitable.

The physical layer covers devices and the infrastructures that are interconnected by CPS networks. In the CPSS physical layer, social world becomes an important part of the system. Hence, the CPSS should use communication techniques that guarantee hyper-connectivity characteristics. There are two different types of communication networks in CPSS: human-type and machine-type communications. MTC is a relatively new type of communication in CPSS, and it faces different issues and challenges compared to human-type communication. In general, MTC consists of a large number of devices, requires a low-latency reaction, transmits a small amount of data, and has little or no mobility. Therefore, the emerging communication technologies, such as 5G communication networks, device to device (D2D), and massive MIMO networks, are crucial for the quality of the MTC. 5G communication networks support human-type, machine-human-type, and machine-type communication. Massive MIMO can be used to improve the spectral efficiency, increase the capacity, and enhance the energy efficiency to ensure good quality of connectivity. D2D supports dynamic hyper-connectivity for faster data collection.

2.2.2 Social Layer

Designing systems such as smart homes, smart cities, smart transportation, smart healthcare, and others must be modeled according to the social human aspects. Social aspect plays an important factor in modeling the CPSSs so that the designers, engineers, and administrators understand how the systems can be improved according to the criteria required by humans.

There are different types of human roles in CPSSs where the role can be as the user, the operator, the decision-maker, and many more. To define the role appropriately in the system, there are key characteristics that need to be considered in modeling the CPSSs: role, responsibility, expertise, and intentionality.

Role
The first role that humans may play is as input providers where the information is given through standard computer-based interface or the information is provided through sensors (directly or indirectly). The information provided to the sensors can be in the forms of voice commands (e.g., turning on/off the lamp or turning on/off the music) or hand gestures (e.g., turning on the water tap). The second role in CPSS is system contributor. Two main categories in the system contributor are information processors and actuators. In the information processing stage, humans observe and analyze data, make a decision according to specific requirements or rules, and validate the decision. In the actuation stage, humans interact with the

environment as required by the CPSS. The third role is service consumer where the service can be passively delivered (e.g., music streaming; heating, ventilation, and air-conditioning (HVAC) technology; automatic light in the smart home; etc.) or where the service is delivered when physical interaction is conducted (e.g., service robot is activated after physical interaction).

Responsibility
There are two types of responsibilities in supporting CPSS: accountable and unaccountable. If humans support CPSS based on a contract or agreement, humans will take accountability for their actions in supporting the CPSS. However, if the involvement is temporarily or anonymously, this is typically categorized as an unaccountable type of responsibility.

Expertise
In a CPSS, it is important to distinguish the expertise of humans in order to develop and maintain the system safely. Different levels of training of the CPSS will be used to validate the level of expertise for the suitable role of those who are involved. Commonly, different levels of authorizations are given according to the level of training. For nonexperts, their interaction with the CPSS may be limited until their expertise reaches a certain level.

Intentionality
There are two types of the intentionality of the humans in CPSSs: cooperative and adversarial human interactions with the system. Many systems are designed to share the control of the system between humans and machines. In the cooperative role, a CPSS is designed to allow the machine to close the feedback control loops, but the system will put humans in the loop at a different level of system architecture depending on the criteria and specification. In the adversarial role, humans may create or remove tasks or control of the CPSS due to a particular specification, rules, or regulations.

2.2.3 Cyber Layer and Computing Techniques

The cyber layer can be viewed as the bridge between the physical layer and the social layer. A WSN is an example of the integration of cyber-physical layers as it consists of wireless communication sensors connected to the Internet to perform ubiquitous monitoring. Computing techniques such as edge computing, machine learning, or deep learning can provide hyper-intelligence in the cyber layer. Using these emerging computing techniques will achieve high efficiency in data processing and intelligent decision-making.

As the future trend leads to distributed computing, edge computing techniques will be briefly discussed here. It is well known that edge computing offers some advantages related to response time, power consumption, bandwidth, and data safety and privacy (Shi et al., 2016). In general, edge-centric architecture consists of four

Fig. 2.2 Information
process in the cyber layer

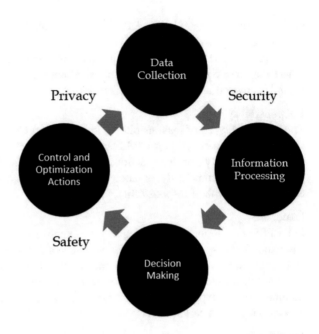

components: the cloud, the end devices, the edge, and the users (Sha et al., 2020).
The edge devices can be a smartphone, a gateway, or a micro data center (Shi et al.,
2016). The end devices can be a controlled lamp, camera, etc. As the cloud is far
away from the end devices, there are some limitations when performing computation
in the cloud. Therefore, the edge becomes the center of the computation, which
supports the cloud and end devices (Sha et al., 2020). The edge computing can also
be improved using machine learning and deep learning algorithms (Lv et al., 2021;
Chen & Ran, 2019).

Further, as illustrated in Fig. 2.2, the central controllers in the cyber layer support
the data collection, information processing, decision-making and optimizing actions.
This way, the cyber layer will provide the intended services or tasks to the users in
the social layers and also distribute commands and authorities to process the
collected information from the physical layers.

2.3 Applications of CPSS

In recent years, CPSS networks have been implemented in various domains to
enhance the system's performance and to create new emerging applications that
are only visible due to the advancement in data speed, communication infrastructure,
ubiquitous access, cloud technologies, pervasive devices, and other supported
technologies.

2.3.1 CPSS in Transportation

Transportation applications are required to be trusted for the safety and reliability of the system. Intelligent urban transport is a representative of CPSS in the transportation domain, which relates to two aspects: engineering complexity and social complexity. Engineering complexity in traffic management includes intelligent infrastructure (e.g., roads and bridges) and traffic control systems. Social complexity in traffic management includes traffic users (e.g., drivers and pedestrians), environment, climate changes, and cultures. There are still some ongoing studies and works to be done, but some countries have started designing and developing intelligent traffic infrastructure and cyber systems that will change the traditional transport system.

Social transportation system usually uses the cloud platform technology as it enables people to connect with the related organization or system. There are four types of data or information that can be collected in the transportation CPSS: emergency events, guidance information (e.g., traffic congestion and road works), travel-related information (e.g., new restaurants and new gas stations), and shared-travel information (e.g., share a ride). These data and information can be distributed to the public, members of social networks, or subscribers of the organization. In addition, the data can be used for travel-related information and shared-travel information as in e-hailing services.

E-hailing is a process of ordering a car, taxi, limousine, or any other form of transportation pickup via virtual devices: computer or mobile device. Compared with the conventional taxi services, e-hailing enables an accurate estimation of cost and online monitoring of driver location prior to arrival. GPS logging provides additional safety features to the passenger. Apart from the convenient and efficient mode of public transportation to the passengers, the equivalent, if not bigger, benefit is being enjoyed by the drivers. When compared with the conventional taxi services, e-hailing drivers enjoy real-time optimal passenger pickup. In an e-hailing driver's point of view, an automated planning system ensures that drivers can optimize passenger pickups and deliveries, thereby enabling a maximum number of passenger pickups.

Further, e-hailing is made possible with the emergence of digital maps and Internet coverage in various cities. The initial business model of e-hailing was to offer transportation service to passengers from a mobile application. However, due to the increasing demand in society, the services have expanded to food delivery, packages, massage services, and other services. This type of transportation service is emerging due to the availability of GPS technology, the ubiquitous access to the Internet, the continuous increase of mobile device users, and, most importantly, the demand for delivery of fast service to their doorstep. The evolution of e-hailing can be seen through the diversification of various companies that leads to even more applications. Figure 2.3 shows some diversification of existing e-hailing companies. These services include e-shopper service, cleaning service, massage service, food

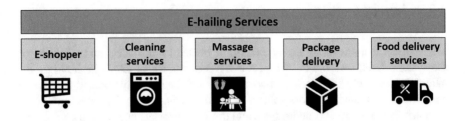

Fig. 2.3 Some diversification of services from existing e-hailing services providers

delivery, and package delivery services. Such services often share a similar social database that was acquired from e-hailing services.

Note that these types of transportation services are emerging due to the availability of GPS technology, the ubiquitous access to the Internet, and the continuous increase of mobile device users. Digital maps have contributed to the possibility of linking the passenger and the driver based on the locality and distances. Most e-hailing apps utilize available digital maps such as Google Maps for navigation. We also notice that most e-hailing technologies depend on GPS locations provided by Internet service providers. The Internet technology coverage and speed enhancement have also enabled the possibility of e-hailing emergence.

E-hailing services connect the passengers to the drivers directly via the application safely, and they create a new type of flexible employment. Such e-hailing services often integrate its large passenger and driver network to leverage on the demand-supply scenario. The advantage of the e-hailing is that it enables tracking of passenger location and tracks the location of drivers to provide better security features for both passengers and drivers. AI is applied to optimize the route efficiency and passenger pickup.

Although navigation maps such as Google Maps have been around for quite some time, some companies have evolved to utilize CPSS concepts in their technology to enhance the driver experience. On top of the existing navigation services, these services include reporting of accidents, road construction, and traffic jams. Various technologies have tried to utilize and optimize sensing technology, such as imaging technology. However, the crowdsourcing method is highly reliable in monitoring road conditions such as accidents, roadblocks, and traffic jams. Crowdsourcing refers to collective information acquired from a network of users for specific purposes. One of the earlier platforms is the Waze application where the Waze platform receives information from "Wazers" and reports the incidents graphically overlaid to existing maps. By using this method, the system can report pothole locations and give warning to other drivers. In 2017, Waze was reportedly collaborating with a state government in Malaysia to enable drivers to report pothole locations so that local authorities may have faster responses (Michael, 2017).

2.3.2 CPSS in Smart City

A smart city can be categorized as a CPSS application since it employs many sensors to sense the environment, such as the weather, the water level in the sinks, traffic congestion, etc. (Cassandras, 2016). The data can be reported on the web and/or physical places so that citizens can view them regularly to get some information. The web can also be accessed anytime and anywhere, even from different cities. In addition, users can also participate in giving some information or inputs to the government using the web or social media.

2.3.3 CPSS in Industry

Many industrial applications belong to CPS implementation, including computer-human communication in factories utilizing advanced sensing and AI technologies to increase efficiency. Recently, the concept of CPSS has been used. In its "Third Industrial Revolution," Special Report on Development and Change (The Economist, 2012), The Economist first explored the idea of collective output in 2012. In the same year, Wang (2012) addressed numerous aspects of social manufacturing, providing a better meaning of the word and its intricacies. Further, a collaborative growth process was discussed by Cao and Jiang (2012). They projected that customers would gain charge of all output-related operations from machining to assembly in an optimized market production system and that they did not need to rely on unsustainable manufacturing processes such as assembly lines.

Social manufacturing has become an emerging technology and market practice in the sense of mass individualization under the phenomena of specialization and socialization, allowing prosumers to produce personalized products and services by their partners via the integration of interorganizational manufacturing service processes. The word *consumer* has developed into *prosumer* in social manufacturing. A *prosumer*, implied in the word itself, helps the user to add to the production phase, thereby being a *producer*, thus, the modern phrase *prosumer*, which is also used in smart grid systems.

Because of the vast flexibility feature of social manufacturing, goods utilizing additive manufacturing (3D printable) will typically be widely relevant to social manufacturing. Currently, numerous industries from computer to military industries have been using additive manufacturing methods for production even though additive manufacturing is considered a niche at this moment. One of the potential candidates in social manufacturing is the garment industry. Even without considering the additive manufacturing approach, the textile industry is often highlighted to be an industry that would benefit from the emergence of social manufacturing due to its high requirement for customization. Users may deploy *smart mirrors*, a technology that enables users to fit the clothes into the body digitally. Digital information may be fed into the manufacturing process for production. With the latest development in 3D printable clothing, this virtual printing technique can be further applied in the context of producing garments. It is believed that this development is only a matter of time before receiving acceptance by user and manufacturer. The takeaway message from this subsection is that one of the greatest benefits of social production disruption is that it encourages customers to engage in generating product inputs. This helps the consumer to perform the producer's role. With this new development, manufacturers are liberated from the restriction of needing processing facilities.

2.3.4   CPSS in Healthcare

CPSS applications for healthcare have been rapidly developed recently. Healthcare applications include two human roles in the technology: service consumers and service providers (Zhou et al., 2020). A patient, as a service consumer, seeks for health services through an ICT platform and interacts with nurses, doctors, or specialists, which act as service providers. Further, CPSS healthcare applications generally can be classified into three categories (Voluntary Organisations Disability Group (VODG), 2013): telehealth, telecare, and assistive technology.

Telehealth refers to a remote patient's health monitoring system that consists of sensors and personalized management features, which may be connected to a hospital and/or doctors. The applications are needed by patients with critical diseases and elderly people who need regular monitoring without going to the hospital. It would be very beneficial for patients who are living remotely in rural or small towns. Wearable sensors are used to collect the patient's physiological data, such as body temperature, blood pressure, etc. The data are then provided to the doctors and nurses for further diagnosis (Zhang et al., 2018). One example of telehealth is a remote cardiac monitoring system (Kakria et al., 2015) where patient's medical data are collected using wearable biosensors and then transmitted wirelessly to a hand-held device to be extracted and processed. The system stores the data on a website portal, which can be accessed by medical staff such as nurses and doctors, and notifies the patient of his/her medical status. This technology has also been implemented for children (Burke & Hall, 2015), remote physiotherapy (Vallati et al., 2019), and controlling infectious diseases (Xu et al., 2018).

Telecare technology provides remote services or monitoring to help elderly people live conveniently at their home or neighborhood. The *SafeNeighborhood* (SN) platform, which was proposed by Garcia et al. (2017), provides a monitoring system for the elderly when they do outdoor activities. The wearable sensors utilize GPS to give information about the route taken by the user. The device also provides information on the physical health of the person, e.g., whether he/she has fallen, weather exposure, and risk of getting lost. Additionally, the mental health of the person can be identified through the walking pattern of the person. On top of that, the system is connected to the trusted neighbors, family, or caregiver to provide this information.

Assistive technology includes a device or platform to facilitate people to fulfill their needs, especially for health needs. This technology can be combined with telehealth and/or telecare technology. For example, a recommender system can be used to recommend a good hospital or doctor based on the patient's preferences (Huang et al., 2012; Jiang & Xu, 2014). The platform is very useful for young or inexperienced patients. It can be extended to a telehealth platform where the patient can do an online consultation with the selected doctor. These kinds of platforms are very useful for the elderly as they are sometimes difficult to leave home due to medical conditions. Another example is medical drones, which are used to deliver medicine to remote areas (Ackerman & Koziol, 2019; Hii et al., 2019).

2.3.5 CPSS in Education

CPSS applications in education are mostly related to moving offline or face-to-face interactions between teachers and students or among students themselves to online modes. The online teaching and learning activities, which use some advanced technologies such as IoT, VR, and AR, are sometimes called Education 4.0. The concept of Education 4.0 has been implemented for manufacturing industry training and workshops (Mourtzis et al., 2018). In particular, an ideal online learning environment should meet the offline teaching and learning requirement such as interactive sessions, assessment tools, pedagogical approach, and student engagement (Santos et al., 2018). Further, the virtual laboratory can also be established to assist students learning in rural areas (Hu et al., 2015; Rong et al., 2015). In addition, social robots can be used as learning tools, especially in science, technology, engineering, and mathematics (STEM) education (Lytridis et al., 2019).

For the past 10 years, massive open online courses (MOOCs) have become increasingly popular due to the development of automatic natural language processing (NLP) assessment tools. Some of the popular examples of MOOCs are created by EdX and Udacity where NLP and machine learning tools are used to grade short-answer and simple essay questions.

2.3.6 CPSS in Entertainment

It is not surprising to find significant enthusiasm with AI-based entertainment, which led to concerns that it reduces real human interactions. Many predicted that people would spend longer hours interacting with a display on their devices than being with others. CPSS enables entertainment (including traditional entertainment) to be more interactive and personalized for an individual or social groups, which are the key factors of the success of any form of entertainment. People also have diverse appeal in entertainment modes, and their preferences change over time.

One of the examples is social robots, which have important roles in entertainment as social robots can be used to perform the theatrical play, music, and stand-up comedy. They may create interaction with the audiences. Another application of CPSS in entertainment is the interactive game using VR technology and Arduino as the sensor interface (Tseng & Chu, 2017).

2.3.7 CPSS in Social Networks

With the advent of cheap smartphones, our culture has developed a vivid social layer unpresented in our past. For the first time in human culture, social networks have breached the limits of each individual's location, scope, and network scale. The CPSS structure is most conveniently demonstrated by social networking platforms, such as Facebook, Instagram, Weibo, Twitter, TikTok, and commonly called as an online community. Online community is where people interact using online social platforms (Xia & Ma, 2011). Generally, in online communities, human and nonhumans communicate using a peer-to-peer (P2P) model by building social relationships autonomously according to the owners' rules. The fundamental role of CPSS in the social community is to exchange information between users where the information can span from important news to leisure activities. By using information exchanged by users, the origin of social relationships and the type of social interaction can be detected and analyzed. One of the challenges using CPPS for social networking is the validity of the broadcasted news. Every individual has an obligation to self-verify the received news before transferring to others. A digital forensics platform for multimedia verification was discussed by Middleton et al. (2018). One example of CPSS application for leisure activities is a platform where the community can share and give recommendations of culinary destinations to users (Utomo & Hendradjaya, 2017). Society contributes to reporting issues in the neighborhood to the authority using a platform that can be considered as CPSS applications in social activities, which is part of smart city, as discussed above (Yetis & Karakose, 2020).

2.3.8 CPSS in Digital Commerce

Other than being used as online community platforms, social media can be used for commercial and marketing platforms. In particular, with social media, businesses can choose the location, demography, and even age group of account bearers to market their product. This enables companies to have better strategies to enhance their services to specific groups. Indeed, social media has effectively created new jobs, like social media marketing officers and influencers.

Inevitably, mainstream networking's most apparent advertisement innovation is the advent of digital ads via social media. In reality, social network marketing has recently proven to be a lucrative career option. The emphasis appears in leveraging new channels to support social media goods and services. We can see interconnectivity and cyber-physical overlap in any industry. Some company owners have also used both physical premise and virtual premise to improve profitability, whereas others focus exclusively on virtual business premise (e-shops) to reduce operational costs. Some sources say that the domination of e-shops significantly affects the physical business such that physical business has little choice but to reinvent to live. E-shop sites, such as LAZADA, Shopee, and Amazon Prime, have made it convenient and simple for vendors to sell their items. With such interconnected partnerships between social networks and trading, consumer interest and knowledge have become valuable assets. How will we be confident that this knowledge would not negatively impact the customer? These advanced data processing techniques may be used against the market by exploiting consumers' psychology. Such large online shopping specifics can use such knowledge to encourage unnecessary and unhealthy shopping lifestyles.

CPSS also provides better coordination for the customers. The introduction of numerous booking sites allowed retailers and service providers to help handle their customers. Nearly all forms of facilities such as dental centers, hairdressers, veterinarians, and restaurants are accessible with booking applications. We may predict that physical facilities are strongly interconnected with digital space, including social media. It is not impossible to envision an environment that eventually links all structures to the cyberspace. This will incorporate location sensors, such as GPS, which would alert the customer to any previous appointments.

2.4 Challenges in CPSSs

2.4.1 Safety and Security

Safety issues in CPSSs can be divided according to its level as threats and attacks. Threats refer to the opportunity of doing attacks. Both threats and attacks can be categorized into two: physical and cyberthreats (Yaacoub et al., 2020). Physical threats are defined as any threats related to physical damage, loss, and repair. Physical damage may be the damage to the electricity source, base stations, etc. Note that these utilities are commonly equipped with strong protection schemes. As a result, when they are damaged, the attack possibility may increase. Loss (e.g., total blackout) and repair (e.g., manual repair of the utilities due to faulty) may increase the attack possibility for the same reason. It is preferable to apply a self-healing process system for speeding the recovery process.

On the other hand, cyberthreats are harmful as they may create several problems (Alguliyev et al., 2018; Wang et al., 2010), such as confidentiality problems (user data leakage), integrity problems (data modification), reliability problems, availability problems, and authenticity problems. It is worth mentioning that cyberthreats are also scalable.

Physical attacks include the attacks on devices (such as USBs, hard drives, CCTV) and communication access (such as cable cut). Meanwhile, cyberattacks in CPSS include information leakage and inference attacks (Zhou et al., 2020). Information leakage can be in the form of eavesdropping, i.e., tapping the information by the adversary (Wang et al., 2010). Eavesdropping is also called passive attack.

Inference attacks include compromised-key attack, man-in-the-middle (MITM) attack, and denial-of-service (DoS) attack. In a compromised-key attack, an attacker obtains a key used to decrypt secure information and may modify the contents of the information without the knowledge of the sender or receiver. In the MITM attack, a fabricated message is sent to an operator, which deceives the target operator to take or to not take a specific function or carry out a certain action. Consequently, an MITM attack may cause undesirable events. A DoS attack is performed by directing a huge amount of network traffic to flood a target network or service, denying the access of legitimate requests.

2.4.2   Privacy and Ethical Issues

In CPSSs, privacy can be a major issue considering the large amount of data being collected and processed. Individual private information may be revealed when machine learning programs are used to make decisions and predictions. In the case where personalized data, such as the location of the device owner, is collected or exchanged by multiple sensory nodes, there should be no way that the owner of the device can be identified. While in certain situations where such information needs to be shared, proper authorization should be given or only in an anonymized fashion (Esterle & Grosu, 2016; Mishra et al., 2018). To ensure that the privacy of device owners is not infringed, CPSSs can implement trust-based security approaches, anonymity approaches, or access control approaches (Esterle & Grosu, 2016; Sharma & Bashir, 2020).

Ethical issues, though, are much more complicated. As human beings, we can differentiate between right and wrong and good and bad decisions. Machines, on the other hand, are usually designed to perform a specific task but will encounter problems when encountering situations that are outside the specified boundaries.

Hence, the integration of artificial moral agents (AMAs) into CPSSs is necessary to make decisions that honor privacy, uphold ethical standards, protect civil rights and individual liberty, and further the welfare of others (Allen et al., 2006). However, the designs of such AMAs will not be easy. The values implemented in AMAs are often common computer ethics such as data privacy, security, and digital rights. On the other hand, CPSSs may encounter situations where a decision made by the system will result in life and death, as often illustrated by trolley cases (Allen et al., 2006). Therefore, the moral or ethical decisions in CPSSs remain a challenge in today's design.

2.4.3 Interdependence and Compatibility

For a CPSS to operate, the integration of multiple devices or systems with different functions is often required. Although these devices or systems need to communicate and are interdependent of each other, their requirements may be different. The web is often used as a platform to integrate systems, but the diversity and heterogeneity of the CPSS limit the capability of the web (Mishra et al., 2018). Furthermore, the network control of a CPSS is different with a conventional network and thus cannot apply the OSI model for the design standards (Zhou et al., 2020; Kim & Kumar, 2013). Hence, CPSS needs to have a standardized protocol for seamless communication between the devices or systems within a CPSS. Web 3.0 or the Semantic Web is also useful as it enhances the CPSS's ability in understanding information from different devices (Mishra & Jain, 2020).

2.5 Conclusion

This chapter has provided an overview of CPSSs that connect humans with physical systems and social networks. It has been discussed that WSNs, 5G, big data, AI, VR, and AR are some of the essential underlying technologies in building the CPSSs. The CPSS architecture consists of three layers, which are the physical layer, cyber layer, and social layer. The physical layer represents the physical environment, and the social layer represents humans that interact with the system. The cyber layer bridges the physical layer and social layer via the Internet using emerging computing techniques. The CPSS has been widely implemented in applications around us. These applications are categorized into eight different domains, namely, transportation, smart city, industry, healthcare, education, entertainment, social networks, and commercial. The implementations and impacts of these CPSS applications have been thoroughly discussed. The integration of CPS into our daily lives (thus, CPSS) has undoubtedly raised concerns, in both social and technical aspects. The associated challenges of CPSS have been presented in three different categories: safety and security, privacy and ethical issues, and interdependence and compatibility.

Review Questions
1. How is CPSS different from IoT?
2. What are the elements that constitute a CPSS? Please elaborate.
3. What are the enablers of CPSS? Please elaborate.
4. What are the applications of CPSS in the medical field?
5. What are the applications of CPSS in education?
6. What are the safety and security issues in CPSS?
7. How can privacy and ethical issues play their roles in CPSS?

Questions for Discussion
1. What are the key issues associated with the current development of the CPSS system?
2. What are the new markets (opportunities) that may arise in the view of the connected world?
3. How can CPSS affect the economy?
4. How can CPSS affect social life?

Problem Statements for Young Researchers
1. There are several safety and security issues that are related to cyberattacks in CPSS. How can the cyberattack be detected and minimized?
2. CPSS will change social life, and it will bring both positive and negative impacts to human lives. What are the positive and negative impacts of CPSS?
3. As CPSS is related to hardware and software, what are the loopholes in the hardware and software that can be discovered in the applications of CPSS? What are the implications of these loopholes?

References

Ackerman, E., & Koziol, M. (2019). In the air with Zipline's medical delivery drones. In *IEEE Spectrum*. Accessed September 1, 2020, from https://spectrum.ieee.org/robotics/drones/in-the-air-with-ziplines-medical-delivery-drones

Aksu, H., Babun, L., Conti, M., Tolomei, G., & Uluagac, A. S. (2018). Advertising in the IoT era: Vision and challenges. *IEEE Communication Magazine, 56*(11), 138–144. https://doi.org/10.1109/MCOM.2017.1700871.

Alguliyev, R., Imamverdiyev, Y., & Sikhostat, L. (2018). Cyber-physical systems and their security issues. *Computers in Industry, 100*, 212–223. https://doi.org/10.1016/j.compind.2018.04.017.

Al-Karaki, J. N., & Kamal, A. E. (2004). Routing techniques in wireless sensor networks: A survey. *IEEE Wireless Communications, 11*(6), 6–28. https://doi.org/10.1109/mwc.2004.1368893.

Allen, C., Wallach, W., & Smit, I. (2006). Why machine ethics? *IEEE Intelligent Systems, 21*(4), 12–17. https://doi.org/10.1109/mis.2006.83.

Andrews, J. G., Buzzi, S., Choi, W., Hanly, S. V., Lozano, A., Soong, A. C. K., & Zhang, J. C. (2014). What will 5G be? *IEEE Journal on Selected Areas in Communications, 32*(6), 1065–1082. https://doi.org/10.1109/jsac.2014.2328098.

Atzori, L., Iera, A., & Morabito, G. (2010). The internet of things: A survey. *Computing Networks, 54*(15), 2787–2805. https://doi.org/10.1016/j.comnet.2010.05.010.

Azuma, R., Baillot, Y., Behringer, R., Feiner, S., Julier, S., & MacIntyre, B. (2001). Recent advances in augmented reality. *IEEE Computer Graphics and Applications, 21*(6), 34–47. https://doi.org/10.1109/38.963459.

Bowman, D. A., & McMahan, R. P. (2007). Virtual reality: How much immersion is enough? *Computer, 40*(7), 36–43. https://doi.org/10.1109/mc.2007.257.

Burke, B. L., & Hall, R. W. (2015). Telemedicine: Pediatric applications. *Pediatrics, 136*(1), 293–308. https://doi.org/10.1542/peds.2015-1517.

Cao, W., & Jiang, P. Y. (2012). Cloud machining community for social manufacturing. *In Applied Mechanics and Materials, 220*, 61–64.

Cassandras, C. G. (2016). Smart cities as cyber-physical social systems. *Engineering, 2*(2), 156–158. https://doi.org/10.1016/J.ENG.2016.02.012.

Chen, X., & Lin, X. (2014). Big data deep learning: Challenges and perspectives. *IEEE Access, 2,* 514–525. https://doi.org/10.1109/ACCESS.2014.2325029.

Chen, J., & Ran, X. (2019). Deep learning with edge computing: A review. *Proceedings of the IEEE, 107*(8), 1655–1674. https://doi.org/10.1109/JPROC.2019.2921977.

Esterle, L., & Grosu, R. (2016). Cyber-physical systems: Challenge of the 21st century. *Elektrotech. Inftech, 133,* 299–303. https://doi.org/10.1007/s00502-016-0426-6.

Garcia, A. C. B., Vivacqua, A. S., Sanchez-Pi, N., Marti, L., & Molina, J. M. (2017). Crowd-based ambient assisted living to monitor the elderly's health outdoors. *IEEE Software, 34*(6), 53–57. https://doi.org/10.1109/MS.2017.4121217.

Hii, M. S. Y., Courtney, P., & Royall, P. G. (2019). An evaluation of the delivery of medicines using drones. *Drones, 3*(3), 52. https://doi.org/10.3390/drones3030052.

Hu, F., Morris, T. H., McCallum, D. M., & Zhou, H. (2015). Towards a multimedia-based virtual classroom on cyber-physical system (CPS) security education for both city and rural schools. In *2015 ASEE Annual Conference & Exposition,* Washington, June 2015.

Huang, Y.-F., Liu, P., Pan, Q., & Lin, J.-S. (2012). A doctor recommendation algorithm based on doctor performances and patient preferences. In *2012 International Conference on Wavelet Active Media Technology and Information Processing (ICWAMTIP),* China, December 2012. IEEE.

Jiang, H., & Xu, W. (2014). How to find your appropriate doctor: An integrated recommendation framework in big data context. In *2014 IEEE Symposium on Computational Intelligence in Healthcare and e-health (CICARE),* USA, December 2014. IEEE.

Kakria, P., Tripathi, N. K., & Kitipawang, P. (2015). A real-time health monitoring system for remote cardiac patients using smartphone and wearable sensors. *International Journal of Telemedicine and Applications.* https://doi.org/10.1155/2015/373474

Kim, K.-D., & Kumar, P. (2013). An overview and some challenges in cyber-physical systems. *Journal of the Indian Institute of Science, 93,* 341–352.

Lv, Z., Chen, D., Lou, R., & Wang, Q. (2021). Intelligent edge computing based on machine learning for smart city. *Future Generation Computer Systems, 115,* 90–99. https://doi.org/10.1016/j.future.2020.08.037.

Lytridis, C., Bazinas, C., Kaburlasos, V. G., Vassileva-Aleksandrova, V., Youssfi, M., Mestari, M., Ferelis, V., & Jaki, A. (2019). Social robots as cyber-physical actors in entertainment and education. In *2019 International Conference on Software, Telecommunications and Computer Networks (SoftCOM),* Croatia, September 2019. IEEE.

Memos, V. A., Psannis, K. E., Ishibashi, Y., Kim, B.-G., & Gupta, B. B. (2018). An efficient algorithm for media-based surveillance system (EAMSuS) in IoT smart city framework. *Future Generation Computer Systems, 83,* 619–628. https://doi.org/10.1016/j.future.2017.04.039.

Michael, K. (2017). *New way to get holes patched.* Accessed September 1, 2020, from https://www.thestar.com.my/metro/metro-news/2017/11/21/new-way-to-get-holes-patched-motorists-can-effectively-use-navigation-apps-to-highlight-potholes-and

Middleton, S. E., Papadopoulos, S., & Kompatsiaris, Y. (2018). Social computing for verifying social media content in breaking news. *IEEE Internet Computing, 22*(2), 83–89. https://doi.org/10.1109/MIC.2018.112102235.

Mishra, S., & Jain, S. (2020). Ontologies as a semantic model in IoT. *International Journal of Computers and Applications, 42*(3), 233–243. https://doi.org/10.1080/1206212X.2018.1504461.

Mishra, S., Jain, S., Rai, C., & Gandhi, N. (2018). Security challenges in semantic web of things. In *International Conference on Innovations in Bio-Inspired Computing and Applications (IBICA)* (Vol. 939, pp. 162–169). Cham: Springer.

Mourtzis, D., Vlachou, E., Dimitrakopoulos, G., & Zogopoulos, V. (2018). Cyber-physical systems and education 4.0 – The teaching factory 4.0 concept. *Procedia Manufacturing, 23,* 129–134. https://doi.org/10.1016/j.promfg.2018.04.005.

Rong, Y., Rajakaruna, S., Murray, I., Mohammadi, N., & Chiong, R. (2015). Transforming the communications engineering laboratory education through remotely accessible software radio platform. In *Proceedings Australasian Association for Engineering Education Conference,* 2016.

Santos, R., Devincenzi, S., Botelho, S., & Bichet, M. (2018). A model for implementation of educational cyber physical systems. *Revista Espacios, 39*(10), 36–53.

Sha, K., Yang, T. A., Wei, W., & Davari, S. (2020). A survey of edge computing-based designs for IoT security. *Digital Communications and Networks, 6*, 195–202. https://doi.org/10.1016/j.dcan.2019.08.006.

Sharma, T., & Bashir, M. (2020). Preserving privacy in cyber-physical-social systems: An anonymity and access control approach. In *Proceedings of the 1st Workshop on Cyber-Physical Social Systems co-located with the 9th International Conference on the Internet of Things (IoT 2019)*, Spain, January 2020.

Sheth, A., Anantharam, P., & Henson, C. (2013). Physical-cyber-social computing: An early 21st century approach. *IEEE Intelligent System, 28*(1), 78–82. https://doi.org/10.1109/MIS.2013.20.

Shi, W., Cao, J., Zhang, Q., Li, Y., & Xu, L. (2016). Edge computing: Vision and challenges. *IEEE Internet of Things Journal, 3*(5), 637–646. https://doi.org/10.1109/jiot.2016.2579198.

The Economist. (2012). *A third industrial revolution*. Accessed September 1, 2020, from http://www.economist.com/node/21552901

Tseng, J.-L., & Chu, C.-W. (2017). Interaction design in virtual reality game using Arduino sensors. In *Simulation and Gaming*.

Utomo, S. B., & Hendradjaya, B. (2017). Usability testing and evaluation of smart culinary system based on cyber-physical-social system. In: *2017 International Conference on Information Technology Systems and Innovation (ICITSI)*, Indonesia, October 2017. IEEE.

Vallati, C., Virdis, A., Gesi, M., Carbonaro, N., & Tognetti, A. (2019). ePhysio: A wearable-enabled platform for the remote management of musculoskeletal diseases. *Sensors, 19*(1), 2. https://doi.org/10.3390/s19010002.

Voluntary Organisations Disability Group (VODG). (2013). Using assistive technology to support personalization in social care. In *The National Care Forum (NCF)*. Accessed September 1, 2020, from https://www.vodg.org.uk/wp-content/uploads/2013-VODG-Assistive-technology-report.pdf

Wang, F.-Y. (2012). From social calculation to social manufacturing: One coming industrial revolution. *Bulletin of the Chinese Academy of Sciences, 27*(6), 658–669.

Wang, E. K., Ye, Y., Xu, X., Yiu, S. M., Hui, L. C. K., & Chow, K. P. (2010). Security issues and challenges for cyber physical system. In *2010 IEEE/ACM International Conference on Green Computing and Communications & International Conference on Cyber, Physical and Social Computing*, China, March 2011. IEEE.

Weiser, M. (1999). The computer for the 21st century. *ACM SIGMOBILE Mobile Computing and Communications Review, 3*(3), 3–11.

Wu, X., Zhu, X., Wu, G., & Ding, W. (2014). Data mining with big data. *IEEE Transactions on Knowledge and Data Engineering, 26*(1), 97–107. https://doi.org/10.1109/tkde.2013.109.

Xia, F., & Ma, J. (2011). Building smart communities with cyber-physical systems. In *Proceedings of 1st International Symposium on From Digital Footprints to Social and Community Intelligence*, China, September 2011. Association for Computing Machinery.

Xu, Q., Su, Z., & Yu, S. (2018). Green social CPS based e-healthcare systems to control the spread of infectious diseases. In: *2018 IEEE International Conference on Communications (ICC)*, USA, May 2018. IEEE.

Yaacoub, J.-P. A., Salman, O., Noura, H. N., Kaaniche, N., Chehab, A., & Malli, M. (2020). Cyber-physical systems security: Limitations, issues and future trends. *Microprocessors and Microsystems, 77*. https://doi.org/10.1016/j.micpro.2020.103201

Yakub, H., & Reine, R. (2018). Performance analysis of green-wall infrastructure using IoT devices. In *IOP Conference Series: Materials Science and Engineering*. Curtin University Technology Science and Engineering (CUTSE) International Conference, Malaysia, November 2018. Vol. 495. IOP Publishing.

Yetis, H., & Karakose, M. (2020). A cyber-physical-social system based method for smart citizens in smart cities. In *2020 24th International Conference on Information Technology (IT)*, Montenegro, February 2020. IEEE.

Zhang, W., Kumar, M., Yu, J., & Yang, J. (2018). Medical long-distance monitoring system based on internet of things. *EURASIP Journal on Wireless Communications and Networking, 176*. https://doi.org/10.1186/s13638-018-1178-2

Zhou, Y., Yu, F. R., & Kuo, Y. (2020). Cyber-physical-social systems: A state-of-the-art survey, challenges and opportunities. *IEEE Communication Surveys & Tutorials, 22*(1), 389–425. https://doi.org/10.1109/COMST.2019.2959013

Regina Reine received the B.Eng. degree in electrical engineering from Trisakti University, Jakarta, Indonesia, in 2000, the M.Sc. degree in computation engineering from UMIST, Manchester, UK, in 2002, the M.Sc. degree in electrical engineering from the University of Aberdeen, Scotland, UK, in 2004, and the Ph.D. degree in electrical engineering from Curtin University Malaysia, in 2016. She was a Lecturer with the Department of Electrical Engineering, Curtin University Malaysia until 2019. She is currently managing research projects in Twigx Research in the United Kingdom. Her research interests include the next generation wireless communications, IoT, power-line communications, and unmanned aerial vehicles.

Filbert H. Juwono received the B.Eng. degree in electrical engineering and the M.Eng. degree in telecommunication engineering from the University of Indonesia, Depok, Indonesia, in 2007 and 2009, respectively, and the Ph.D. degree in electrical and electronic engineering from The University of Western Australia, Perth, WA, Australia, in 2017. He is currently a Lecturer with the Department of Electrical and Computer Engineering, Curtin University Malaysia. His research interests include signal processing for communications, wireless communications, power-line communications, IoT, and biomedical engineering. He was a recipient of the prestigious Australian Awards Scholarship, in 2012. He serves as an Associate Editor for IEEE ACCESS and a Review Editor for Frontiers in Signal Processing.

Zee Ang Sim received the B.Eng. degree in electronic and communications engineering and the Ph.D. degree in electrical and computer engineering from Curtin University Malaysia, Miri, Malaysia, in 2015 and 2020, respectively. He is currently an Assistant Professor with the School of Engineering and Physical Sciences, Heriot-Watt University Malaysia, Putrajaya, Malaysia. His research interests include signal processing for communications, wireless communications, and filter design for communication systems.

W. K. Wong received the M.Eng. and Ph.D. degrees from Universiti Malaysia Sabah in 2012 and 2016, respectively. Prior to joining academia, he was with the telecommunication and building services industry. He is currently serving as a Senior Lecturer with the Department of Electrical and Computer Engineering, Curtin University Malaysia. His research interests include embedded system development, machine learning applications, and image processing.

Chapter 3
The Web of Things Ecosystem

Anindita Saha, Mayurakshi Jana, Chandreyee Chowdhury, Suparna Biswas, and Diptangshu Pandit

Abstract The Internet of Things (IoT) ecosystem is gradually changing our activities and social interactions through the wide scale of applications it offers. However, these applications rely on the networking protocol stack where the application layer of the stack is implemented differently by different applications. As a result, a variety of data representation and diverse application layer protocols can be found in place adopted by a range of IoT-based services. This creates the issue of interoperability and scalability. Web of Things is a concept that interestingly applies the Web technologies to IoT-based applications. This chapter introduces the concept of the Web of Things, reviews its application potential, and discusses the details of forming such an ecosystem.

Keywords IoT · WoT · Semantics · Web · Crowdsourcing · Semantic computing · Ontology

Key Points
- Briefly introduces the concept of WoT and smart connected web along with IoT-WoT convergence
- Discusses the architecture of WoT such as REST (Representational State Transfer) and WS-*

A. Saha (✉)
Department of Information Technology, Techno Main Salt Lake, Kolkata, West Bengal, India

M. Jana · S. Biswas
Computer Science and Engineering, Maulana Abul Kalam Azad University of Technology, Kolkata, India

C. Chowdhury
Computer Science and Engineering, Jadavpur University, Kolkata, India

D. Pandit
Teesside University, Middlesbrough, UK
e-mail: D.Pandit@tees.ac.uk

- Explains several crowdsourced applications of WoT with real-life implementations
- Discusses several challenges of the WoT ecosystem and how they can be handled
- Narrates the existing semantic approaches along with their integration with WoT

3.1 Introduction

In recent years, rapid and comparatively successful advancements in communication technologies have resulted in an upsurge of smart sensors, and smart applications. Lifestyles are changing at a faster rate and the Internet of Things (IoT) plays a major role in creating a new shift toward urbanizing several applications through pervasive computing. IoT may be defined as a systematic network of "things" or physical objects, powered by embedded technology to communicate over several networking interfaces, that can sense as well as interact with the external environment, and the entire system can eventually be connected to the Internet on a wider scale (https:// www.gartner.com/en/information-technology/glossary/internet-of-things). Things refer to real-life physical objects (such as electronic appliances) which are digitally enhanced with wireless sensors and actuators and other embedded technologies such as RFID and WSN.

IoT has been the driving force behind the evolution of the Web of Things (WoT). WoT refers to the software architecture that integrates real-life "things" into the web. While IoT creates a network of things, devices, objects, and applications manifesting the functionalities of a network layer, WoT integrates them into the web, exhibiting the functionalities of an application layer over it through main-stream Web technologies. This application layer simplifies the complex working principles of IoT, provides URLs to connected objects on the web, and makes them linkable and interoperable for users through APIs and standard data models (Guinard & Trifa, 2009). Web servers can be embedded inside smart things and the web architectural style of REST is applied, which is implemented by URIs to identify resources on the web, and languages such as XML and HTML along with traditional HTTP, thus creating simple, scalable, loosely coupled, and reusable Web services.

As a result, clients can interact with smart things through a web browser to create applications with real-world physical objects involving virtual Web services with ample possibilities for customization and flexibility (Guinard et al., 2011a). Thus, WoT allows everything to be connected to the web, and with Web services it is possible to have open access to information that can be reused across independent platforms. Due to the reuse of HTTP standards, it will be easier to treat every object as a resource on the web and to integrate these objects with web content.

From the above discussion, it is evident that IoT is a network of physical devices, digitally augmented and connected to the Internet through sensors, actuators, communication, and computational interfaces. Each device has its own protocols and this makes IoT platforms difficult to program, as the protocols and standards are not publicly accessible but funded privately, which is why IoT is tightly coupled with connecting networks and applications. WoT, on the other hand, is a network of the web created specifically to leverage the IoT platforms, adding a software layer to it to connect the "things" to the web. WoT deals with Web servers, and due to a common API to handle multiple protocols of IoT, it is easy to program the loosely coupled application layer of WoT. Thus, a convergence of these two platforms enables the digitally enhanced "things" to implement "smart connected Web" without any human intervention, which not only guarantees an adaptive synchronization between these devices but also allows the creation of new services with these heterogeneous device networks. The smart connected web platform has three layers: IoT-WoT networking layer, platform layer, and application/service layer. The networking layer is responsible for interconnection between several IoT and WoT things, providing real-time monitoring of network functions. The platform layer synchronizes web resources with the "things" and the application layer, and through its open API, creates a mashup of services of IoT-WoT applications. Thus, the IoT-WoT convergence platform or "smart connected Web" provides global inter-compatibility to users for easy communication with all "things" connected via the web (Yu et al., 2016).

3.2 Architecture of WoT

In comparison to traditional client server architecture, WoT has a flat model and aims to integrate physical "things" into the web so that they can provide interoperable and composable Web services. Integration may be done either directly, for example for a home appliance, or indirectly, for example for an RFID through a server-embedded RFID reader. For direct integration, it is mandatory for the "Thing" to have an IP address so that direct communication is possible through the Web browser from any terminal. For indirect integration, there is an intermediate proxy between the Thing and the Web, popularly known as a smart gateway. This functions as a mediator between the smart thing to understand its protocols and APIs, and creates an abstraction for them and provides uniform access to the web via standard web APIs. As the integration of smart things is possible, it is imperative to abstract these Things into reusable Web services, which are software systems designed for interoperable communication within machines connected via a network, as per W3C (World Web Consortium) (Zeng et al., 2011).

There are two major approaches for the development of the Web services REST (Representational State Transfer) and WS-*, where the former is considered to be the best architecture for WoT. In simple terms, a Web service is a network-accessible interface to an application functionality, and acts as an abstraction layer between the application code and the application user. WS-*are known to provide mechanisms to use resources for distributed applications on remote devices in a similar manner to local devices (Guinard et al., 2011b). Functionalities available on one server may be used as a method call for specific applications running on remote servers, which is done through network protocols, and packet formats by the Web service protocol stack. For example, a server meant to forecast weather may provide a method to access temperature which can be called by any application running on a remote device connected to the Internet. Hence, ports and bindings are the two important components of WS-* that provide the required application layer and network layer support respectively. For application data to be carried over a network by transport layer there is a need for packaging the same in a common format; SOAP (Mitra & Lafon, 2003) is a common packaging format consolidated over XML and, following that, WS-* provides a set of protocols, allowing servers and clients to communicate with each other. Users can request services which can be encapsulated using SOAP and transmitted over the network with the help of HTTP protocol. There is a machine-readable description for the ports and bindings of a Web service to be specified using WSDL or Web Services Description Language, and if the functionality of a sensor node is expressed using this, it is easier to access it through specified method calls.

REST, on the other hand, is lightweight in comparison to WS-*, which is based on SOAP-based messages with XML and HTTP protocol for Remote Procedure Call (RPC). In REST, URIs or Uniform Resource Identifiers are used to represent each Thing and the content of that Thing can be obtained by using simple HTTP methods such as GET and PUT. REST emphasizes simple point-to-point HTTP communication using conventional XML or JSON. This makes REST less complex, easily mashed up or integrated ad hoc with Web services, and ideal for devices with constrained resources. REST provides loosely coupled Web services to clients through a ubiquitous API for smart things, in addition to being robust and scalable in comparison to SOAP-based WS-* standards. In comparison, REST is more acceptable nowadays for a number of reasons. SOAP uses standard message formats for communication and produces greater network traffic with higher latency. This affects performance metrics such as throughput and response time. Furthermore, SOAP messages require larger bandwidth and message encoding consumes resources, which leads to high performance overheads (Mumbaikar & Padiya, 2013).

Interestingly, in direct integration of Things onto the Web, smart things can directly access their RESTful APIs because Web servers are embedded, which eliminates the need to convert HTTP requests of different clients into the exact protocols of heterogeneous smart devices. In case of indirect integration, the proxy or smart gateways act as a Web server to abstract the communication with RESTful API using drivers. When a request to a smart device comes from the web across the RESTful API, the gateway converts the request to the device-understandable API, and communication is carried out using the protocol recognized by the same, as shown in Fig. 3.1 (Guinard et al., 2010).

3.3 Web of Things Applications

The Web of Things has several applications. The main goal of these applications is to facilitate the appropriate deployment of multiple and heterogeneous systems with simultaneous provision of cost effectiveness and time management. The WoT group (WOT GROUP, n.d.) is working to standardize efficient communication protocols between inter-IoT devices as well as between these devices and the Internet.

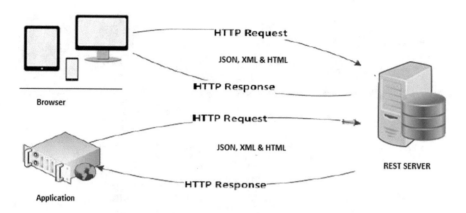

Fig. 3.1 RESTful architecture of the Web of Things

3.3.1   Crowdsourced Applications

Crowdsourcing has gained popularity due to its potential to incorporate human intelligence in order to accumulate heterogeneous data collected from various sensors in a ubiquitous environment. In active crowdsourcing, as shown in Fig. 3.2, individuals with varied domains of knowledge voluntarily undertake a task given to them by an institution or an organization, entailing mutual benefits among them (Chowdhury & Roy, 2017). Crowdsourcing can be applied to several areas, as discussed below.

Smart Transportation With the emergence of IoT, there is a huge demand for connected vehicles that are well equipped with smart devices to provide information-related transportation of the same. With crowdsourcing, vehicles can collect data related to traffic or road safety, road maps, traffic congestion, and accidents much more effectively in comparison to conventional methods which require various resources to accomplish the task. The crowdsourced applications provide real-time data without delay in the complex and complicated vehicular environment and can give accurate information on sudden changes of vehicular data at any point in time during the trip. This data can be used for active decision making for safety and intelligence of the traffic system. Research reveals that by using crowdsourcing, vehicles can be tracked through the smartphone GPS, and road conditions detected and road surfaces monitored with more accuracy or even understand the intersection of roads across, generated through crowdsourcing (Li et al., 2020). One of the most popular crowdsourced traffic and navigation apps used in practice is Waze (https://digital.hbs.edu/platform-rctom/submission/how-crowdsourcing-is-changing-the-waze-we-drive/, n.d.), providing a database of traffic and road condition information which is publicly available and shared with the government as a stream of constantly updated data in real time. Authorities within cities, such as traffic engineers/municipal personnel, may be able to receive crowdsourced data from users about updated

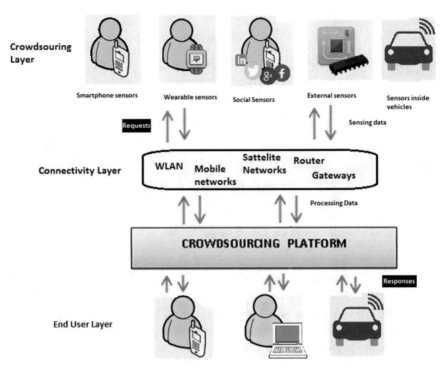

Fig. 3.2 Crowdsourcing architecture

traffic conditions or live information about congestion or even accidents, and may take necessary actions providing targeted solutions.

Smart Parking With the emergence of smart devices, intelligent transportation systems have become the essence of smart cities. Machine learning approaches such as spatial-temporal CNN-based classifiers (Saif et al., 2020) can be used to collect parking experiences from different vehicles in context, through GPS, and recommendations may be made to vehicles to figure out parking lots even without real-time data. This crowdsourcing method of detecting parking lots is novel and encouraging for individuals to find easy parking by sharing their parking experience with others (Nie et al., 2019). To facilitate autonomous parking in urban areas, crowdsourcing and fog computing can be used to assist AVs to collect parking information, locate free space, and find a relation with nearby traffic conditions, which might have an effect on the estimation of parking availability in that area (Zhu et al., 2019). There are several real-life applications that entail infrastructure-based smart parking, such as the San Francisco-based project SFPark (SFMTA, n.d.), which demands high initial investments and substantial maintenance cost. There are also a few pure crowdsourced-based solutions such as Open Spot (Kincaid, 2010) which are also effective in the real world.

Smart Environment Ensuring a smart environment is essential for a smart city, and crowdsourcing has ample scope in this regard. Air pollution is hazardous to human health, and handheld devices are proposed by researchers (Munasinghe et al., 2017) that can collect levels of poisonous gases in the atmosphere using sensors to monitor air quality in real time. The system can also collect, transmit, store, analyze, process, and give feedback through Android applications and visual platforms. Here, crowdsourcing can aid in superior data collection through the general public better than conventional approaches, and allows for greater accuracy with low cost and more coverage area. In large cities air pollution has a greater impact on inhabitants, and crowdsourcing can be leveraged to collect data from quality sensors inside floating vehicles from all across the city as the air quality is measurable inside them when the windows are open. Thus, the air quality of the area of the moving vehicle can be crowdsensed and analyzed, and a fine-grained air quality map can be prepared for public benefit (Huang et al., 2018). AirVisual, one of the most well-known social enterprises for air quality data and its forecasting, may be considered as a first-of-its-kind crowdsourced air pollution measurement system. It hosts the largest global dataset for air quality, from approximately 9000 cities in 70 countries, and provides all of the information people need to combat polluted environments (AirVisual).

Smart Waste Management Waste management is an important aspect of a smart city, and garbage collection is a major issue in this regard. It is possible to apply crowdsourcing concepts by involving citizens in uploading images to a server through mobile apps. These images can be analyzed through computer vision techniques to estimate garbage volumes, which enables the municipality to collect it efficiently across the city (Suresh et al., 2016). Images were taken from eight perspectives and the system achieved an overall accuracy of 85%. Researchers have revealed that citizens can be empowered to report to the higher authorities about uncollected garbage through mobile applications. Complaints made by the "crowd" are then verified and necessary actions can be taken by authorities to maintain the cleanliness of the smart city (Singh et al., 2017). In recent years, Crowdsourcing has emerged out as a valuable mechanism to involve the general public in collecting information about solid waste landfills in urban cities like Kinshasa where, as per Mavakala et al. (2017). In this participatory project, a spatial and temporal database is created through information collected from citizens, and visualizing it through an interactive map. The project has also resulted in disposal of solid waste amounting to approximately 600,000 m^3, including 61 public disposals, and 151 wild dumps.

Smart Home Crowdsourcing has ample opportunities to be used in a smart home, especially for data-driven devices used there, where datasets of real-world network traffic have been constructed from these smart home devices within home networks, by crowdsourcing through an open source tool called IoT inspector. This ensures the security and privacy of these devices at home, which are often susceptible to attacks and tracking due to weak TLS implementations (Huang et al., 2020).

Smart Health Various kinds of research has revealed that crowdsourcing can be an effective tool in global health care as it can be leveraged to collect a huge amount of data from a wide range of individuals across the globe (Wazny, 2018). Studies have reported that it can be used to perform medical diagnosis and surveillance, and can be used in many other medical disciplines, such as genetics, nutrition, psychology, and general medicine. Applying crowdsourcing in smart health care can be cost effective and flexible, can improve accuracy through gamification, and can also raise public awareness toward medical criticality. Some of the real-life examples of crowdsourcing in digital health may be seen in Crowdsourcing in Healthcare (n.d.).

Smart Agriculture Several initiatives have been taken in the field of agriculture to utilize the concept of crowdsourcing that can generate data from farmers related to agricultural applications. The data can be about agricultural land use, soil, weather, phenology, crop calendar, weeds, diseases and pests, yield and vegetation status, and price. Farming practices can be improved by farmers sharing information, and these inputs help agricultural researchers, practitioners, and scientists to develop applications for better farming (Minet et al., 2017). Yield gap analysis is an important aspect of agriculture and it can be conducted appropriately through crowdsourced data from farmers to use field observation as an alternative to data collected through remote and on-field sensors, as depicted in Beza et al. (2017). Weed management is a crucial aspect of agriculture, and smartphone applications can be successfully used to capture weed images, to be processed through image processing algorithms at the backend. Two levels of crowdsourcing can be composed of experts and non-experts who can contribute substantially to identification of weeds at a much lower cost, and thus it is easier to impose quick remedial measures to prevent infestations (Rahman et al., 2015). In real life, Mutembesa et al. (2018) present a mobile ad hoc surveillance system that can monitor pests as well as viral diseases through crowdsourcing with farmers via mobile phones. The system was deployed in Uganda for 76 weeks and was found to be effective in harnessing widespread use among the farming community to provide real-time surveillance of viral disease in cassava plants.

Smart Education Crowdsourcing concepts are equally relevant in the field of education to develop a smart learning environment, where teachers, students, and administrators can contribute knowledge to improve the teaching-learning process. Through crowdsourcing, the points of view of the team members, including students, are collected, and with the help of a thorough panel discussion several possible solutions are brainstormed to choose the best. Students not only listen to the lectures but can also evaluate the quality and content of the classes, give suggestions for improvement, rate the teaching skills, and eventually contribute to creating teaching materials (Simic et al., 2015). Some real-life examples of crowdsourced applications in smart education may be seen in WTF Columbia, a Website created by students to voice their suggestions about improving the campus (Crowdsourcing in Education, n.d.). In addition, several other universities such as the University of Calgary have turned to crowdsourcing in order to generate measures for cost savings and revenue generation.

Smart Industry In the era of Industry 4.0, there is a close connection between customers, workers, and employers in several aspects, such as decision making, performance metrics, and feedback collection. With crowdsourcing, an impressive amount of data can be collected from individuals which can prove beneficial for Industry 4.0, for efficient production, cost effectiveness, quality control, product customization, product availability, as well as work environment and safety (Pilloni, 2018). In addition, process monitoring, asset tracking, customer feedback, logistic tracking etc. can be successfully accomplished for industrial spaces through crowdsensing by integrating human intellect into machine intelligence and information sharing (Shu et al., 2017). According to Crowdsourcing in Industry (n.d.), companies such as Lego have successfully implemented crowdsourcing to improve their revenue by allowing users to design new products which are opened to all for voting. Those with the maximum number of votes are sent to production. Other companies such as Lays, one of the world's leading chip manufacturers, encourages customers to create their own flavors for innovative ideas on the company's behalf.

3.3.2 Conventional IoT Applications

IoT has an immensely bright future around the world and is going to be the pioneer of crucial innovations and major investments in the near future (Dutta et al., 2019). There is a wide scope of heterogeneous applications of IoT generating a massive amount of data that needs to be analyzed and processed through data science, and smart cities are the best manifestation of this. There are various components that contribute toward making a city "smart." Smart transportation must be ensured in such cities to control and manage traffic during busy hours of work days. In contrast to the traditional centralized traffic management approach, IoT can be applied to develop a system that can sense the ongoing road traffic through sensors, cameras, and RFIDs on the roadside, and govern these in a decentralized fashion. The data collected from sensors are processed by local servers and cumulative traffic density is calculated at a given time (Javaid et al., 2018). IoT also enables device-to-device communication without any human intervention through the Internet, using ultrasonic sensors in devices that collect data about traffic density which is then transmitted to the other devices using an Android application (Mahalank et al., 2016). This helps users to take alternative routes, avoiding congestion and ensuring better traffic management.

Smart parking IoT can be a solution to limited car parking spaces in urban areas. Real-time parking systems are developed (Lookmuang et al., 2018) that can not only inform drivers about an empty parking space but also help to locate that particular space to minimize congestion in the adjoining area. Users obtain information about the parking area, parking slots as well as several relevant information through appropriate applications. Usage of computer vision can help drivers to detect a vehicle in huge parking areas and also monitor the parked vehicle to ensure security.

Smart cities must also ensure a *smart environment*, which is highly affected by air pollution. IoT can facilitate integrating sensor-collected data remotely with an application for real-time monitoring of pollution levels to reduce risk factors (Alshamsi et al., 2017). Especially for city dwellers, air pollution can be measured by a wearable smartwatch that can detect concentration of air pollutants such as CO and CO_2 through embedded sensors at a low cost and cast these data to a smartphone application to present them to the wearer in an appropriate manner (Kodali et al., 2020).

Smart waste management is essential to the novelty of a smart city. Smart waste collection is possible using smart waste bins that have embedded ultrasonic sensors and gas sensors to automatically detect the maximum level of waste and the presence of hazardous gases. The collected data is sent to the municipality after processing via the cloud server and concerned authorities can check the current status of the bin (whether it has crossed the threshold level of waste or gas) online. The shortest routes can then be adopted to reach to the appropriate location to collect waste using less fuel for economic gains (Misra et al., 2018).

Conventional homes can be transformed into *smart homes* where sensor-embedded devices (light, fans, etc.) may be controlled remotely through the user's Smartphone, and the sensor's data is stored in the cloud and can be accessed using mobile applications (Govindraj et al., 2017). Security is a big concern in smart homes as IoT devices are susceptible to attacks, which have been challenged by recent advancements in technology that have enhanced security features behind such automation. A low-cost security system of Smartdoor sensors can be developed using Raspberry Pi along with RESTful API, which can detect door open actions and dwellers are notified by Smartphone applications immediately (Hoque & Davidson, 2019).

Probably the most important application of IoT has been *smart health care* where automatic monitoring of patients is carried out to avoid unprecedented medical situations (Saha et al., 2020). With emerging technologies such as RFID, WSN, and smartphones, it is possible to collect real-time data which can be further processed by medical applications for users' easy access via the REST Web service. The infrastructure is complex and uses CoAP, 6LoWPAN, and HSN, and is suitable for a hospital/nursing center where doctors can connect to RFID readers through their smartphone and connect to patients through mobile applications for routine consultations (Catarinucci et al., 2015). IoT can be leveraged to prioritize patients as per their disease, and also minimize response time by medical practitioners, by adopting a hash polynomial decision tree, a scheduling algorithm that categorizes patients as being critical or stable (Manikandan et al., 2020).

The rapid emergence and acceptance of IoT has a significant impact on *smart agriculture* to create better opportunities for farmers. Sensors are deployed for specific applications in agricultural activities such as preparation of soil, the status of crops, insect and infestation detection, UAV for crop surveillance, and facilitation of optimized crop yield (Ayaz et al., 2019). Irrigation is an important aspect of agriculture, and IoT can successfully establish automated solutions for a smart irrigation system, by sensing real-time data on ambient temperature, adjoining humidity, the moisture content in soil, and water level through smartphones using a cloud-based communication system (Saraf & Gawali, 2017).This helps to enhance the quantity as well as the quality of agricultural land without any human intervention.

IoT has a profound effect on higher education, and several universities have adopted this paradigm shift to *smart education* to urge Internet-based interaction among objects and people (students, teachers, and staff members). Smart classrooms with sensors, face recognition algorithms, and cameras can be provided to both learners and lecturers to improve traditional teaching-learning methodologies (Majeed & Ali, 2018). Moreover, IoT applications can ensure security through NFC and RFID, which is essential today for larger campus areas of modern universities, in addition to delivering smart education to students, monitoring students' health care, enabling smart parking, and observing the real-time eco-system of the campus area.

IoT has been the driving force behind the rise of Industry 4.0, and the concept of a smart factory with vertical networks connecting all components of a firm is a reality today. Smart labels, which are module-embedded context-aware tags, enable items to sense, identify, track, and interact with each other as well as with machines, computers, and even employees in an industry using RFID technology (Fernández-Caramés & Fraga-Lamas, 2018).

3.4   Challenges of the Web of Things Ecosystem

However, the development of WoT is still at a nascent state and is not devoid of challenges that hinder developers from fully exploiting the complete potential of WoT (Mishra et al., 2018). Being a web-based architecture, WoT integrates numerous small devices across the globe. An increase in the number of devices enhances the concerns of WoT, and some of these are listed below.

Heterogeneity Due to the large number of heterogeneous devices being integrated in WoT, diversity in data-communication methods and capabilities such as data rate, protocol stack, and reliability may exist among them. There can also be a mismatch in terms of computational power, storage capacity, mobility, and energy availability, and this heterogeneity among devices is a major challenge in ubiquitous implementation of WoT. Furthermore, the data requirements of consumers are also heterogeneous in terms of quality, sampling rates, spatial resolution, and volume. In addition, several applications can also be diverse in characteristics such as latency, bandwidth, and reliability. Thus, handling such diversity while designing a unifying framework like WoT and communication protocol is undoubtedly a challenging task.

Scalability Scalability is a major issue in WoT, especially in a large distributed environment which eventually becomes complex, and optimum solutions are needed to handle performance degradation. Since the devices are heterogeneous in functionality, with a substantial increase in their number, graceful management becomes a cumbersome task. Furthermore, these resource-constrained devices are limited in terms of handling the increasing number of public requests, even with embedded Web servers. Hence, it is challenge to coordinate the large number of smart things in the WoT ecosystem without an appropriate design mechanism.

Search Engine Search engines are crucial for WoT. On the traditional web, search queries are static or slowly changing and are manually typed by users, whereas WoT content is dynamic since it is produced automatically by smart things. Hence, a search engine for the WoT ecosystem should be designed to search rapidly changing content. This is a major challenge as existing search engines assume slow change of web content so that they can update an index at lower frequencies, which is impossible in WoT, because the state of heterogeneous devices changes at a high frequency. Furthermore, some web content is time-specific in WoT. The dynamic feature of WoT needs a search engine that supports dynamic and real-time search for queries, which is a big challenge in the WoT ecosystem.

Device Security As far as smart health care is concerned, personalized information should be protected in an efficient manner. WoT is a new technology which requires a great deal of effort to solve security issues. Classical cryptographic algorithms such as AES, RSA, and SHA are not supported by many embedded devices in the WoT network. Therefore, the popular HTTPS scheme cannot be applied in this scenario. The web authentication technique OAuth (Leiba, 2012) is not enough to take all security measures. In Barka et al. (2015), the researchers have shown the role-based access control of connected things. The cryptographic key generation and encryption technique verifies the user as well as data. A large amount of data on the web can be protected by this technique if the proper implementation is carried out.

Encryption and Authentication The two cryptographic methods Encryption and Authentication are implemented together. Generally, Transport Layer Security (TLS) protocol is used to incorporate HTTP service with encryption in the transport layer and authentication in the application layer protocol. The Datagram Transport Layer Security Protocol (DTLS) and the Constrained Application Protocol (COAP) are used to reduce the energy in 6LowPAN. This works against data traffic and can provide a solution. But the problem lies in the encryption method used in the transport layer. In the transport layer, there is no user intervention. Therefore, it is difficult to identify if a user is initiating any processing or not. The authentication process including servers and clients can involve initiation operations using many web clients and it is difficult to keep track of these. Therefore, the data in Web service remains in a vulnerable condition.

Authorization and Ownership Transfer It is a difficult task to manage the user's privacy in the WoT system. Authorization and ownership transfer are the two effective techniques to protect user data. WoT architecture provides some basic rules to protect authorization and ownership issues, as proposed in Oh and Kim (2014). It works on the Internet address of a device with its resource-oriented working principles. The things in web architecture have to publish their web resources in the web architecture, which can be accessed by an HTTP client with due permission. According to the researchers, the architecture is classified into five filters. The first filter deals with unallowable domain access that filters out the TCP/IP packets, which are not allowed to access the web resource. The second step involves identifying the invalid request or abnormal parameters which are made by HTTP/REST (REpresentational state transfer). In the third step HTTP headers are identified to verify the client to detect a valid user. In the fourth step, the web resources are validated. The request is checked for availability and relevance and rejected if the criterion is not satisfied. In the final step it verifies that the objects requesting access to the web resources are really assigned to operate these web resources or not, and are not allowed if found unassigned. The authors need to follow all of the rules when they propose the criteria for the architecture. Once the permission is granted it can access multiple resources. Generally, IP address, domain, device id, etc. are included for access with necessary conditions such as how much time it takes to operate or the CPU access time. This architecture provides a decentralized and flexible web access mechanism in the Web of Things (WoT). The freely available web resources can be copied and shared using the transmission medium. The user's authentication and authorization should be carried out, but in case of ownership transfer there are no such proper techniques to execute this job. However, the ownership of web resources is mandatory.

Network Security The WoT is a combination of heterogeneous physical devices with several transmission protocols such as Zigbee, Bluetooth, 6LoWPAN, IPv4, IPv6, TCP/IP, HTTP, and many more. The protocols should run accurately to get the real-time data. But the problem lies in the security of protocols. The messages which are shared by this medium can be easily tapped if proper security measures are not taken. In Xie et al. (2016), the authors have shown that smart gateways are employed to take all security measures.

3.5   Existing Semantic Approaches

The Internet of Things (IoT) can connect numerous sensors and edge devices via a communication medium which may be wired or wireless transmission, as shown in Fig. 3.3. IoT generally follows a particular domain. On the other hand, the Web of Things (WoT) can provide web-based technologies to the billions of interconnected IoT networks. But at the same time the WoT platform has to handle extreme workload and scalability. Web 2.0 provides the versatility and high availability of web content in addition to the participation of users with standardized protocols. The main objective of WoT is to combine the heterogeneous IoT architectures to exchange information among data and ontologies (Mishra & Jain, 2020).

In Wu et al. (2016), WoT is classified as Plain WoT (P-WoT), which is the atomic resource present in web-based technologies. It can be accessed manually by web developers through some web-based applications. The second classification is domain-specific WoT (D-WoT). As the name suggests, the data are available in a

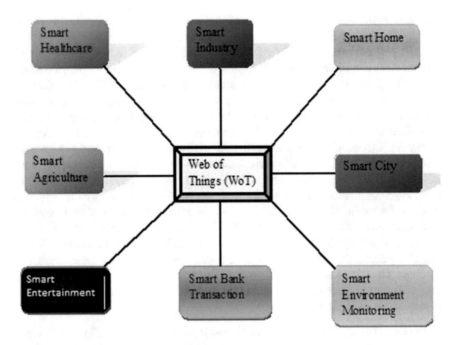

Fig. 3.3 Web of Things (WoT) applications

particular domain-centric manner and represent some specific schemas, vocabularies, and ontologies. The Web of Things (WoT) framework has been categorized into three components: Manual Annotator, Semi-automatic Annotator, and Semantic Search Engine. P-WoT is the input of the Manual Annotator. The model is based on machine learning and message passing algorithms in order to verify the D-WoT. Semantic Web technologies provide web-enabled services in a WoT-based scenario (Klinov & Mouromtsev, 2015). The existing research attributes are considered sufficient to do all the jobs. The RDF data model, OWL ontologies, and various techniques are involved in conducting Web services which connect the health care sector to industrial fields.

It is very important to build a web-based ontology using existing ones. Here three existing real-world ontologies are considered. The first is an Arduino-based weather station, the second is a wall or ceiling exhaust bath fan, and the third is an electric meter in a residential building. These three groups collect three completely different kinds of parameters. Sensors are the basic components of a weather station. It can measure the temperature and humidity. The exhaust bath fan can also switch off or on based on humidity level. If it crosses the threshold, it automatically starts working. The electric meter can pass various measuring parameters to the company using a transmission medium like a gateway. These three real-world ontologies are now considered and divided into three groups. The first group consists of sensors, actuators, and systems which work according to their respective jobs. The second group maintains the latitude and longitude, as the devices are working in local and global systems as well. Standard communication protocols with their latest versions are maintained, and these can connect physical devices in a cyber physical world. The sensors are further classified into groups based on their units of measurement and dimensions. Finally, a group is maintained for sensor and actuator manufacturer vendors to store information such as Websites, contacts, responsible persons, date, place, and time. Finally, from the above-mentioned information a web-enabled tool is developed, i.e., the Web of Things Semantic Description Helper, which can provide the necessary information regarding these concepts. Thus, the Web of Things (WoT) can adopt different architectures and their multiple purposes to provide a common platform.

In Hoyos et al. (2017), a smart agriculture scenario has been shown. The things of the WoT network are controlled by a software artifact called an avatar. The research aims to water a vineyard from local water bodies. Drones equipped with a GPS sensor, camera, wifi, and Bluetooth are used to identify the lack of water in the fields and generate the necessary reports. The weather conditions are measured to generate a forecast. Certain conditions are created in this scenario, and based on these conditions decisions are taken by the drones with the help of domain experts, users, appliance vendors, and Web services. These decisions or activities are used to build a context model and further transformation rules. Finally, the software artifact, the avatar, is used to retrieve the best adaptation possibilities. These adaptation rules are based on contextual information, that is, data source, raw data value, and contextual information thresholds. Therefore, the WoT system can adapt several adaptation rules among various devices and application domains. In the most recent era of technology, both IoT and WoT are used to connect every device, which create a new platform to work on. IoT and WoT are mixed together dynamically without any intervention by users (Yu et al., 2016). We already know that IoT can provide smart enabling technologies like sensing, visualization, and analysis. However, the Web of Things (WoT) provides web-enabled technologies over various IoT domains. The whole paradigm is divided into layers. The accessibility layer accesses transmission protocols and mediums and is connected to edge devices via Web services. The findability layer finds the services, such as query extraction and content extraction. The sharing layer shares physical data to social networking sites via a social network aggregator. In the next layer, certain data are mixed up for composition and, finally, with the help of specific application software developed by the web developer, they are provided to users.

Hence, the diverse fields of IoT and WoT generate different kinds of things and data, and various ontologies provide inputs to the semantic translator. They further classify them based on transition rules and provide services in a cyber physical medium. This platform mixed with IoT and WoT can provide a stable semantic environment which presents new services without the intervention of users. In this global pandemic situation caused by COVID-19, it is inevitable that we are using contactless payment methods. The existing mobile wallet applications are gaining popularity. This idea is focused on in Grønli et al. (2015), where emerging technologies such as IoT and WoT are used. The Web of Things (WoT) architecture is divided into various forms. The first form is IoT. An IoT architecture is composed of lightweight sensors which take part in machine-to-machine communication. Here, REpresentational State Transfer (RESTful) approaches are used by traditional Web services such as SOAP and UDDI. Cloud technology is one of the important forms where information is communicated with more resources and WoT solutions, to provide better flexibility and scalability. Cloud computing has become the backbone of Web of Things architecture. Node.js (Joyent Inc, 2013) is one of the most commonly used frameworks where modern services of WoT are provided. The Near Field Communication or NFC technique is used as a backbone for Cloud Payment. NFC is available in the form of applications for both customers and retailers. User sensitive information is stored in the cloud and is accessed only when it is required, and this increases the manageability of the NFC ecosystem. Some popular mobile wallet applications are Google Wallet (Google Wallet, 2013), MasterPass (MasterPass, 2013) and PayPass Wallet Services (MasterCard PayPass, 2013). These provide secure transaction, dynamic demand of resources, real-time operation of transaction, and interoperable communication of data.

The whole framework is divided into layers where the Things Interface Layer directly communicates with sensor devices or smart objects which collect information. The Things Management Layer manages the collected information with the user interface via Web services. Lastly, the Things Service Layer provides the services, stores the data, and supplies necessary information to implement a transaction. The User or Application Layer checks information or requests services. In Serena et al. (2017), a semantic discovery of the Web of Things (WoT) has been described. The WoT ontology is divided into concepts such as Thing, interaction pattern, data format, and endpoint. Thing defines the things which are used in the context of WoT. The interaction among the things is defined by interaction patterns. Data format is defined as how the data is generated and stored. Finally, the endpoint is web applications accessed by respective users. In WoT architecture another highly important parameter is mapping ontology, which provides communication between data available in an online resource to the target object. Therefore, WoT provides a common data model and interoperability to the IoT platform. It provides the best possible solutions to the IoT environment by mapping various core ontologies. The existing ontologies are mashed up to deliver a new platform where web solutions are provided with some generalized approaches (Jain et al., 2016; Patel & Jain, 2019).

3.6   Open Issues

- As it is dealing with heterogeneous devices, the security of WoT architecture is a primary concern. It is obvious that the hardware devices can break down at any point in time. The security checking should be done at several points in the architecture.
- The quality of data should be maintained and proper standardization techniques must be adapted.

- The generated data from each IoT device should be linked to an open IoT platform to maintain the reliability and scalability of a high amount of real-time data processing. Moreover, it must be kept in mind that the IoT data will come to the platform using various transmission protocols.
- Existing semantic web-based architectures communicate, exchange, merge, and re-use numerous IoT based architectures. Interoperability of smart data between IoT domains in this case becomes crucial to handle.
- Including or excluding rules for WoT services is important to make the system more adaptable over time.
- The Web services should be unified to give accessibility to cross-domain applications.
- Sensor devices can generate large amount of data. Therefore, to handle complex events in a real-time scenario, it is necessary to implement machine learning algorithms and further deep learning algorithms.
- The whole framework of WoT should be designed in such a way that it can be re-used properly.

3.7 Conclusion

This chapter provides an overview of WoT, the relation between IoT and WoT, and the need for WoT for integrating diverse IoT applications and things under one umbrella. WoT is regarded as the next big possibility for the future as it will greatly increase the scope and size of the current Internet to a substantial extent, with concerns such as security and scalability being sufficiently addressed in future.

Questions for Review
- What is the penetration of smartphones? How many and what different types of contact tracing apps and methodologies exist? Why are their results in many cases still inadequate?
- What is an alternative that can also be used in parallel to mitigation after a positive case is found? What are some possible ways to facilitate this—and how has this been done so far?
- How is prevention viewed from the individual viewpoint? What are the associated risks of infection, and its costs given the individual and his cohabitants? To what extent can the individual self-reflect on these, and how could ICT and AI help in this direction?
- How is prevention viewed from the activity organizer's viewpoint? What are the associated personalized risks of infection transmission in a specific activity? What are its costs given the individual participants and their cohabitants, and also given the activity context? To what extent can the organizer and the individual participants self-reflect on these, and how could ICT and AI help in this direction, and toward optimizing the activity?

- What is the concept of "Pandemic Cohort Management" and where can it be helpful? How is the calculation of risks and benefits at the individual as well as collective level performed? How are self-determination and privacy preserved, and what are the benefits of this concept?
- What are some fundamental ethical questions regarding the pandemic and vaccinations, and what answers have different parties and public personalities provided, using which arguments?
- Can these answers be evaluated on the basis of fundamental bio-ethics principles, and if so, with what kinds of computational models?
- What is "privacy by design"? What are some of its constituent technologies, and how can it be applied in pandemic cohort management and other pandemic-related systems?
- How can prevention during execution be informed and optimized through such systems?
- How can health care departments as well as medical research benefit too?

Questions for Discussion
- How can individuals be incentivized to enter data into their pandemic wallet enough, often, and accurately enough?
- How would citizens, other stakeholders, and governments view such systems, and how can their presentation and the relevant narratives be tailored in order to incentivize their adoption?
- What are potential difficulties and/or opportunities for the application of such systems in different countries and/or contexts and settings?
- What are the main ethical questions that have been featured in the media regarding the pandemic?
- What other questions exist which have not received publicity, and what other questions might arise in the future?
- How have these questions been answered by different entities, and what was the argumentation?
- How does this relate to specific systems of bio-ethics principles and their various philosophical interpretations (e.g., in terms of distributive justice)?
- What does the analysis of the answers given by specific entities, as well as their argumentation, reveal about their hidden (or even unconscious) preferences and assumptions, when they are viewed in light of the computational models built on the basis of specific bio-ethics principles?
- How can we create a democratic yet robust and rational use of computational ethical models in practice?

Problem Statements for Young Researchers
- What would be the effect of partial completeness and measurable inaccuracies and biases in the data entered into the pandemic wallet app?
- How much is enough for pre-specified levels of accuracy and effectiveness of the collective risk assessments and meeting optimizations?

- What are different types of security "attacks" that can happen in a pandemic cohort management system? What are ways to estimate their probability, to detect them, and to minimize the potential harms of each?
- How can the security- and privacy-related aspects of the system be further improved?
- How can the tunable parameters of the individual and collective risk calculators be empirically adjusted?
- How can models for large seating arrangements be tackled (e.g., through hierarchical decompositions), and how can we optimize increasingly different types of activities, beyond business meetings?
- How can we estimate the opinions and attitudes about a pandemic wallet before it is released?
- How can we create a strategic plan for increased adoption?
- How can we strategize the political issues that might arise?
- What innovative media-driven and/or incentivization techniques can be utilized?
- How do perceived and actual values and legal and ethical systems interact with the pandemic management technologies of this chapter, and how can they be custom-tailored on a country-by-country basis?
- How can we use computational models and automated reasoning systems grounded in established bio-ethical principles in order to analyze existing answers to questions regarding the pandemic and their argumentation, and in order to derive more precise decisions after informed fixing of appropriate weights and priorities?

References

AirVisual. Retrieved from https://www.prnewswire.com/news-releases/crowdsourced-air-quality-monitoring-network-revolutionizes-environmental-reporting-through-distributed-sensors-producing-the-worlds-largest-air-pollution-dataset-300443335.html

Alshamsi, A., Anwar, Y., Almulla, M., Aldohoori, M., Hamad, N., & Awad, M. (2017, November). Monitoring pollution: Applying IoT to create a smart environment. In *2017 International Conference on Electrical and Computing Technologies and Applications (ICECTA)* (pp. 1–4). IEEE.

Ayaz, M., Ammad-Uddin, M., Sharif, Z., Mansour, A., & Aggoune, E. H. M. (2019). Internet-of-Things (IoT)-based smart agriculture: Toward making the fields talk. *IEEE Access, 7*, 129551–129583.

Barka, E., Mathew, S. S., & Atif, Y. (2015, May). Securing the web of things with role-based access control. In *International Conference on Codes, Cryptology, and Information Security* (pp. 14–26). Cham: Springer.

Beza, E., Silva, J. V., Kooistra, L., & Reidsma, P. (2017). Review of yield gap explaining factors and opportunities for alternative data collection approaches. *European Journal of Agronomy, 82*, 206–222.

Catarinucci, L., De Donno, D., Mainetti, L., Palano, L., Patrono, L., Stefanizzi, M. L., & Tarricone, L. (2015). An IoT-aware architecture for smart healthcare systems. *IEEE Internet of Things Journal, 2*(6), 515–526.

Chowdhury, C., & Roy, S. (2017). Mobile crowd-sensing for smart cities. In *Smart cities: Foundations, principles and applications* (pp. 125–154). Wiley. ISBN: 978-1-119-22639-0.

Crowdsourcing in Education. Retrieved from https://ideascalenation.medium.com/three-real-world-examples-of-crowdsourcing-in-education-ae470d3a8ef6

Crowdsourcing in Healthcare. Retrieved from https://medicalfuturist.com/crowdsourcing-in-digital-health/

Crowdsourcing in Industry. Retrieved from https://tweakyourbiz.com/marketing/9-great-examples-crowdsourcing-age-empowered-consumers

Dutta, J., Roy, S., & Chowdhury, C. (2019). Unified framework for IoT and smartphone based different smart city related applications. *Microsystem Technologies, 25*(1), 83–96.

Fernández-Caramés, T. M., & Fraga-Lamas, P. (2018). A review on human-centered IoT-connected smart labels for the industry 4.0. *IEEE Access, 6*, 25939–25957.

Google Wallet. (2013). Google Wallet 2013. Retrieved from http://www.google.com/wallet/

Govindraj, V., Sathiyanarayanan, M., & Abubakar, B. (2017, August). Customary homes to smart homes using Internet of Things (IoT) and mobile application. In *2017 International Conference On Smart Technologies For Smart Nation (SmartTechCon)* (pp. 1059–1063). IEEE.

Grønli, T. M., Pourghomi, P., & Ghinea, G. (2015). Towards NFC payments using a lightweight architecture for the Web of Things. *Computing, 97*(10), 985–999.

Guinard, D., & Trifa, V. (2009, April). Towards the web of things: Web mashups for embedded devices. In *Workshop on Mashups, Enterprise Mashups and Lightweight Composition on the Web (MEM 2009), in proceedings of WWW (International World Wide Web Conferences), Madrid, Spain* (Vol. 15, p. 8).

Guinard, D., Trifa, V., & Wilde, E. (2010, November). A resource oriented architecture for the web of things. In *2010 Internet of Things (IOT)* (pp. 1–8). IEEE.

Guinard, D., Trifa, V., Mattern, F., & Wilde, E. (2011a). From the Internet of Things to the web of things: Resource-oriented architecture and best practices. In *Architecting the Internet of Things* (pp. 97–129). Berlin: Springer.

Guinard, D., Ion, I., & Mayer, S. (2011b, December). In search of an internet of things service architecture: REST or WS-*? A developers' perspective. In *International Conference on Mobile and Ubiquitous Systems: Computing, Networking, and Services* (pp. 326–337). Berlin: Springer.

Hoque, M. A., & Davidson, C. (2019). Design and implementation of an IoT-based smart home security system. *International Journal of Networked and Distributed Computing, 7*(2), 85–92.

Hoyos, J. R., Preuveneers, D., & García-Molina, J. J. (2017, June). Quality parameters as modeling language abstractions for context-aware applications: An AAL case study. In *International and Interdisciplinary Conference on Modeling and Using Context* (pp. 569–581). Cham: Springer.

https://digital.hbs.edu/platform-rctom/submission/how-crowdsourcing-is-changing-the-waze-we-drive/

Huang, J., Duan, N., Ji, P., Ma, C., Ding, Y., Yu, Y., Zhou, Q., & Sun, W. (2018). A crowdsource-based sensing system for monitoring fine-grained air quality in urban environments. *IEEE Internet of Things Journal, 6*(2), 3240–3247.

Huang, D. Y., Apthorpe, N., Li, F., Acar, G., & Feamster, N. (2020). IoT inspector: Crowdsourcing labeled network traffic from smart home devices at scale. *Proceedings of the ACM on Interactive, Mobile, Wearable and Ubiquitous Technologies, 4*(2), 1–21.

Jain, S., Gupta, C., & Bhardwaj, A. (2016, December). Research directions under the parasol of ontology based semantic web structure. In *International Conference on Soft Computing and Pattern Recognition* (pp. 644–655). Cham: Springer.

Javaid, S., Sufian, A., Pervaiz, S., & Tanveer, M. (2018, February). Smart traffic management system using Internet of Things. In *2018 20th International Conference on Advanced Communication Technology (ICACT)* (pp. 393–398). IEEE.

Joyent Inc. (2013). Node.js: Evented I/O for JavaScript. Retrieved from: http://nodejs.org/

Kincaid, J. (2010). *Googles open spot makes parking a breeze, assuming everyone turns into a Good Samaritan*. Retrieved from https://techcrunch.com/2010/07/09/google-Parking-Open-Spot/

Klinov, P., & Mouromtsev, D., (Eds.). (2015). *Knowledge Engineering and Semantic Web: 6th International Conference, KESW 2015, Moscow, Russia, September 30-October 2, 2015, Proceedings* (Vol. 518). Springer.

Kodali, R. K., Rajanarayanan, S. C., & Boppana, L. (2020, January). IoT based smart wearable for air quality monitoring. In *2020 International Conference on Computer Communication and Informatics (ICCCI)* (pp. 1–5). IEEE.

Leiba, B. (2012). Oauth web authorization protocol. *IEEE Internet Computing, 16*(1), 74–77.

Li, H., Pei, L., Liao, D., Zhang, M., Xu, D., & Wang, X. (2020). Achieving privacy protection for crowdsourcing application in edge-assistant vehicular networking. *Telecommunication Systems: Modelling, Analysis, Design and Management*, 1–14.

Lookmuang, R., Nambut, K., & Usanavasin, S. (2018, May). Smart parking using IoT technology. In *2018 5th International Conference on Business and Industrial research (ICBIR)* (pp. 1–6). IEEE.

Mahalank, S. N., Malagund, K. B., & Banakar, R. M. (2016, March). Device to device interaction analysis in IoT based smart traffic management system: An experimental approach. In *2016 Symposium on Colossal Data Analysis and Networking (CDAN)* (pp. 1–6). IEEE.

Majeed, A., & Ali, M. (2018, January). How Internet-of-Things (IoT) making the university campuses smart? QA higher education (QAHE) perspective. In *2018 IEEE 8th Annual Computing and Communication Workshop and Conference (CCWC)* (pp. 646–648). IEEE.

Manikandan, R., Patan, R., Gandomi, A. H., Sivanesan, P., & Kalyanaraman, H. (2020). Hash polynomial two factor decision tree using IoT for smart health care scheduling. *Expert Systems with Applications, 141*, 112924.

MasterCard PayPass. (2013). *Just tap and go 2013*. Retrieved from https://www.paypass.com/

MasterPass. (2013). *Introducing MasterPass 2013*. Retrieved from https://masterpass.com/

Mavakala, B., Mulaji, C., Mpiana, P., Elongo, V., Otamonga, J. P., Biey, E., Wildi, W., Pote-Wembonyama, J., & Giuliani, G. (2017). Citizen sensing of solid waste disposals: Crowdsourcing as tool supporting waste management in a developing country. In *Proceedings Sardinia 2017/Sixteenth International Waste Management and Landfill Symposium*.

Minet, J., Curnel, Y., Gobin, A., Goffart, J. P., Melard, F., Tychon, B., Wellens, J., & Defourny, P. (2017). Crowdsourcing for agricultural applications: A review of uses and opportunities for a farmsourcing approach. *Computers and Electronics in Agriculture, 142*, 126–138.

Mishra, S., & Jain, S. (2020). Ontologies as a semantic model in IoT. *International Journal of Computers and Applications, 42*(3), 233–243.

Mishra, S., Jain, S., Rai, C., & Gandhi, N. (2018, December). Security challenges in semantic Web of Things. In *International Conference on Innovations in Bio-Inspired Computing and Applications* (pp. 162–169). Cham: Springer.

Misra, D., Das, G., Chakrabortty, T., & Das, D. (2018). An IoT-based waste management system monitored by cloud. *Journal of Material Cycles and Waste Management, 20*(3), 1574–1582.

Mitra, N., & Lafon, Y. (2003). Soap version 1.2 part 0: Primer. *W3C Recommendation, 24*, 12.

Mumbaikar, S., & Padiya, P. (2013). Web services based on soap and rest principles. *International Journal of Scientific and Research Publications, 3*(5), 1–4.

Munasinghe, M. I. N. P., Perera, G. I. U. S., Karunathilaka, J. K. W. D. B., Cooray, B. C. S., & Manupriyal, K. G. D. (2017). Air pollution monitoring through crowdsourcing. In *111th annual sessions of the IESL*, Colombo.

Mutembesa, D., Omongo, C., & Mwebaze, E. (2018, June). Crowdsourcing real-time viral disease and pest information: A case of nation-wide cassava disease surveillance in a developing country. In *Proceedings of the AAAI Conference on Human Computation and Crowdsourcing* (Vol. 6, no. 1).

Nie, Y., Xu, K., Chen, H., & Peng, L. (2019, October). Crowd-parking: A new idea of parking guidance based on crowdsourcing of parking location information from automobiles. In *IECON 2019-45th Annual Conference of the IEEE Industrial Electronics Society* (Vol. 1, pp. 2779–2784). IEEE.

Oh, S. W., & Kim, H. S. (2014, February). Decentralized access permission control using resource-oriented architecture for the Web of Things. In *16th International Conference on Advanced Communication Technology* (pp. 749–753). IEEE.

Patel, A., & Jain, S. (2019). Present and future of semantic web technologies: A research statement. *International Journal of Computers and Applications*, 1–10.

Pilloni, V. (2018). How data will transform industrial processes: Crowdsensing, crowdsourcing and big data as pillars of industry 4.0. *Future Internet, 10*(3), 24.

Rahman, M., Blackwell, B., Banerjee, N., & Saraswat, D. (2015). Smartphone-based hierarchical crowdsourcing for weed identification. *Computers and Electronics in Agriculture, 113*, 14–23.

Saha, A., Chowdhury, C., Jana, M., & Biswas, S. (2020). IoT sensor data analysis and fusion applying machine learning and meta-heuristic approaches. In *Enabling AI applications in data science* (pp. 441–469).

Saif, S., Datta, D., Saha, A., Biswas, S., & Chowdhury, C. (2020). Data science and AI in IoT based smart healthcare: Issues, challenges and case study. In *Enabling AI Applications in Data Science* (pp. 415–439). Cham: Springer.

Saraf, S. B., & Gawali, D. H. (2017, May). IoT based smart irrigation monitoring and controlling system. In *2017 2nd IEEE International Conference on Recent Trends in Electronics, Information & Communication Technology (RTEICT)* (pp. 815–819). IEEE.

Serena, F., Poveda-Villalón, M., & García-Castro, R. (2017, June). Semantic discovery in the web of things. In *International Conference on Web Engineering* (pp. 19–31). Cham: Springer.

SFMTA. SFPark-About the Project. Retrieved from https://www.sfmta.com/demand-responsive-parking-pricing

Shu, L., Chen, Y., Huo, Z., Bergmann, N., & Wang, L. (2017). When mobile crowd sensing meets traditional industry. *IEEE Access, 5*, 15300–15307.

Simic, K., Despotovic-Zrakic, M., Đuric, I., Milic, A., & Bogdanovic, N. (2015). A model of smart environment for e-learning based on crowdsourcing. *RUO. Revija za Univerzalno Odlicnost, 4* (1), A1.

Singh, S., Mehta, K. S., Bhattacharya, N., Prasad, J., Lakshmi, S. K., Subramaniam, K. V., & Sitaram, D. (2017, July). Identifying uncollected garbage in urban areas using crowdsourcing and machine learning. In *2017 IEEE Region 10 Symposium (TENSYMP)* (pp. 1–5). IEEE.

Suresh, S., Sharma, T., & Sitaram, D. (2016, December). Towards quantifying the amount of uncollected garbage through image analysis. In *Proceedings of the Tenth Indian Conference on Computer Vision, Graphics and Image Processing* (pp. 1–8).

Wazny, K. (2018). Applications of crowdsourcing in health: An overview. *Journal of Global Health, 8*(1).

WOT GROUP. Retrieved from https://www.w3.org/WoT/wg/

Wu, Z., Xu, Y., Zhang, C., Yang, Y., & Ji, Y. (2016, July). Towards semantic web of things: From manual to semi-automatic semantic annotation on web of things. In *International Conference on Big Data Computing and Communications* (pp. 295–308). Cham: Springer.

Xie, W., Tang, Y., Chen, S., Zhang, Y., & Gao, Y. (2016, September). Security of web of things: A survey (short paper). In *International Workshop on Security* (pp. 61–70). Cham: Springer.

Yu, J., Bang, H. C., Lee, H., & Lee, Y. S. (2016). Adaptive Internet of Things and Web of Things convergence platform for Internet of reality services. *The Journal of Supercomputing, 72*(1), 84–102.

Zeng, D., Guo, S., & Cheng, Z. (2011). The web of things: A survey. *JCM, 6*(6), 424–438.

Zhu, C., Mehrabi, A., Xiao, Y., & Wen, Y. (2019, September). CrowdParking: Crowdsourcing based parking navigation in autonomous driving era. In *2019 International Conference on Electromagnetics in Advanced Applications (ICEAA)* (pp. 1401–1405). IEEE.

Anindita Saha is an Assistant Professor in the Department of Information Technology at Techno Main SaltLake, formerly known as Techno India, West Bengal, India. She completed her B-Tech in Information Technology from Institute of Engineering and Management (IEM), Kolkata, in 2003, and M-Tech in Computer Science and Application from Calcutta University in 2012. She has also successfully completed her MBA from ICFAI University, Hyderabad in 2008. Her research interests include Wireless Sensor Networks, Wireless Body Area Networks, Human Activity Recognition using Machine Learning, Deep Learning and Crowd-sourcing.

Mayurakshi Jana received M.Sc. degree in Computer Science from West Bengal State University (India) in 2016 and B.Sc. degree in Computer Science (Honours) from University Of Calcutta in 2014. She is currently teaching at the Department of Computer Science, Bijoy Krishna Girls' College, Howrah as State Aided College Teacher (CAT-1). Her research interests are Artificial Intelligence, Applications of Machine learning and Deep learning in Healthcare sectors.

Dr. Chandreyee Chowdhury is a faculty in the department of Computer Science and Engineering at Jadavpur University, India. She received Ph.D. in Engineering from Jadavpur University in 2013 and M.E. in Computer Science and Engineering from Jadavpur University in 2005. Her research interests include routing issues of Wireless Sensor Networks and its variants, mobile crowd-sensing, and applications of mobile agents in mobile ad-hoc networks. She has published more than 60 papers in reputed journals and international peer reviewed conferences. She is a member of IEEE and IEEE Computer Society.

Dr. Suparna Biswas is working as an Associate Professor in the Department of Computer Science and Engineering in Maulana Abul Kalam Azad University of Technology, WB. She has received ME and Ph.D from Jadavpur University, West Bengal in 2004 and 2013 respectively. She has been an ERASMUS MUNDUS Post Doctoral research fellow in cLINK project in Northumbria University, Newcastle, UK during 2014–2015. She is currently handling two funded research projects in the capacity of PI and Co-PI in the area of IoT based remote healthcare. She has co-authored a number of research papers published in journals, conferences and as book chapters of international repute. Her areas of research interests are Internet of Things, Network Security, Mobile Computing and Remote Healthcare.

Dr Diptangshu Pandit (Max) is a Senior Lecturer in Computer Game Design. He focuses teaching mainly the technical side of the games development using Unreal Engine and visual scripting. He has a PhD in applied artificial intelligence for biomedical signal processing. He holds both bachelors and masters degree in Computer Science and Engineering. Before joining Teesside, he was teaching at Northumbria University for 2 years in computer and information sciences department. His work is mostly focused on machine learning and evolutionary optimisation algorithms and their use in various domains including game development. His research interests include, but not limited to the following areas; Machine Learning and its applications, AI in computer games, Bio-medical signal processing, Evolutionary optimization, Brain Computer Interface, Deep learning.

Chapter 4
Semantic Intelligence in Big Data Applications

Valentina Janev

Abstract Today, data are growing at a tremendous rate, and according to the International Data Corporation, it is expected they will reach 175 zettabytes by 2025. The International Data Corporation also forecasts that more than 150B devices will be connected across the globe by 2025, most of which will be creating data in real time, while 90 zettabytes of data will be created by Internet of things (IoT) devices. This vast amount of data creates several new opportunities for modern enterprises, especially for analyzing enterprise value chains in a broader sense. In order to leverage the potential of real data and build smart applications on top of sensory data, IoT-based systems integrate domain knowledge and context-relevant information. Semantic intelligence is the process of bridging the semantic gap between human and computer comprehension by teaching a machine to think in terms of object-oriented concepts in the same way as a human does. Semantic intelligence technologies are the most important component in developing artificially intelligent knowledge-based systems, since they assist machines in contextually and intelligently integrating and processing resources. This chapter aims at demystifying semantic intelligence in distributed, enterprise, and Web-based information systems. It also discusses prominent tools that leverage semantics, handle large data at scale, and address challenges (e.g., heterogeneity, interoperability, and machine learning explainability) in different industrial applications.

Keywords Semantic intelligence · Big data applications · Knowledge graphs · Artificial intelligence · Interoperability

Key Points
- Semantic intelligence is the process of bridging the semantic gap between human and computer comprehension.

V. Janev (✉)
Institute Mihajlo Pupin, University of Belgrade, Belgrade, Serbia
e-mail: valentina.janev@institutepupin.com

© The Author(s), under exclusive license to Springer Nature Switzerland AG 2021   71
S. Jain, S. Murugesan (eds.), *Smart Connected World*,
https://doi.org/10.1007/978-3-030-76387-9_4

- There is a need for semantic standards to improve the interoperability of complex systems.
- The semantic data lakes supply the data lake with a semantic middleware that allows uniform access to original heterogeneous data sources.
- Knowledge graphs are a solution that allows the building of a common understanding of heterogeneous, distributed data in organizations and value chains, and thus provision of smart data for artificial intelligence applications.
- The goal of semantic intelligence is to make business intelligence solutions accessible and understandable to humans.

4.1 Introduction

Both researchers and information technology (IT) professionals have to cope with a large number of technologies, frameworks, tools, and standards for the development of enterprise Web-based applications. This task has become even more cumbersome as a result of the following events:

- The emergence of the Internet of things (IoT) in 1999 (Rahman & Asyhari, 2019)
- The development of Semantic Web (SW) technologies as a cornerstone for further development of the Web (Berners-Lee, 2001; Bizer et al., 2009)
- The development of big data solutions (Laney, 2001; Firican, 2017; Patrizio, 2018)

Hence, topics such as smart data management (Alvarez, 2020), linked open data (Auer et al., 2007a), semantic technologies (Janev & Vraneš, 2009), and smart analytics have spawned a tremendous amount of attention among scientists, software experts, industry leaders, and decision-makers. Table 4.1 defines a few terms related to data, such as open data, big data, linked data, and smart data.

Table 4.1 Definitions

Term	Definition
Open data	"The data available for reuse free of charge can be observed as open data" (Janev et al., 2018)
Big data	"'Big data' are high-volume, velocity, and variety information assets that demand cost-effective, innovative forms of information processing for enhanced insight and decision making" (Laney, 2001)
	"Big data are high volume, high velocity, and/or high variety information assets that require new forms of processing to enable enhanced decision making, insight discovery, and process optimization" (Manyika, 2011)
Linked data	The term "linked data" refers to a set of best practices for publishing structured data on the Web. These principles have been coined by Tim Berners-Lee in the design issue note Linked Data[a] (Berners-Lee, 2006)
Smart data	"Simply put, if big data are a massive amount of digital information, smart data are the part of that information that is actionable and makes sense. It is a concept that developed along with, and thanks to, the development of algorithm-based technologies, such as artificial intelligence and machine learning" (Dallemand, 2020)

[a]https://www.w3.org/DesignIssues/LinkedData

Despite the fact that the term IoT ("sensors and actuators embedded in physical objects and connected via wired and wireless networks") is 20 years old, the actual idea of connected devices is older and dates back to the 1970s. In the last two decades, with the advancement in ITs, new approaches have been elaborated and tested for handling the influx of data coming from IoT devices. On one side, the focus in industry has been on manufacturing and producing the right types of hardware to support IoT solutions. On the other, the software industry is concerned with finding solutions that address issues with different aspects (dimensions) of data generated from IoT networks, including (1) the *volume* of data generated by IoT networks and the methods of storing data, (2) the *velocity* of data and the speed of processing, and (3) the *variety* of (unstructured) data that are communicated via different protocols and the need for adoption of standards. While these three Vs have been continuously used to describe big data, additional dimensions have been added to describe data integrity and quality, such as (4) *veracity* (i.e., truthfulness or uncertainty of data, authenticity, provenance, and accountability), (5) *validity* (i.e., correct processing of data), (6) *variability* (i.e., context of data), (7) *viscosity* (i.e., latency data transmission between the source and destination), (8) *virality* (i.e., speed of the data sent and received from various sources), (9) *vulnerability* (i.e., security and privacy concerns associated with data processing), (10) *visualization* (i.e., interpretation of data and identification of the most relevant information for the users), and (11) *value* (i.e., usefulness and relevance of the extracted data in making decisions and capacity to turn information into action).

With the rapid development of the IoT, different technologies have emerged to bring the knowledge (Patel et al., 2018) within IoT infrastructures to better meet the purpose of the IoT systems and support critical decision-making (Ge et al., 2018; Jain, 2021). While the term "big data" refers to datasets that have large sizes and complex structures, the term "big data analytics" refers to the strategy of analyzing large volumes of data which are gathered from a wide variety of sources, including different kind of sensors, images/videos/media, social networks, and transaction records. Aside from the analytic aspect, big data technologies include numerous components, methods, and techniques, each employed for a slightly different purpose, for instance for pre-processing, data cleaning and transformation, data storage, and visualization.

In addition to the emergence of big data, the last decade has also witnessed a technology boost for artificial intelligence (AI)-driven technologies. A key prerequisite for realizing the next wave of AI application is to leverage data, which are heterogeneous and distributed among multiple hosts at different locations. Consequently, the fusion of big data and IoT technologies and recent advancements in machine learning have brought renewed visibility to AI and have created opportunities for the development of services for many complex systems in different industries (Mijović et al., 2019; Tiwari et al., 2018). Nowadays, it is generally accepted that AI methods and technologies bring transformative change to societies and industries worldwide. In order to reduce the latency, smart sensors (sensor networks) are empowered with embedded intelligence that performs pre-processing, reduces the volume, and reacts autonomously. Additionally, in order to put the data in context, standard data models are associated with data processing services, thus facilitating the deployment of sensors and services in different environments.

This chapter explains the need for semantic standards that improve interoperability in complex systems, introduce the semantic lake concept, and demystify the semantic intelligence in distributed, enterprise, and Web-based information systems (see the following section). In order to select an appropriate semantic description, processing model, and architecture solution, data architects and engineers need to become familiar with the analytical problem and the business objectives of the targeted application. Therefore, the authors describe four eras of data analytics and introduce different big data tools.

4.2 From Data to Big Data to Smart Data Processing

Data-driven technologies such as big data and the IoT, in combination with smart infrastructures for management and analytics, are rapidly creating significant opportunities for enhancing industrial productivity and citizen quality of life. As data become increasingly available (e.g., from social media, weblogs, and IoT sensors), the challenge of managing them (i.e., selecting, combining, storing, and analyzing them) is growing more urgent (Janev, 2020). Thus, there is a demand for development of computational methods for the ingestion, management, and analysis of big data, as well as for the transformation of these data into knowledge.

From a data analytics point of view, this means that data processing has to be designed taking into consideration the diversity and scalability requirements of the targeted domain. Furthermore, in modern settings, data acquisition occurs in near real time (e.g., IoT data streams), and the collected and pre-processed data are combined with batch loads by different automated processes. Hence, novel architectures are needed; these architectures have to be "flexible enough to support different service levels as well as optimal algorithms and techniques for the different query workloads" (Thusoo et al., 2010).

4.2.1 Variety of Data Sources

The development of big data-driven pipelines for transforming big data into actionable knowledge requires the design and implementation of adequate IoT and big data processing architecture, where, in addition to volume and velocity, the variety of available data sources should be considered. The processing and storage of data which are generated by a variety of sources (e.g., sensors, smart devices, and social media in raw, semi-structured, unstructured, and rich media formats) is complicated. Hence, different solutions for distributed storage, cloud computing, and data fusion are needed (Liu et al., 2015). In order to make the data useful for data analysis, companies use different methods to reduce complexity, downsize the data scale (e.g., dimensional reduction, sampling, and coding), and pre-process the data (i.e., data extraction, data cleaning, data integration, and data transformation) (Wang, 2017). Data heterogeneity can thus be defined in terms of several dimensions:

- *Structural variety*, which refers to data representation and indicates multiple data formats and models. For instance, the format of satellite images is very different from the format used to store tweets which are generated on the Web.
- *Media variety*, which refers to the medium in which data get delivered. For instance, the audio of a speech vs. the transcript of the speech may represent the same information in two different media.
- *Semantic variety*, which refers to the meaning of the units (terms) used to measure or describe the data that are needed to interpret or operate on the data. For instance, a standard unit for measuring electricity is the kilowatt; however, the electricity generation capacity of big power plants is measured in multiples of kilowatts, such as megawatts and gigawatts.
- *Availability variations*, which mean that the data can be accessed continuously (e.g., from traffic cameras) or intermediately (e.g., only when the satellite is over the region of interest).

In order to enable broad data integration, data exchange, and interoperability, and to ensure extraction of information and knowledge, standardization at different levels (e.g., metadata schemata, data representation formats, and licensing conditions of open data) is needed. This encompasses all forms of (multilingual) data, including structured and unstructured data, as well as data from a wide range of domains, including geospatial data, statistical data, weather data, public sector information, and research data, to name a few.

4.2.2 The Need for Semantic Standards

In 1883, Michel Bréal, a French philologist, coined the term "semantics" to explain how terms may have various meanings for different people, depending on their experiences and emotions. In the information processing context, semantics refers to the "meaning and practical use of data" (Woods, 1975), namely, the efficient use of a data object for representing a concept or object. Since 1980, the AI community has promoted the concept of providing general, formalized knowledge of the world to intelligent systems and agents (see also the panel report from the 1997 *Data Semantics: what, where and how?*) (Sheth, 1997).

In 2001, Sir Tim Berners-Lee, Director of the World Wide Web Consortium (W3C), presented his vision for the SW, describing it as an expansion of the traditional Web and a global distributed architecture where data and services can easily interact. In 2006, Berners-Lee also introduced the basic (linked data) principles for interlinking datasets on the Web via references to common concepts. The Resource Description Framework (RDF) norm is used to reflect the knowledge that defines the concepts. Parallel to this, increased functionalities and improved

Table 4.2 An overview of (recommended) Semantic Web technologies

Technology	Definition
RDF, 2004	RDF is a general-purpose language for encoding and representing data on the Internet The RDF Schema is used to represent knowledge in terms of objects ("resources") and relationships between them
RDFS, 2004	RDF Schema serves as the meta language or vocabulary to define properties and classes of RDF resources
SPARQL, 2008	SPARQL Query Language for RDF is a standard language for querying RDF data
OWL, 2004	OWL is a standard Web Ontology Language that facilitates greater machine interpretability of Web content than that supported by XML, RDF, and RDF-S by providing additional vocabulary along with a formal semantics
SWRL, 2004	SWRL aims to be the standard rule language of the Semantic Web. It is based on a combination of the OWL DL, OWL Lite, RuleML, etc.
WSDL, 2007	WSDL provides a model and an XML format for describing Web services
SAWSDL, 2007	SAWSDL (Semantic Annotations for WSDL and XML Schema) explains how to apply semantic annotations to WSDL and XML Schema documents
RDFa, 2008	A collection of attributes and processing rules for extending XHTML to support RDF
GRRDL, 2007	A mechanism for Gleaning Resource Descriptions from Dialects of Languages (e.g., microformats)
OWL 2, 2012	OWL 2 extends the W3C OWL Web Ontology Language with a small but useful set of features (EL, QL, RL) that enable effective reasoning
DQV, 2015	Data Quality Vocabulary is an extension to the DCAT vocabulary to cover the quality of the data
SHACL, 2017	Shapes Constraint Language is a language for validating RDF graphs against a set of conditions
DCAT, 2020	Data Catalog Vocabulary is an RDF vocabulary for facilitating interoperability between Web-based data catalogs

robustness of modern RDF stores, as well as wider adoption of standards for representing and querying semantic knowledge, such as RDF(s) and SPARQL, have adopted linked data principles and semantic technologies in data and knowledge management tasks. Table 4.2 gives an overview of (recommended) SW technologies by the W3C.[1]

Aside from the W3C, there are a few international organizations (associations or consortia) that are important for assessing and standardizing ITs, such as IEEE-SA (see The Institute of Electrical and Electronics Engineers Standards Association[2]), OASIS (see The Organization for the Advancement of Structured Information Standards[3]), and a number of others.

---

[1]http://www.w3.org/.

[2]http://standards.ieee.org/.

[3]http://www.oasis-open.org/.

4.2.3 Semantic Integration and Semantic Data Lake Concept

In Tim Berners-Lee's vision, the Web is a massive platform-neutral engineering solution that is service-oriented, with service specified by machine-processable metadata, formally defined in terms of messages which are exchanged between provider and requester agents, rather than the properties of the agents themselves. In the last 10 years, businesses have embraced Tim Berners-Lee's vision and the linked data approach, and cloud computing infrastructures have enabled the emergence of semantic data lakes.

The following are some of the ways by which computer scientists and software providers have tackled the emerging problems in the design of end-to-end data/ knowledge processing pipelines:

- In addition to operational database management systems (present on the market since the 1970s), different NoSQL stores appeared that lack adherence to the time-honored SQL principles of ACID (i.e., atomicity, consistency, isolation, and durability) (Table 4.3).
- Cloud computing emerged as a paradigm that focuses on sharing data and computations over a scalable network of nodes including end user computers, data centers, and Web services (Assunção et al., 2015).
- The concept of open data emerged ("data or content that anyone is free to use, reuse and redistribute") as an initiative to enable businesses to use open data sources to improve their business models and drive a competitive advantage (see an example of integrating open data in end-to-end processing in modern ecosystem in Fig. 4.1).
- The concept of data lake as a new storage architecture was promoted; in it, raw data can be stored regardless of source, structure, and (usually) size. As a result, the data warehousing method (which is built on a repository of centralized, filtered data that have already been processed for a particular purpose) is seen as obsolete, as it causes problems with data integration and adding new data sources.

The development of business intelligence services is simple, when all data sources collect information based on unified file formats and the data are uploaded to a data warehouse. However, the biggest challenge that enterprises face is the undefined and unpredictable nature of data appearing in multiple formats. Additionally, in order to gain competitive advantage over their business rivals, the companies utilize open data resources that are free from restrictions, can be reused and redistributed, and can provide immediate information and insights. Thus, in a modern data ecosystem, data lakes and data warehouses are both widely used for storing big data. A data warehouse (Kern et al., 2020) is a repository for structured, filtered data that have already been processed for a specific purpose. A data lake is a large, raw data repository that stores and manages the company's data bearing any format. Moreover, recently, *semantic data lakes* (Mami et al., 2019) were introduced as an extension of the data lake supplying it with a semantic middleware, which

Table 4.3 Semantic intelligence in the drug domain (example)

	Step	Description
1	Identification of datasets	The data architect first identifies the existing company data sources, as well as available open data sources (e.g., DrugBank and DBpedia)
	Elaboration of business questions	The business users specify questions to be answered with a unified access interface to a set of autonomous, distributed, and heterogeneous data sources, as well as with AI-based business intelligence services
2	Development of semantic models	In the case of the drug domain, the drug dataset has properties such as generic drug name, code, active substances, non-proprietary name, strength value, cost per unit, manufacturer, related drug, description, URL, and license. Hence, ontology development can leverage reuse of classes and properties from existing ontologies and vocabularies including Schema.org vocabulary[a], DBpedia Ontology[b], UMBEL (Upper Mapping and Binding Exchange Layer)[c], DICOM (Digital Imaging and Communications in Medicine)[d], and DrugBank
3	Elaboration of extraction rules	The data administrator runs the extraction process using software tools, such as OpenRefine (which the authors used), RDF Mapping Language[e], and XLWrap[f], which is a Spreadsheet-to-RDF Wrapper, among others
	Elaboration of mapping rules	For the identified datasets (i.e., Excel, XLS data, and MySQL store), the data administrator can specify and run mapping rules in order to query the data on-the-fly without data transformation or materialization
4	Elaboration of quality assessment services	The business user/data architect specifies models for describing the quality of the semantic (big linked) data which are needed. Zaveri et al. (2016), for instance, grouped the dimensions into: • *Accessibility*: availability, licensing, interlinking, security, and performance • *Intrinsic*: syntactic validity, semantic accuracy, consistency, conciseness, and completeness • *Contextual*: relevancy, trustworthiness, understandability, and timeliness • *Representational*: representational conciseness, interoperability, interpretability, and versatility
5	Standardization of interlinking	Specialized tools are used to help the interlinking and to discover links between the source and target datasets. Since the manual mode is tedious, error-prone, and time-consuming, and the fully automated mode is currently unavailable, the semi-automated mode is preferred and reliable. Link generation application yields links in RDF format using *rdfs:seeAlso* or *owl:sameAs* predicates
	Standardization of data querying connectors	The data administrator specifies connectors as standardized components for interoperability between different solutions. Once the datasets are prepared based on standard vocabularies, the next step is to provide standard querying mechanisms. To this aim, vocabularies such as DCAT and DQV are used to

(continued)

Table 4.3 (continued)

	Step	Description
		describe the datasets and standardize the access to data. SPARQL is one of the standard querying languages for RDF KGs
6	Exploration via federated querying	Intelligently searching vast datasets of drug data (i.e., patents, scientific publications, and clinical trials) data will help, for instance, accelerate the discovery of new drugs and gain insights into which avenues are likely to yield the best results. Federated query processing techniques (Endris et al., 2020) provide a solution to scale up to large volumes of data distributed across multiple data sources. Source details are used to find efficient execution plans that reduce the overall execution time of a query while increasing the completeness of the answers
7	Advanced Data Analytics Services	Drug data aggregated with other biomedical data often display different levels of granularity, that is, a variety of data dimensionalities, sample sizes, sources, and formats. In order to support human decision-making, different widgets are needed for visualization and tracing the results of interactive analysis
	Advanced Business Intelligence Services	Algorithm-based techniques (i.e., machine learning and deep learning algorithms) have already been used in drug discovery, bioinformatics, and cheminformatics. What is new in semantic intelligence-based systems is that contextual information from the KG can be used in machine learning, thus improving, for instance, the recommendation and explainability capabilities (Fletcher, 2019; Patel et al., 2020)
8	Integration in big data ecosystem	There are multiple ways of exposing and exploring the KGs-based services to public and other businesses, for instance, using the *data-as-a-service* or *software-as-a-service* concept

[a]https://schema.org/
[b]https://wiki.dbpedia.org/services-resources/ontology
[c]http://umbel.org/
[d]https://www.dicomstandard.org/
[e]https://github.com/RMLio
[f]http://xlwrap.sourceforge.net/

allows uniform access to original heterogeneous data sources. *Semantic data lakes* integrate knowledge graphs (KGs), a solution that allows the building of a common understanding of heterogeneous, distributed data in organizations and value chains, and thus provision of smart data for AI applications.

In 2012, the announcement of the Google Knowledge Graph drew much attention to graph representations of general world knowledge. In the last decade, enterprise settings have shown a tendency to collect and encapsulate metadata in a form of corporate knowledge (or smart data) using semantic technologies, while the data are stored or managed via an enterprise KG. However, many factors have prevented effective large-scale development and implementation of complex knowledge-based

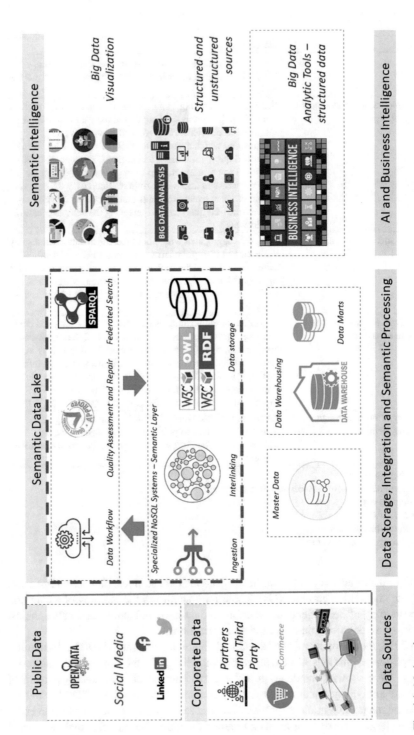

Fig. 4.1 Modern data ecosystem

scenarios because of the inability to cope with the rising challenges coming from big data applications, the rigidity of existing database management systems, the inability to go beyond the standard requirements of query answering, and the lack of knowledge languages expressive enough to address real-world cases. Despite the challenges, the voluntary created KGs such as DBpedia (Auer et al., 2007a, b) motivated many big companies (e.g., Google, Facebook, and Amazon) to explore the benefits of using semantic technologies for profit.

4.3   Semantics and Data Analytics

Data analytics is a concept that refers to a group of technologies that are focused on data mining and statistical analysis. Data analytics has grown in popularity as a field of study for both practitioners and academics over the last 70 years. The Analytics 1.0 era started in the 1950s and lasted roughly 50 years. With the advent of relational databases in the 1970s and the invention of the Web by Sir Tim Berners-Lee in 1989, the data analytics progressed dramatically as a new software approach, and AI was developed as a separate scientific discipline.

The Analytics 2.0 era began in the 2000s with the introduction of Web 2.0-based social and crowdsourcing systems. Although business solutions in the Analytics 1.0 era were focused on relational and multidimensional database models, the Analytics 2.0 era introduced NoSQL and big data database models, which opened up new goals and technological possibilities for analyzing large volumes of semi-structured data. Before big data and after big data are terms companies and data scientists use to describe these two spans of time (Davenport, 2013).

The fusion of internal data with externally sourced data from the Internet, different types of sensors, public data projects (e.g., the human genome project), and captures of audio and video recordings were made possible by a new generation of tools with fast-processing engines and NoSQL stores. The data science area (a multifocal field consisting of an intersection of mathematics and statistics, computer science, and domain specific knowledge) also advanced significantly during this period, delivering scientific methods, exploratory processes, algorithms, and resources that can be used to derive knowledge and insights from data in various forms. The IoT and cloud computing technologies ushered in the Analytics 3.0 era, allowing for the creation of hybrid technology environments for data storage, real-time analysis, and intelligent customer-oriented services. After the countless possibilities for capitalizing on analytics resources, Analytics 3.0 is also known as *the era of impact* or *the era of data-enriched offerings* after the endless opportunities for capitalizing on analytics services. For creating value in the data economy, Davenport (2013) suggested that the following factors need to be properly addressed:

- Combining multiple kinds of information
- Adoption of novel information management tools

- Introduction of "agile" analytical methods and machine-learning techniques to generate insights at a much faster rate
- Embedding analytical and machine learning models into operational and decision processes
- Development of skills and processes for data exploration and discovery
- Requisite skills and processes to develop prescriptive models that involve large-scale testing and optimization and are a means of embedding analytics into key processes
- Leveraging new approaches to decision-making and management

The aim of the Analytics 4.0 era, also known as *the era of consumer-controlled data*, is to give consumers complete or partial control over data. There are various possibilities for automating and augmenting human/computer communications by integrating machine translation, smart reply, chat-bots, and virtual assistants, all of which are associated with the Industry 4.0 trend.

The selection of an appropriate semantic processing model (i.e., vocabularies, taxonomies, and ontologies that facilitate interoperability) (Mishra & Jain, 2020) and analytical solution is a challenging problem and depends on the business issues of the targeted domain, for instance, e-commerce, market intelligence, e-government, healthcare, energy efficiency, emergency management, production management, and/or security.

4.4 Semantics and Business Intelligence Applications

The topic semantic intelligence brings together the efforts of AI, machine learning, and SW communities. The choice of an effective processing model and analytical approach is a difficult task that is influenced by the business concerns of the targeted domain, for instance, risk assessment in banks and the financial sector, predictive maintenance of wind farms, sensing and cognition in production plants, and automated response in control rooms. The integration of advanced analytical services with semantic data lakes is a complex and hot research topic (see the eight-step process in Fig. 4.2). Although the aim of semantics is to make data and processes understandable to machines, the goal of semantic intelligence is to make business intelligence solutions accessible and understandable to humans. Natural language processing and semantic analysis, for example, are used to understand and address posted questions while incorporating semantic knowledge in human-machine interfaces (digital assistants). In this case, natural language processing methods combine statistical and linguistic methods with graph-based AI.

Example This example presents the process of creating and publishing a linked drug dataset based on open drug datasets from selected Arabic countries. The drug dataset has been integrated in a form of a materialized KG (Lakshen et al., 2020). The overall goal is to allow the business user to retrieve relevant information about

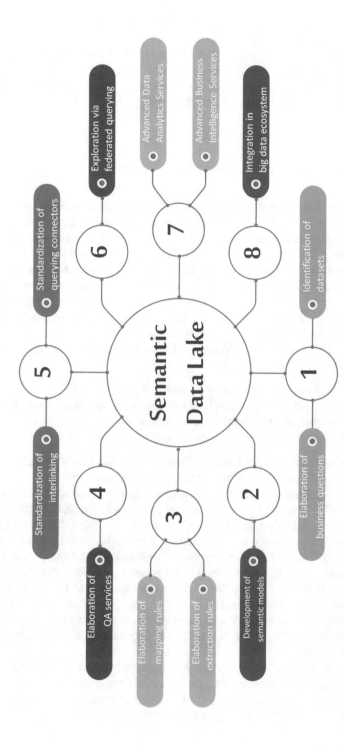

Fig. 4.2 Semantic intelligence driven by KGs

drugs from the local company data store and other open-source datasets. To this aim, an intelligent digital assistant is needed.

The pharmaceutical/drug industry was among the first that validated linked data principles and standards recommended by the W3C consortium and used the approach for precise medicine. Table 4.3 briefly describes the necessary tasks for development of a semantic data lake and leveraging AI with KGs.

4.5   Role of Semantics in (Big) Data Tools

Different keywords are used to name semantic techniques and technologies in the literature and in practice: semantic annotation tools and content indexing and categorization tools; semantic data processing and integration platforms; RDF triple storage systems; SW services (Patel & Jain, 2019) and SOA middleware platforms; semantic annotation tools, content indexing, and categorization tools; semantic search and information retrieval technologies; semantic textual similarity methods, linguistic analysis and text mining algorithms, and ontology-mediated portals; ontological querying/inference engines and rule-based engines; ontology learning methods; and ontology reasoners. In their study of the market value of semantic technologies, Davis et al. (2004) defined the following four major functions 50 commercial companies offered in 2004:

- Discover, acquire, and create semantic metadata
- Represent, organize, integrate, and inter-operate meanings and resources
- Reason, interpret, infer, and answer using semantics
- Provision, present, communicate, and act using semantics

Based on the analysis of the functionalities of more than 50 SW tools, Janev and Vraneš (2011) classified main semantic technology segments into semantic modeling and creation, semantic annotation, semantic data management and integration, semantic search and retrieval, semantic collaboration including portal technologies, and learning and reasoning. Furthermore, Janev et al. (2020) discussed challenges related to big data tools and points to a repository of big data tools; see the results of the project LAMBDA—Learning, Applying, Multiplying Big Data (Janev, 2020). We have categorized the tools into 12 categories (see also Table 4.4): Cloud Marketplaces, Hadoop as a Web Service/Platform, Operational Database Management Systems, NoSQL/Graph databases, Analytics Software/System/Platform, Data Analytics Languages, Optimization Library for Big Data, Library/API for Big Data, ML Library/API for Big Data, Visualization Software/System, and Distributed Messaging System.

The authors' analysis highlights that it is important to distinguish between big data processing, where the size (volume) is one of many important aspects of the data, and big data analytics, where semantic processing and use of semantic standards can improve the analysis and produce explainable results.

Table 4.4 Big data tools[a]

Category	Tools
Cloud marketplaces	Alibaba Cloud; IBM Cloud; Google Cloud Platform; Oracle Cloud Marketplace; CISCO Marketplace; Microsoft Azure Marketplace; AWS Marketplace
Hadoop as a Web service/ platform	HDInsight; IBM InfoSphere BigInsights; MapR; Cloudera CDH; Amazon EMR
Operational database management systems	IBM (DB2); SAP (SAP HANA); Microsoft (SQL Server); ORACLE (Database)
NoSQL/graph databases	Hadoop Distributed File System (hdfs); Amazon Neptune neo4j; TigerGraph; Mapr database; OntoText GraphDB; AllegroGraph; Virtuoso; Apache Jena; MarkLogic JanusGraph; OrientDB; Microsoft Azure Cosmos DB; Apache Hbase; Apache Cassandra; MongoDB
Stream processing engines	Apache Flume; Apache Apex; Amazon Kinesis Streams; Apache Flink; Apache Samza; Apache Storm; Apache Spark
Analytics software/system/ platform	SAS Analytics Software & solutions; MatLab; H2O.ai; Accord framework; Apache Hadoop; Cloudera data platform; VADALog system; Semantic Analytics Stack (SANSA)
Data analytics languages	Scala; Julia; SPARQL; SQL; R; Python package index (PyPI); Python
Optimization library for big data	Facebook ax; Hyperopt; IBM ILOG CPLEX optimization library
Library/API for big data	TensorFlow serving; MLLIB; BigML; Google Prediction API; Azure machine learning; Amazon machine learning API; IBM Watson programming with Big Data in R
ML library/API for big data	Caffe.ai; Apache MXNet; Xgboost; PyTorch; Keras; TensorFlow
Visualization software/ system	Oracle Visual Analyzer; Microsoft Power BI; DataWrapper; QlikView; Canvas.js; HighCharts; Fusion Chart; D3; Tableau; Google chart
Distributed messaging system	Apache Kafka

[a]LAMBDA Catalogue available at https://project-lambda.org/tools-for-experimentation

4.6 Summary

Advances in hardware and software technology, such as the IoT, mobile technologies, data storage and cloud computing, and parallel machine learning algorithms, have allowed the collection, analysis, and storage of large volumes of data from a variety of quantitative and qualitative domain-specific data sources over the last two decades. As the authors presented in this chapter, interoperable data infrastructure and standardization of data-related technology, including the creation of metadata standards for big data management, are needed to simplify and make big data processing more efficient. Semantics play an important role, particularly when it comes to harnessing domain information in the form of KGs. As the authors' analysis showed, in the last decade, especially after the announcement of the Google Knowledge Graph, large corporations introduced semantic processing technologies to provide scalable and flexible data discovery, analysis, and reporting. The semantic data lake approach has been exploited to allow uniform access to original heterogeneous data, while the semantic standards and principles are used for:

- Representing (schema and schema-less) data
- Representing metadata (about documentation, provenance, trust, accuracy, and other quality properties)
- Modeling data processes and flows (i.e., representing the entire pipeline making data representation shareable and verifiable)
- Implementing standard querying and analysis services

However, transforming big data into actionable big knowledge demands scalable methods for creating, curating, querying, and analyzing big knowledge. The authors' study on big data tools reveals that there are still open issues that impede a prevalence usage of graph-based frameworks over more traditional technologies such as relational databases and NoSQL stores. For instance, tools are needed for federations of data sources represented using the RDF graph data model for ensuring efficient and effective query processing while enforcing data access and privacy policies. Next, the integration of analytic algorithms over a federation of data sources should be assessed and evaluated. Finally, quality issues that are more likely to be present, such as inconsistency and incompleteness, should be properly addressed and integrated in the reasoning processes.

Along with the discussion of the emerging big data tools on the market (categorized into 12 groups), in this chapter, the authors summarized an eight-step approach for the utilization of KGs for semantic intelligence. Hence, it is possible to conclude that there is a broad spectrum of applications in different industries where semantic technologies and machine-learning methods are used for managing actionable knowledge in real-world scenarios.

Once the abovementioned issues are effectively addressed, promising results from semantic intelligence services and applications are expected, for instance, for personalized healthcare, financial portfolio optimization and risk management, and big data-driven energy services.

Review Questions
- What is the difference between open data, big data, linked data, and smart data?
- What are the biggest challenges that enterprises face nowadays?
- What are key requirements for development of big data-driven pipelines for transforming big data into actionable knowledge?
- How does the data analytics field develop over time?
- What is the process of development of a semantic data lake?

Discussion Questions
- How can we categorize big data tools? Which technologies are needed for transforming big data into actionable big knowledge?
- Elaborate challenges for big data ecosystems, e.g., energy domain.

- How stable are W3C standards? How often are they used for building semantic intelligence applications? Do you know other standards for building semantic applications?
- Discuss extraction rules and standards for different data sources.

Problem Statements for Young Researchers
- Compare the data warehousing and data lakes concepts.
- Discover different ways for building semantic data lakes.
- How can we leverage AI with KGs?
- How can quality issues in big data (inconsistency and incompleteness) be addressed and integrated in the reasoning processes?
- How can we improve the explainability of AI systems with knowledge graphs?

Acknowledgments The research the authors presented in this chapter is partly financed by the European Union (H2020 PLATOON, Pr. No: 872592; H2020 LAMBDA, Pr. No: 809965; H2020 SINERGY, Pr. No: 952140) and partly by the Ministry of Science and Technological Development of the Republic of Serbia and Science Fund of Republic of Serbia (Artemis).

References

Alvarez, E. B. (2020). Editorial: Smart data management and applications. *Special Issues on Mobility of Systems, Users, Data and Computing, Mobile Networks and Applications.*

Assunção, M. D., Calheiros, R. N., Bianchi, S., Netto, M. A. S., & Buyya, R. (2015). Big data computing and clouds: Trends and future directions. *Journal of Parallel and Distributed Computing, 79–80,* 3–15. https://doi.org/10.1016/j.jpdc.2014.08.003.

Auer, S., Bryl, V., & Tramp, S. (2007a) *Linked open data – Creating knowledge out of interlinked data* (Vol. 8661). Springer International Publishing. https://doi.org/10.1007/978-3-319-09846-3

Auer S., Bizer C., Kobilarov G., Lehmann J., Cyganiak R., & Ives Z. (2007b). DBpedia: A nucleus for a web of open data. In Aberer K. et al. (Eds.), *The semantic web.* ISWC, ASWC 2007. Lecture notes in computer science (Vol. 4825). Berlin: Springer. https://doi.org/10.1007/978-3-540-76298-0_52.

Berners-Lee, T. (2001). The semantic web. *Scientific American, 284,* 34–43.

Berners-Lee, T. (2006). *Design issues: Linked data.* Retrieved from http://www.w3.org/DesignIssues/LinkedData.html

Bizer, C., Heath, T., & Berners-Lee, T. (2009). Linked data – The story so far. *International Journal on Semantic Web and Information Systems, 5*(3), 1–22.

Dallemand, J. (2020). Smart data; How to shift from Big Data. In *How can travel companies generate better customer insights?* Retrieved from https://blog.datumize.com/smart-data-how-to-shift-from-big-data

Davenport, T. H. (2013). Analytics 3.0. Retrieved from https://hbr.org/2013/12/analytics-30

Davis, M., Allemang, D., & Coyne, R. (2004). Evaluation and market report. IST Project 2001-33052 WonderWeb: Ontology Infrastructure for the Semantic Web.

Endris, K. M., Vidal, M. E., & Graux, D. (2020). Federated query processing. In V. Janev, D. Graux, H. Jabeen, & E. Sallinger (Eds.), *Knowledge graphs and big data processing. Lecture notes in computer science* (Vol. 12072). Cham: Springer. https://doi.org/10.1007/978-3-030-53199-7_5.

Firican, G. (2017). *The 10 vs of big data*. Retrieved from https://tdwi.org/articles/2017/02/08/10-vs-of-big-data.aspx

Fletcher, J (2019, March 6). KGCNs: Machine learning over knowledge graphs with tensor flow. *TowardsDataScience.com*. Retrieved from https://towardsdatascience.com/kgcns-machine-learning-over-knowledge-graphs-with-tensorflow-a1d3328b8f02

Ge, M., Bangui, H., & Buhnova, B. (2018). Big data for Internet of Things: A survey. *Future Generation Computer Systems, 87*, 601–614.

Jain, S. (2021). *Understanding semantics-based decision support*. New York: Chapman and Hall/CRC. https://doi.org/10.1201/9781003008927.

Janev, V. (2020). Ecosystem of big data. In V. Janev, D. Graux, H. Jabeen, & E. Sallinger (Eds.), *Knowledge graphs and big data processing* (pp. 3–19). Springer International Publishing. https://doi.org/10.1007/978-3-030-53199-7_1.

Janev, V., & Vraneš, S. (2009). *Semantic Web technologies: Ready for adoption?* IEEE IT Professional, September/October, 8–16. IEEE Computer Society.

Janev, V., & Vraneš, S. (2011). Applicability assessment of semantic web technologies. *Information Processing & Management, 47*, 507–517. https://doi.org/10.1016/j.ipm.2010.11.002.

Janev, V., Mijović, V., & Vraneš, S. (2018). Using the linked data approach in European e-government systems. *International Journal on Semantic Web and Information Systems, 14*(2), 27–46. https://doi.org/10.4018/IJSWIS.2018040102.

Janev, V., Paunović, D., Sallinger, E., & Graux, D. (2020). LAMBDA learning and consulting platform. In *Proceedings of 11th International Conference on eLearning*, 24–25 September 2020, Belgrade, Serbia, Belgrade Metropolitan University.

Kern, R., Kozierkiewicz, A., & Pietranik, M. (2020). The data richness estimation framework for federated data warehouse integration. *Information Sciences, 513*, 397–411. ISSN: 0020-0255. https://doi.org/10.1016/j.ins.2019.10.046.

Lakshen, G., Janev, V., & Vraneš, S. (2020). Arabic Linked Drug Dataset Consolidating and Publishing. Computer Science and Information Systems. Retrieved from http://www.comsis.org/archive.php?show=ppr751-2005

Laney, D. (2001). *3D data management: controlling data volume, velocity, and variety*. Application Delivery Strategies, Meta Group.

Liu, Y., Wang, Q., & Hai-Qiang, C. (2015). Research on it architecture of heterogeneous big data. *Journal of Applied Science and Engineering, 18*(2), 135–142.

Mami, M. N., Graux, D., Scerri, S., Jabeen, H., Auer, S., & Lehmann, S. (2019). Uniform access to multiform data lakes using semantic technologies. In *Proceedings of the 21st International Conference on Information Integration and Web-based Applications & Services* (pp. 313–322). https://doi.org/10.1145/3366030.3366054

Manyika, J. (2011). *Big data: The next frontier for innovation, competition, and productivity*. The McKinsey Global Institute (pp. 1–137).

Mijović, V., Tomasević, N., Janev, V., Stanojević, M., & Vraneš, S. (2019). Emergency management in critical infrastructures: A complex-event-processing paradigm. *Journal of Systems Science and Systems Engineering, 28*(1), 37–62. https://doi.org/10.1007/s11518-018-5393-5.

Mishra, S., & Jain, S. (2020). Ontologies as a semantic model in IoT. *International Journal of Computers and Applications, 42*(3), 233–243.

Patel, A., & Jain, S. (2019). Present and future of semantic web technologies: A research statement. *International Journal of Computers and Applications*, 1–10.

Patel, A., Jain, S., & Shandilya, S. K. (2018). Data of semantic web as unit of knowledge. *Journal of Web Engineering, 17*(8), 647–674.

Patel, L., Shukla, T., Huang, X., Ussery, D. W., & Shanzhi Wang, S. (2020). Machine learning methods in drug discovery. *Molecules, 25*, 5277.

Patrizio, A. (2018, December 03). IDC: Expect 175 zettabytes of data worldwide by 2025. *Network World*. https://www.networkworld.com/article/3325397/idc-expect-175-zettabytes-of-data-worldwide-by-2025.html

Rahman, M. A., & Asyhari, A. T. (2019). The emergence of Internet of Things (IoT): Connecting anything, anywhere. *Computers, 8*, 40. https://doi.org/10.3390/computers8020040.

Sheth, A. (1997). Panel: Data semantics: What, where and how? In R. Meersman & L. Mark (Eds.), *Database applications semantics. IAICT* (pp. 601–610). Boston, MA: Springer. https://doi.org/10.1007/978-0-387-34913-826.

Thusoo, A., Borthakur, D., & Murthy, R. (2010). Data warehousing and analytics infrastructure at Facebook. In *Proceedings of the 2010 ACM SIGMOD International Conference on Management of Data SIGMOD 2010* (pp. 1013–1020). ACM.

Tiwari, S. M., Jain, S., Abraham, A., & Shandilya, S. (2018). Secure semantic smart HealthCare (S3HC). *Journal of Web Engineering, 17*(8), 617–646.

Wang, L. (2017). Heterogeneous data and big data analytics. *Automatic Control and Information Sciences, 3*(1), 8–15.

Woods, W. (1975). What's in a link: Foundations for semantic networks. In *Representation and understanding* (pp. 35–82).

Zaveri, A., Rula, A., Maurino, A., Pietrobon, R., Lehmann, J., & Auer, S. (2016). Quality assessment for linked data: A survey. *Semantic Web – Interoperability, Usability, Applicability, 7*(1), 63–93. https://doi.org/10.3233/SW-150175

Valentina Janev is a Senior Researcher at the Mihajlo Pupin Institute, University of Belgrade, Serbia. She received the PhD degree in the field of Semantic Web technologies from the University of Belgrade, School of Electrical Engineering. Since 2006, she has taken part in many research projects funded by the European Commission (LAMBDA, SINERGY, SLIDEWIKI, LOD2, MOVECO, EMILI, GEO-KNOW, GENDERTIME, HELENA, SHARE-PSI, PACINNO, FORSEE, Web4Web and others), coordinating two of them (see LAMBDA and SINERGY). She has published 1 authored book, 1 edited book and around 90 papers as journal, book, conference, and workshop contributions in these fields. She serves as an expert evaluator of EC Framework Programme Projects; as a reviewer and an Editorial Board Member of respectable international journals; as well as a member of the Program Committees several International Conferences including ESWC, ISWC, SEMANTiCS, CENTERIS, and ICIST.

Chapter 5
Securing Smart Connected World: Key Challenges and Possible Solutions

Yang Lu ⬤

Abstract To build fully functional smart applications, critical challenges need to be properly addressed for user privacy, system availability, and cyber resilience. In this chapter, we identify the challenges in privacy, security, and trust aspects and review existing solutions adopted to protect IoT systems from malicious attacks, unauthorized access, and privacy breaches. Due to a high volume of interconnected devices raising scalability, heterogeneity, and interoperability issues, we propose semantic-enabled solutions to protect sensitive data shared for clinical collaboration, such as record linkage. As semantic reasoning allows effective management of user privileges and anonymity schemes, both privacy and utility can be ensured in the release of record linkage.

Keywords IoT · Access control · Trust · Ontology · Semantic reasoning · e-Health

Key Points
- Review of the concepts being used to support smart connected web applications (such as IoT, WoT, and SWoT) and security models proposed for IoT systems
- Content broken down into three sections to review identified challenges and technical solutions related to privacy, authentication, and access control, as well as trust
- Demonstration of how semantic methods can be designed for security and privacy purposes within the example scenarios of clinical collaboration
- Summary of the challenges of securing smart web applications and the benefits of using Semantic Web technologies to protect heterogeneous content from security issues

Y. Lu (✉)
School of Science, Technology and Health, York St John University, York, UK
e-mail: y.lu@yorksj.ac.uk

© The Author(s), under exclusive license to Springer Nature Switzerland AG 2021
S. Jain, S. Murugesan (eds.), *Smart Connected World*,
https://doi.org/10.1007/978-3-030-76387-9_5

5.1   Introduction

The Internet of Things (IoT) refers to connecting devices to the Internet to be able to exchange information anytime from anywhere to any device. Challenges are being faced by those who create applications that span many IoT platforms. To ensure interoperability among devices, the Web of Things (WoT) framework was suggested to enable worldwide discovery by exposing these platforms through web applications (Guinard et al., 2011). The Semantic Web of Things (SWoT) refers to a service infrastructure where semantic applications are used to improve the accessibility and utility of connected sensors (Pfisterer et al., 2011; Gyrard et al., 2017). For instance, data collected from smart devices is considered highly heterogeneous, which can add difficulties to knowledge sharing and information extraction and integration. To address these issues, IoT data can be modeled in the form of ontologies to serve as the knowledge base for efficient reasoning (Mishra & Jain, 2020).

While building a smart application, security and privacy requirements of IoT should be considered and satisfied. For instance, IoT systems may have unpatched vulnerabilities in their hardware and software; they are exposed to larger attack surfaces, and thus cyber-attacks are possible to the entire network due to the connected devices; IoT clients may not have enough knowledge, etc. To ensure security and privacy, Fabian and Gunther (2007) described *data authentication*, *user privacy*, *access control*, and *resilience to network attacks* as the requirements of using IoT technology. In addition, Nzabahimana (2018) proposed the CIA triad for IoT infrastructures. As shown in Fig. 5.1, *confidentiality* requires that IoT manufacturers and vendors ensure only authorized consumers have access to data transmitted by connected devices; in regard to *integrity*, data must remain intact when it is transmitted among IoT systems; and for *availability*, single points of failure should be avoided, and downtime should be minimized in critical systems. Based on the Internet standards, Seliem et al. (2018) stated that cyber-attacks could happen at the device layer, network/platform layer, and application layer, and suggested that the mechanisms could be adopted to protect IoT data.

Once the concept of the Web was proposed, it soon became an information space that reflects human knowledge and relationships, adding complexity to trust relationships among humans, computers, and organizations. As a result, trusted computing has been developed as a new paradigm in the security community, discussing the protection mechanisms for open, decentralized computer systems (Golbeck, 2008). Trust management is found useful to overcome the uncertainty about security and privacy risks, and engage in the consumption of IoT services and applications (Yan et al., 2014). According to Gu et al. (2014), trusted computing mechanisms are significant in IoT environments since they can address the uncertainty and heterogeneity in collaboration, improve flexibility and efficiency, as well as make them compatible with other security mechanisms. As the WoT framework was proposed as a guarantee of interoperability among IoT systems, trust models can be built with trustworthiness among service consumers, based on the opinions of friends and service seekers (Javaid et al., 2018).

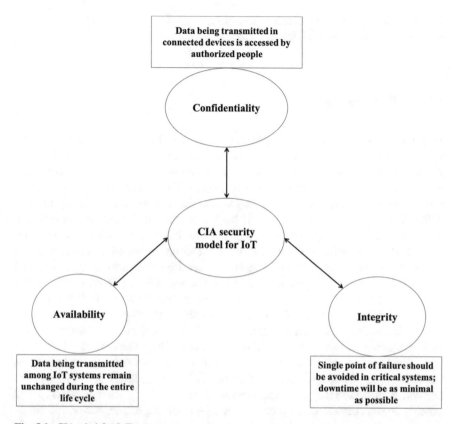

Fig. 5.1 CIA triad for IoT system

To guide software engineers to consider such issues, this chapter investigates privacy and security requirements based on IoT system features. In Sects. 5.2–5.4, we review and discuss technical solutions for *privacy, authentication, access control,* and *trust management* adopted in IoT platforms. Based on the example scenarios in Sect. 5.5, we discuss potential challenges of protecting smart web applications designed for clinical collaboration. To ensure heterogeneity and scalability of distributed systems, we provide semantic-enabled solutions with efficient reasoning to support automated policy composition and enforcement.

5.2 Privacy

Privacy means that personal information should not be disclosed without explicit consent. In other words, data subjects have the right to decide who can access their data. For example, Nikhil should be the only one who can share his real-time locations with the coronavirus contact tracing app to receive real-time self-isolating tips. To ensure privacy in smart environments, there are solutions designed to protect various IoT data types in different contexts.

5.2.1 Data Privacy

With the widespread use of IoT services, personal data has been collected, analyzed, and sold to data consumers such as service providers, due to the usefulness in presenting value-added services such as recommendation and customization. (Oh et al., 2019). To use personalized services, IoT customers are willing to share their personal information even though this can put personal privacy at risk. Although the perceived privacy risk is high in general healthcare environments, it shows that people are generally willing to share data to use health services (Kim et al., 2019). In addition, different privacy concerns can be found regarding personal sensing types. For example, customers are less sensitive to wearing devices installed with accelerometers or barometers than microphones or GPS (Klasnja et al., 2009).

Identifiable information generated from sensor networks can facilitate service automation such as payment tokens, proximity cards, and toll-payment transponders. For instance, the e-passport represents the initial deployment of biometrics and radio-frequency identification (RFID) technology. Regardless of the benefit of auto-authenticating travelers, releasing biometric data can cause new risks such as identity forgery, theft, tracking, and hotlisting (Juels et al., 2005). As RFID tags are embedded in personal belongings, pockets, and even body sensors, privacy and security issues stimulated research on privacy-preserving authentication/identification. For instance, with item-level RFID tagging, retailers can monitor stock levels and prevent out-of-stock issues. However, it can betray the competitive intelligence if the stock turnover rates are disclosed to competitors (Juels, 2006). In case of a certain level of emergency, Hu et al. (2011) proposed a location system to confirm user identities through authentication. As shown in Fig. 5.2, the location system is built on subsystems for registration, authentication, as well as policy compliance. To

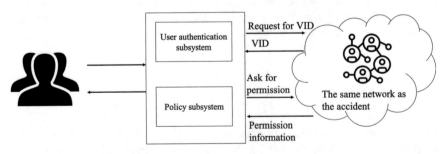

Fig. 5.2 Locating users in IoT environments (Hu et al., 2011)

ensure privacy while providing user locations, it ensures that location information can only be accessed by authorized users.

5.2.2   Contextual Privacy

Contextual information can be used to characterize the situation of entities (such as a person, an object, or a place) related to the interaction of an application (Abowd et al., 1999). To raise awareness of privacy risks existing in IoT data collection practices, Onu et al. (2020) proposed a framework to contextualize privacy policies within IoT domains. Apart from conventional elements, the proposed policy model also specifies the *frequency of collection*, *sensor activation*, and *context* to enrich privacy requirements of data collection. To satisfy the domain-specific needs in terms of privacy and quality, Sicari et al. (2016) designed the framework with annotated IoT data representation coming from heterogeneous technologies.

Special needs for privacy were studied in certain application domains. For instance, it was shown that security and privacy behaviors in the multi-user smart home can be influenced by the limited usage of access control, concern regarding social norms, and the trade-off between privacy and utility (Zeng & Roesner, 2019). To avoid competitive risks in sharing transport data among private and public operators, a k-anonymous diffusion mechanism was proposed to ensure privacy in network data management (He & Chow, 2019). In the smart healthcare system, sensitive data is generated from, aggregated, and exchanged among a huge number of interactive nodes. To satisfy the context-aware privacy requirements, Zemmoudj et al. (2019) suggested an identity-based encryption scheme to be applied in the communication scenarios. In the mobile health paradigm, wearables collect a wide variety of data through interfacing with smartphones and computers. To ensure privacy in data collection from wearable devices and eliminate errors incurred by perturbation, Kim et al. (2020) proposed a solution through leveraging differential privacy on a small number of salient data samples.

5.2.3   Privacy-Preserving Data Processing

With database operations and machine learning techniques utilized for IoT data analytics, it is necessary to assess potential risks and address users' privacy concerns. Given that statistical anomalies in sensor data may cause privacy breaches, Ukil et al. (2014) proposed a scheme that enables data owners to quantify the privacy risk of data disclosure, with the deployment of statistical disclosure control and information theoretic models. Range queries in IoT applications could improve efficiency while also allowing device identification and query result disclosure. To ensure data and location privacy, a privacy-preserving database query (PPDQ) protocol was designed with hashing and bitwise exclusive OR operations to support the MIN,

MAX, and MAX/MIN range queries (Sciancalepore & Di Pietro, 2020). Privacy may not be guaranteed as sensitive data can be generated from interactive nodes and exchanged through IoT platforms. To address this, Boussada et al. (2019) provided a privacy-preserving data transmission solution with an identity-based encryption scheme and communication scheme. To maintain data privacy while analyzing IoT data for intrusion detection, Rahman et al. (2020) proposed a federated learning-based scheme to perform training and inference of intrusion detection models locally.

5.3   Authentication and Access Control

Security and privacy policies are defined to protect sensitive information. According to Abouelmehdi et al. (2018), IoT security refers to protecting data, devices, and connections against the risks of unauthorized access, malicious attacks, and stealing for profit. Due to the explicit requirements regarding integrity and availability, it is insufficient to secure smart web applications by only addressing privacy issues. Specifically, the authentication and access control methods need to ensure the security of heterogeneous data in various IoT scenarios (Weber, 2010). To address the lack of security from traditional methods, a key-changed authentication protocol was designed with an integrated random number generator (Peng et al., 2013). In the wireless sensor network (WSN), the usage of one-way hash function, real-time key update, and backup can guarantee mutual authentication and minimize risks of key exposure during communication. To protect heterogeneous IoT nodes and networks, the authentication protocol was designed based on the heterogeneous fusion mechanism (Wan et al., 2020). Considering the limited resources and energy in unmanned aerial vehicle (UAV) networks, Nikooghadam et al. (2020) devised an efficient authentication method for smart city surveillance. Since the denial-of-service (DoS) attack can be a significant threat for consuming energy of IoT nodes, Ghahramani et al. (2020) suggested a received signal strength (RSS) method to resist DoS attacks imposed by humans and ensure the availability requirements. IoT applications may rely on real-time communication for decision-making. As a consequence, a cloud-based identity management system may not be appropriate for heterogeneous devices. To solve this issue, Sadique et al. (2020) proposed an edge-fog-based identity management scheme for IoT devices and edge IoT gateways (EIoTG), which includes the protocols of authentication, authorization, secure communication, and key distribution.

In the light of confidentiality and integrity, access control models can be designed to manage different access requests. Specifically, there are conventional access control models, such as role-based access control (RBAC) and attribute-based access control (ABAC), tailored to protect IoT entities from unexpected access (Pal et al., 2017; Bonatti et al., 2013; Bezawada et al., 2018). Due to the lack of scalable mechanisms that can protect distributed systems of dynamicity needs, Gusmeroli et al. (2013) proposed a capability-based access control method for organizations or individuals to customize their own requirements in terms of services and information access. To support the interoperability among standardized communication protocols, a flexible framework, OAuth-IoT, was designed to facilitate authentication and authorization in the IoT contexts (Sciancalepore et al., 2017). While serving an open ecosystem such as Web of Things (WoT), it is crucial to have finer-grained access control to verify different parties and evaluate access requests (Mishra et al., 2018). For instance, Barka et al. (2015) introduced an architecture allowing WoT service prescribers to manage who can access what content and how this access can be continued or terminated.

5.4 Trust Management

IoT trust issues are derived from two facets: *transparency*, meaning that IoT users are informed about what data is collected, for what purposes, and how it will be processed; and *consistency*, meaning that IoT devices should meet users' expectations. Since IoT information is provided by electronic tags and sensors, it is possible for a malicious party to inject false information into devices and affect other parties (Javaid et al., 2018). One solution to this issue can be building trusted virtual domains in which users trust each other by sharing a common policy enforced (Joshi & Mishra, 2016). Meanwhile, intrusion detection systems (IDS) tailored for IoT applications can be set up to detect adversarial activities (Raza et al., 2013). Based on the indirect and direct trust relations, Bao and Chen (2012) suggested a genetic algorithm for a SOA-based, social WoT system. In addition, reputation architectures were built to coordinate data processing (Cuomo et al., 2017), resource sharing (De Meo et al., 2017), and cross-domain authorization (Chen et al., 2019; El Jaouhari et al., 2020). As for IoT availability and accountability, distributed ledgers and encryption techniques can be adopted to identify malicious objects (Boudguiga et al., 2017) and secure communication between devices (Kumar et al., 2019).

5.5 Securing Collaboration with Semantic Solutions

The rapid growth of IoT and WoT applications has given rise to a proliferation of information sources accessible via the Internet. However, without a standardized, machine-readable representation, it is often difficult to deal with device information to meet the myriad user demands. To accommodate the scaling resources in dynamic smart environments, security models were formed by leveraging domain-specific ontologies (Finin et al., 2008; Knechtel et al., 2008; Sinnott et al., 2009). In the following example scenarios, we show that semantic-enabled solutions can be implemented for multi-domain authentication, trust, and privacy-aware access control so as to facilitate clinical collaboration.

Table 5.1 Role definition in INPDR (Lu & Sinnott, 2015)

Role names	Privileges
Clinician	Create/Edit/Delete data of his/her center
	Read data tagged as his/her center/country
	Read data tagged as all
Collaborator	Create/Edit data of his/her center
	Read data tagged as his/her center/country
	Read data tagged as all
Researcher	Read data tagged of his/her center/country
	Read data tagged as all
External Researcher	Read data tagged as all

Registration is typically the first step of requesting to access data. For instance, the International Niemann-Pick Disease Registry (INPDR, https://inpdr.org/) relies on one authority for user authentication and authorization. Table 5.1 shows the role names and corresponding privileges supported in the INPDR. In addition to matching privileges, data in request should be verified based on the "access level" and users' geolocations. After registering, all users are assigned a centralized username and password. As shown in Fig. 5.3a, through enrolling at the INPDR system and receiving the pre-agreed credentials from the centralized INPDR administrator, both Dr. Müller and Dr. Smith can apply to view or request certain NPD patient information in the roles of *Clinician* and *Researcher*, respectively. Alternatively, Fig. 5.3b shows a semantic-based, federated identity management solution for supporting trusted communication between identity providers and associated services, with users being directed to their home sites to authenticate (Lu & Sinnott, 2015). Through the leverage of existing security information, the impact of increased number of users as well as up-to-date privileges can be minimized. In this case, common elements (such as *Role* and *Country*) are represented by *Classes* and specific instances by *Individuals*, such as *Clinician* (*Role*) and *Berlin03* (*Centre*). With a federated identity management system like Shibboleth (Jie et al., 2011), Dr. Müller can select *Berlin03* to verify his identity, bb@berlin3.gr. After authenticating, the identity provider sends identity certificates and potentially local attributes, e.g., the clinical role of pediatrician (in German *Pädiatrisch*, center *Berlin03*, and country *Deutschland*). Based on agreed mappings, Dr. Müller can be automatically granted with the privileges mapped to the central role of *Clinician* and country *Germany*. Inspired by the Circle-of-Trust (CoT) model designed for resource sharing in decentralized environments (Ajayi et al., 2008), a certain degree of trust can be achieved based on the length of a trust route. For instance, Fig. 5.4 shows a cross-domain authentication paradigm where IdP_5 is allowed to request services provided by SP_1 according to the trust transitivity, even though it is not in the federation at the beginning. This trust model can be implemented to authenticate external users automatically. In Fig. 5.3b, a medico verified by a trusted center *Udine02* should be able to read all NPD patient information, given the role definition of *External Researcher*.

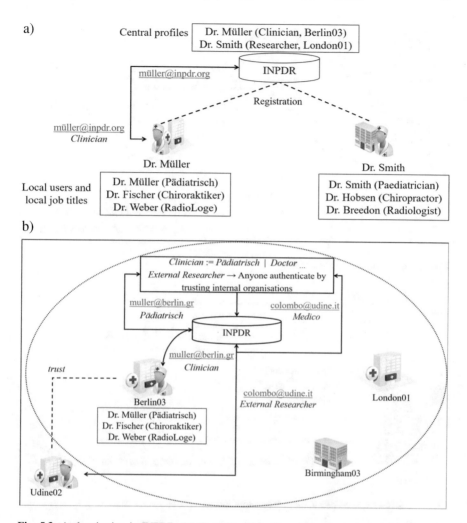

Fig. 5.3 Authentication in INPDR. (**a**) Centralized identity management system. (**b**) Semantic-enabled federated identity management system

Another example scenario requiring "data access" is record linkage, as shown in Fig. 5.5. Record (data) linkage refers to the process through which information recorded in discrete sources can be matched to identify the same individuals or properties related to those individuals (Fellegi & Sunter, 1969). For instance, to request the record linkage produced with datasets maintained by *Centre01* and *Centre02*, users are required to pass the policy checks at both sides. In this case, this involves presenting the role of *Arzt* (German for doctor), which corresponds with the local role of *Doctor*. Achieving such correspondences involves:

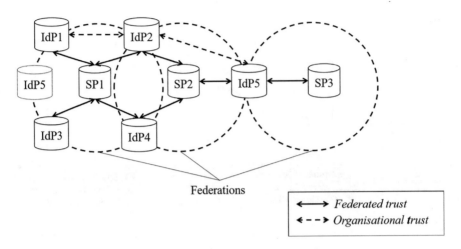

Fig. 5.4 Cross-domain authentication

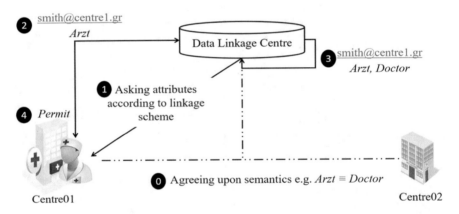

Fig. 5.5 Semantic interoperability in requesting linked records

- Step 0. Building the domain knowledge based on agreement of attribute metadata and attribute relations.
- Step 1. Based on the linkage scheme and data requests, the relevant policies (for datasets) are located and triggered to ask for more attributes (where needed).
- Step 2. The requestor submits the attributes.
- Step 3. According to the policies and domain knowledge, e.g., "Arzt *sameAs* Doctor," the user can get authorized by *Centre02*.
- Step 4. After verifying the collected attributes and evaluating their use in the composite policies, the linkage center can make the final access decision, e.g., permit to the current request.

Through leveraging the eXtensible Access Control Markup Language (XACML) policy framework with obligation components for tackling privacy issues in target

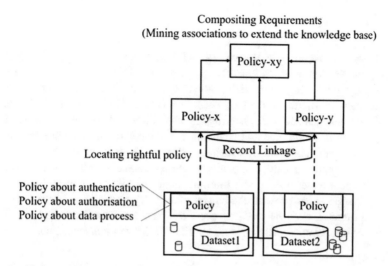

Fig. 5.6 Composing policies in the linkage unit

resources (Lu & Sinnott, 2016), semantic access control methods can deal with more complex scenarios such as ongoing (repeated) record linkage access requests by policy composition (Lu et al., 2018a). Flexible decentralized authentication and authorization cannot address the challenges associated with data privacy, however, since inferences and risk disclosure issues can still arise. For a better trade-off between privacy and utility, a semantic linkage k-anonymity (SLKA) algorithm was designed based on the "unknown presence" of individuals among the linkage cohort (Lu et al., 2017). To avoid unnecessary information loss, accumulative associations mined from historical releases should be mapped to authorized users (groups) and to different linkage schemes. In addition, less transformed anonymity schemes from historical releases should be specified for authorized users (groups) and for different linkage schemes. Through reasoning predefined semantic relations and rules, the SLKA can locate the associated attribute pairs to verify the linkage content (Lu et al., 2018b). For instance, Fig. 5.6 shows that localized policies, *Policy-x* and *Policy-y*, are composed as *Policy-xy* to protect $Linkage_{1-2}$ (i.e., matched records between $Dataset_1$ and $Dataset_2$). With the SLKA, it is not necessary to generalize all values to meet the new requirement such as K_{x-y}. Instead, only the risky associations mined from the historical releases of $Linkage_{1-2}$ will be processed. For complete and sound policy enforcement, *Policy-xy* is generated based on reasoning and inference of risks involving all protagonists, which can deliver more flexible protection for arbitrary combinations.

5.6   Summary

In this chapter, we review the current advancements in securing IoT systems, focusing on the solutions designed for privacy, authentication, access control, and trust management. Regarding the challenges in clinical collaboration scenarios, semantic-enabled methods are suggested to address identity management, access control, and anonymization for heterogeneous entities and contents. Through specifying policies in ontologies and semantic rules, we show how authentication and access control are supported in distributed systems by efficient reasoning. In addition, the automated policy composition can guarantee baseline governance for privacy in the release of data with minimal changes. As well as these issues, smart web applications also present challenges of security and privacy, which demand future exploration, such as profiling users of smart services (Kumar et al., 2016), compliance checking for data ethics, as well as IoT data monetarization.

Review Questions
- How would you explain the concepts of *Internet of Things*, *Web of Things*, and *Semantic Web of Things* and the differences among them?
- What security and privacy technologies might be adopted to meet the confidentiality requirement in a smart healthcare system?
- What essential knowledge and skills are required for cyber security analysts working in IoT-based smart systems?

Discussion Questions
- What is "privacy by design," and how can it be implemented in smart healthcare systems?
- What role do people play in the future cyber security paradigms?
- How can one get adaptive personalization while ensuring privacy?
- How might digital transparency influence privacy?
- How can a trade-off be achieved between "risk" and "benefits"?

Problem Statements for Young Researchers
- What ethical regulations apply to biometric data collection and application? What are the technological and societal challenges in smart surveillance systems (e.g., coronavirus contact-tracing apps, face recognition cameras, immunity passports)? What privacy and security issues could arise if they are built on a centralized/decentralized architecture?
- How could security- and privacy-related aspects of these systems be further improved? Which AI technologies can be adopted to improve existing solutions and how?

References

Abouelmehdi, K., Beni-Hessane, A., & Khaloufi, H. (2018). Big healthcare data: Preserving security and privacy. *Journal of Big Data, 5*(1), 1–18.

Abowd, G. D., Dey, A. K., Brown, P. J., Davies, N., Smith, M., & Steggles, P. (1999). Towards a better understanding of context and context-awareness. In *International Symposium on Hand-held and Ubiquitous Computing* (pp. 304–307). Springer.

Ajayi, O., Sinnott, R., & Stell, A. (2008). Dynamic trust negotiation for flexible e-health collaborations. In *Proceedings of the 15th ACM Mardi Gras Conference: From Lightweight Mash-ups to Lambda Grids: Understanding the Spectrum of Distributed Computing Requirements, Applications, Tools, Infrastructures, Interoperability, and the Incremental Adoption of Key Capabilities* (pp. 1–7). ACM.

Bao, F., & Chen, R. (2012). Trust management for the internet of things and its application to service composition. In *2012 IEEE International Symposium on a World of Wireless, Mobile and Multimedia Networks* (pp. 1–6). IEEE.

Barka, E., Mathew, S. S., & Atif, Y. (2015). Securing the web of things with role-based access control. In *International Conference on Codes, Cryptology, and Information Security* (pp. 14–26). Cham: Springer.

Bezawada, B., Haefner, K., & Ray, I. (2018). Securing home IoT environments with attribute-based access control. In *Proceedings of the Third ACM Workshop on Attribute-Based Access Control* (pp. 43–53). ACM.

Bonatti, P., Galdi, C., & Torres, D. (2013). ERBAC: Event-driven RBAC. In *Proceedings of the 18th ACM Symposium on Access Control Models and Technologies* (pp. 125–136). ACM.

Boudguiga, A., Bouzerna, N., Granboulan, L., Olivereau, A., Quesnel, F., Roger, A., & Sirdey, R. (2017). Towards better availability and accountability for iot updates by means of a blockchain. In *2017 IEEE European Symposium on Security and Privacy Workshops* (pp. 50–58). IEEE.

Boussada, R., Hamdane, B., Elhdhili, M. E., & Saidane, L. A. (2019). Privacy-preserving aware data transmission for IoT-based e-health. *Computer Networks, 162*, 106866.

Chen, J., Tian, Z., Cui, X., Yin, L., & Wang, X. (2019). Trust architecture and reputation evaluation for internet of things. *Journal of Ambient Intelligence and Humanised Computing, 10*(8), 3099–3107.

Cuomo, S., De Michele, P., Piccialli, F., Galletti, A., & Jung, J. E. (2017). IoT-based collaborative reputation system for associating visitors and artworks in a cultural scenario. *Expert Systems with Applications, 79*, 101–111.

De Meo, P., Messina, F., Postorino, M. N., Rosaci, D., & Sarné, G. M. (2017). A reputation framework to share resources into iot-based environments. In *2017 IEEE 14th International Conference on Networking, Sensing and Control* (pp. 513–518). IEEE.

El Jaouhari, S., Bouabdallah, A., & Corici, A. A. (2020). SDN-based security management of multiple WoT smart spaces. *Journal of Ambient Intelligence and Humanized Computing*, 1–16.

Fabian, B., & Gunther, O. (2007). Distributed ONS and its impact on privacy. In *2007 IEEE International Conference on Communications* (pp. 1223–1228). IEEE.

Fellegi, I. P., & Sunter, A. B. (1969). A theory for record linkage. *Journal of the American Statistical Association, 64*(328), 1183–1210.

Finin, T., Joshi, A., Kagal, L., Niu, J., Sandhu, R., Winsborough, W., & Thuraisingham, B. (2008). ROWLBAC: Representing role-based access control in owl. In *Proceedings of the 13th ACM Symposium on Access Control Models and Technologies* (pp. 73–82). ACM.

Ghahramani, M., Javidan, R., Shojafar, M., Taheri, R., Alazab, M., & Tafazolli, R. (2020). RSS: An energy-efficient approach for securing IoT service protocols against the DoS attack. *IEEE Internet of Things Journal, 8*, 3619–3635.

Golbeck, J. (2008). Weaving a web of trust. *Science, 321*(5896), 1640–1641.

Gu, L., Wang, J., & Sun, B. (2014). Trust management mechanism for Internet of Things. *China Communications, 11*(2), 148–156.

Guinard, D., Trifa, V., Mattern, F., & Wilde, E. (2011). From the Internet of Things to the Web of Things: Resource-oriented architecture and best practices. In *Architecting the Internet of Things* (pp. 97–129). Berlin: Springer.

Gusmeroli, S., Piccione, S., & Rotondi, D. (2013). A capability-based security approach to manage access control in the internet of things. *Mathematical and Computer Modelling, 58*(5–6), 1189–1205.

Gyrard, A., Patel, P., Datta, S. K., & Ali, M. I. (2017). Semantic web meets Internet of Things and Web of Things. In *Proceedings of the 26th International Conference on World Wide Web Companion* (pp. 917–920).

He, B. Y., & Chow, J. Y. (2019). Optimal privacy control for transport network data sharing. *Transportation Research Procedia, 38*, 792–811.

Hu, C., Zhang, J., & Wen, Q. (2011). An identity-based personal location system with protected privacy in IoT. In *2011 4th IEEE International Conference on Broadband Network and Multimedia Technology* (pp. 192–195). IEEE.

Javaid, S., Afzal, H., Arif, F., & Iltaf, N. (2018). Trust management for SOA based social WoT system. In *2018 20th International Conference on Advanced Communication Technology* (pp. 387–392). IEEE.

Jie, W., Arshad, J., Sinnott, R., Townend, P., & Lei, Z. (2011). A review of grid authentication and authorization technologies and support for federated access control. *ACM Computing Surveys, 43*(2), 1–26.

Joshi, S., & Mishra, D. K. (2016, November). A roadmap towards trust management & privacy preservation in mobile ad hoc networks. In *2016 International Conference on ICT in Business Industry & Government* (pp. 1–6). IEEE.

Juels, A. (2006). RFID security and privacy: A research survey. *IEEE Journal on Selected Areas in Communications, 24*(2), 381–394.

Juels, A., Molnar, D., & Wagner, D. (2005). Security and privacy issues in e-passports. In *First International Conference on Security and Privacy for Emerging Areas in Communications Networks*. IEEE.

Kim, D., Park, K., Park, Y., & Ahn, J. H. (2019). Willingness to provide personal information: Perspective of privacy calculus in IoT services. *Computers in Human Behavior, 92*, 273–281.

Kim, J. W., Moon, S. M., Kang, S. U., & Jang, B. (2020). Effective privacy-preserving collection of health data from a user's wearable device. *Applied Sciences, 10*(18), 6396.

Klasnja, P., Consolvo, S., Choudhury, T., Beckwith, R., & Hightower, J. (2009). Exploring privacy concerns about personal sensing. In *International Conference on Pervasive Computing* (pp. 176–183). Berlin: Springer.

Knechtel, M., Hladik, J., & Dau, F. (2008). Using OWL DL reasoning to decide about authorization in RBAC. *In OWLED, 8*, 30.

Kumar, R., Gupta, P., & Jain, S. (2016). Ensuring user security against Internet. Scholars Press. ISBN: 978-3-659-83704-3.

Kumar, S., Hu, Y., Andersen, M. P., Popa, R. A., & Culler, D. E. (2019). JEDI: Many-to-many end-to-end encryption and key delegation for IoT. In *28th USENIX Security Symposium* (pp. 1519–1536).

Lu, Y., & Sinnott, R. O. (2015). Semantic security for e-health: A case study in enhanced access control. In *12th International Conference on Autonomic and Trusted Computing* (pp. 407–414). IEEE.

Lu, Y., & Sinnott, R. O. (2016). Semantic-based privacy protection of electronic health records for collaborative research. In *2016 15th IEEE International Conference on Trust, Security and Privacy in Computing and Communications* (pp. 519–526). IEEE.

Lu, Y., Sinnott, R. O., & Verspoor, K. (2017). A semantic-based K-anonymity scheme for health record linkage. *Studies in Health Technology and Informatics, 239*, 84–90.

Lu, Y., Sinnott, R. O., & Verspoor, K. (2018a). Semantic-based policy composition for privacy-demanding data linkage. In *2018 17th IEEE International Conference on Trust, Security and Privacy in Computing and Communications* (pp. 348–359). IEEE.

Lu, Y., Sinnott, R. O., Verspoor, K., & Parampalli, U. (2018b). Privacy-preserving access control in electronic health record linkage. In *17th IEEE International Conference on Trust, Security and Privacy in Computing and Communications* (pp. 1079–1090). IEEE.

Mishra, S., & Jain, S. (2020). Ontologies as a semantic model in IoT. *International Journal of Computers and Applications, 42*(3), 233–243.

Mishra, S., Jain, S., Rai, C., & Gandhi, N. (2018). Security challenges in semantic web of things. In *International Conference on Innovations in Bio-Inspired Computing and Applications* (pp. 162–169). Cham: Springer.

Nikooghadam, M., Amintoosi, H., & Kumari, S. (2020). A provably secure ECC-based roaming authentication scheme for global mobility networks. *Journal of Information Security and Applications, 54*, 102588.

Nzabahimana, J. P. (2018). Analysis of security and privacy challenges in Internet of Things. In *2018 IEEE 9th International Conference on Dependable Systems, Services and Technologies* (pp. 175–178). IEEE.

Oh, H., Park, S., Lee, G. M., Heo, H., & Choi, J. K. (2019). Personal data trading scheme for data brokers in IoT data marketplaces. *IEEE Access, 7*, 40120–40132.

Onu, E., et al. (2020). Contextual privacy policy modelling in IoTs. In *2020 IEEE International Conference on Dependable, Autonomic and Secure Computing* (pp. 94–102). IEEE.

Pal, S., Hitchens, M., Varadharajan, V., & Rabehaja, T. (2017). On design of a fine-grained access control architecture for securing IoT-enabled smart healthcare systems. In *Proceedings of the 14th EAI International Conference on Mobile and Ubiquitous Systems: Computing, Networking and Services* (pp. 432–441).

Peng, L., Ru-chuan, W., Xiao-yu, S., & Long, C. (2013). Privacy protection based on key-changed mutual authentication protocol in internet of things. In *China Conference Wireless Sensor Networks* (pp. 345–355). Berlin: Springer.

Pfisterer, D., Romer, K., Bimschas, D., Kleine, O., Mietz, R., Truong, C., Richardson, R., et al. (2011). SPITFIRE: Toward a semantic web of things. *IEEE Communications Magazine, 49*(11), 40–48.

Rahman, S. A., Tout, H., Talhi, C., & Mourad, A. (2020). Internet of Things intrusion detection: Centralized, on-device, or federated learning? *IEEE Network, 34*(6), 310–317.

Raza, S., Wallgren, L., & Voigt, T. (2013). SVELTE: Real-time intrusion detection in the Internet of Things. *Ad Hoc Networks, 11*(8), 2661–2674.

Sadique, K. M., Rahmani, R., & Johannesson, P. (2020). IMSC-EIoTD: Identity management and secure communication for edge IoT devices. *Sensors, 20*(22), 6546.

Sciancalepore, S., & Di Pietro, R. (2020). PPRQ: Privacy-preserving MAX/MIN range queries in IoT networks. *IEEE Internet of Things Journal*.

Sciancalepore, S., Piro, G., Caldarola, D., Boggia, G., & Bianchi, G. (2017). OAuth-IoT: An access control framework for the Internet of Things based on open standards. In *2017 IEEE Symposium on Computers and Communications* (pp. 676–681). IEEE.

Seliem, M., Elgazzar, K., & Khalil, K. (2018). Towards privacy preserving iot environments: A survey. *Wireless Communications and Mobile Computing*.

Sicari, S., Cappiello, C., De Pellegrini, F., Miorandi, D., & Coen-Porisini, A. (2016). A security-and quality-aware system architecture for Internet of Things. *Information Systems Frontiers, 18*(4), 665–677.

Sinnott, R. O., Doherty, T., Gray, N., & Lusted, J. (2009). Semantic security: Specification and enforcement of semantic policies for security-driven collaborations. *Studies in Health Technology and Informatics, 147*, 201–211.

Ukil, A., Bandyopadhyay, S., & Pal, A. (2014, April). IoT-privacy: To be private or not to be private. In *2014 IEEE Conference on Computer Communications Workshops* (pp. 123–124). IEEE.

Wan, Z., Xu, Z., Liu, S., Ni, W., & Ye, S. (2020). An Internet of Things roaming authentication protocol based on heterogeneous fusion mechanism. *IEEE Access, 8*, 17663–17672.

Weber, R. H. (2010). Internet of Things–New security and privacy challenges. *Computer Law & Security Review, 26*(1), 23–30.

Yan, Z., Zhang, P., & Vasilakos, A. V. (2014). A survey on trust management for Internet of Things. *Journal of Network and Computer Applications, 42*, 120–134.

Zemmoudj, S., Bermad, N., & Omar, M. (2019). CAPM: Context-aware privacy model for IoT-based smart hospitals. In *2019 15th International Wireless Communications & Mobile Computing Conference* (pp. 1139–1144). IEEE.

Zeng, E., & Roesner, F. (2019). Understanding and improving security and privacy in multi-user smart homes: A design exploration and in-home user study. In *28th USENIX Security Symposium* (pp. 159–176).

Yang Lu is currently working as a lecturer (assistant professor) in computer science at School of Science, Technology and Health, York St John University. She received the Ph.D. degree from the School of Computing and Information Systems, University of Melbourne. Her Ph.D. thesis, completed in 2018, focused on developing policy frameworks with semantic web technologies to ensure the security and privacy of aggregated datasets. Her ongoing research projects involve privacy by design, machine learning and artificial intelligence, data ethics and compliance, ontology, access control and trust in distributed systems.

Chapter 6
Ontology for Data Analytics

Fatmana Şentürk

Abstract Nowadays, with the development of technology, storage, processing, and information extraction of data have become important. Thus, while a system is generated, it should be designed in such a way that works in harmony with each of these data processing steps. Data analytics is one of the methods used to develop such a system. Data analytics applications are used in many different areas such as increasing market shares of a firm, customer behavior analysis, predicting the life of an electronic device, detection of the anomaly on a network, social network analysis, healthcare systems, chemical component interactions, and bank operations. These data analytics applications can obtain data from different sources, and these sources must interact with each other. It is not always easy to design this interactive architecture. These difficulties can be overcome by using ontologies. For data analytics, ontologies can be used for facilitating data collection, improving the quality of the data used, analyzing data, showing the obtained results, and ensuring the reusability of the designed system. In this study, we introduce an overview of data analytics and explain data analytics steps; in addition, we seek to answer the question of how to enrich and improve a data analytics system by using ontologies. We give different examples of how to use ontologies in different steps in the systems. Moreover, we emphasize the pros and cons of using ontologies in data analytics. We then discuss the future outlook for these ontologies for data analytics.

Keywords Data analytics · Data analytics processes · Semantic Web · Ontologies · Ontology-based data analytics

F. Şentürk (✉)
Engineering Faculty, Computer Engineering Department, Pamukkale University, Denizli, Turkey
e-mail: fatmanas@pau.edu.tr

© The Author(s), under exclusive license to Springer Nature Switzerland AG 2021
S. Jain, S. Murugesan (eds.), *Smart Connected World*,
https://doi.org/10.1007/978-3-030-76387-9_6

Key Points

In this chapter you will learn:

- The definition of data analytics
- The subprocesses of data analytics
- The importance of ontologies for data analytics
- How to use ontologies for data analytics
- Examples of data analytics using ontologies for different domains
- The pros and cons of using ontologies for data analytics
- How ontologies can be used for data analytics in the future

6.1 What Is Data Analytics?

Nowadays, we are faced with rapidly increasing data sizes with the development of technology. Storing, processing, and making meaning of these data is very important in terms of information technologies. Especially extracting meaningful information from these data is one of the most basic features that should be obtained quickly and accurately. Data analytics methods are used in order to provide these features and to obtain meaningful information.

Data analytics is a process that enables the analysis of raw data to find potential hidden trends and to extract information through the methods it uses. Data analytics techniques enable organizations to make more informed decisions to improve themselves. For example, in commercial industries, data analytics is widely used for purposes such as increasing the market share of companies, modeling customer behavior, and estimating the life span of an electronic component. Data analytics techniques are used not only by commercial companies but also by different industries. There are many applications of data analytics in the health field, in the estimation of chemical component interactions, and in the banking sector.

6.1.1 Types of Data Analytics

Data analytics is a very broad concept that covers a variety of data analyses. It allows the processing of data in any format, and can be used for purposes such as data changes over time, finding the source of a problem, and customer churn analysis. Considering these purposes, there are four different types: descriptive, diagnostic, predictive, and prescriptive analytics. Different methods are applied for each of these four different types of objectives.

6.1.1.1 Descriptive Analytics

Descriptive analytics is a type of data analytics that is used to find solutions to questions about the process of changing data over a period of time. Descriptive analytics aims to present an understandable summary view required to extract information from or present data to be used in a decision-making process for business intelligence. Company reports produced for purposes such as the amount of increase or decrease in the sales of a company, financial status, and continuity of its customers can be given as examples of descriptive analytics. In addition, descriptive analytics methods are used to find answers to questions such as "By how much has the sales amount increased in the last month?", "How loyal are the company customers?", and "How much has the market share of the firm increased or decreased in the last 1 year?" For descriptive analytics, statistical tools such as averages, percentage changes, and simple mathematical and arithmetic operations are used.

6.1.1.2 Diagnostic Analytics

Diagnostic analytics are methods used to answer questions to determine the cause of a problem. These methods are used in conjunction with descriptive analytics methods. That is, diagnostic analytics methods are used to deal with the reasons for inferences obtained with descriptive analytics. For example, when a decline in a company's air conditioner sales is detected, diagnostic analytics are used to determine whether the decline is due to a seasonal transition. For diagnostic analytics, techniques such as data discovery, drill down, data mining, and correlation are used.

6.1.1.3 Predictive Analytics

Predictive analytics are methods used to predict future conditions. These methods use historical data for predicting trends and determining whether these trends are likely to recur. For example, the predictive analytics method is used to search for an answer to questions such as "What percentage of sales will be this summer?" When searching for answers to these questions, a variety of methods are used for predictive analytics, such as neural networks, decision trees, and regression analysis.

6.1.1.4 Prescriptive Analytics

Prescriptive analytics offers different solutions to improve the path followed in the execution of a process. In this method, past events are analyzed and an attempt is made to predict the probability of realization of different results. For example, if a company predicts that sales will decrease in the summer period, prescriptive analytics can determine what methods to follow to prevent this decrease. Combinations of

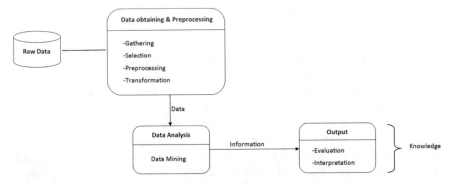

Fig. 6.1 Steps of KDD (Tsai et al., 2015)

techniques such as business rules, business-specific algorithms, machine learning, and computational modeling methods are used for prescriptive analytics.

6.1.2 Processes of Data Analytics

Data analytics generally consists of three stages—data acquisition (data collection and selection), preprocessing and transformation, and analysis—which are given in Fig. 6.1. Selection, preprocessing, transformation, data mining, and interpretation or evaluation processes are also used for knowledge discovery in databases (KDD) (Fayyad et al., 1996). KDD means analyzing the data stored in databases and extracting previously unknown information stored in the data. Data analytics includes the process of extracting hidden information from existing data. In addition, data mining techniques used for KDD are also implemented for certain problems for which data analytics find solutions. In summary, data analytics and KDD are alike in both the similarity of the process followed for KDD and the use of the techniques used in KDD. Considering all these similarities, data analytics can be thought of as KDD (Tsai et al., 2015).

The first stage in data analytics is that of collecting data and making it ready for processing and analysis. Data is obtained from different sources as a result of developing technological infrastructures and easier access to data. For example, a company collects and processes many types of data, such as the products that its customers have reviewed, the duration of the customer's review of that product, and whether the customer has purchased that product or not. The company may also collect data from platforms such as social media or the Internet, and the collected data is used for data analysis. Therefore, this company has more than one source from which to obtain data, and these resources should be brought into a regular format. For this reason, the useful parts of the collected data must first be selected and then converted into a specific format for analysis. If the same company carries out a comparison based on the product review times of the customers, the customers should keep the time they spend on that product in a single type such as seconds or minutes.

After the data is collected, selected, and transformed, the next step is its analysis. In the data analysis phase, a process is carried out according to the decisions that companies should take in order to progress. That is, if the company wants to forecast the number of sales the following year, the predictive analytics method is applied for data analytics. For this purpose, the collected data by the company is analyzed by applying statistical methods, artificial neural networks, or machine learning-based algorithms.

The last step is the interpretation of the data obtained as a result of the analysis. During the interpretation step, the numerical values obtained are supported by graphics and figures and transformed into a form that makes them easier for end-users to understand. In addition, determining the accuracy of the inferences obtained as a result of the analysis is handled in this step. The reasons for the decrease in the sales rates of the company are obtained with diagnostic analytics methods, and later the comparison of the accuracy of the obtained reasons is evaluated in this step.

Data analytics has a wide perspective that can be used in many areas. Therefore, different methods are needed to transform data from different sources into a processable format, operating the proper algorithms for the researched information and showing the result of the analysis. One of these methods is ontologies. The following sections discuss the correlation between data analytics and ontologies.

6.2   What are Ontologies?

Today's technologies can process different types of data such as images, sound, video, and text. The heterogeneous structure of these data should be transformed into a structure that can be processed by the computer. This structure can be provided via the Semantic Web.

The Semantic Web is defined as a structure that aims to interpret Internet pages by computers like a human and develop computers that will understand people's requests (Berners-Lee & Fischetti, 2001). Through the Semantic Web, information is transformed into a format that can be processed not only by humans but also by computers. Metadata models are defined so that computers can automatically detect and process data. These metadata model definitions are provided via ontologies.

Ontologies are metadata in which the concepts specific to a domain, the relationships between these concepts, and the instances of the concepts are defined together. The relationships between concepts and beings in the real world also represent semantic connections between these entities. In other words, an ontology is a collection of data items that helps in storing and representing data in a way that preserves its patterns and the semantic relationship between the items (Malik & Jain,

2021). Ontologies have a wide range of uses, and for this reason various ontologies are created automatically or semiautomatically for many fields.

Ontologies provide a framework for data integration from heterogeneous sources. This framework can be used in many areas, such as data representation, information extraction and combining information, information management, database integration, data transformation, natural language processing, digital libraries, geographic information systems, visual information access, and multi-agent systems (Kolli, 2008).

6.2.1 Ontologies and Their Applications

Since ontologies can convert data from heterogeneous sources into a standard format, they can be used in many areas, such as data representation, information finding and combining, information management, database integration, data transformation, natural language processing, digital libraries, geographic information systems, visual information access, and multi-agent systems.

Ontologies can store the desired information in structures called triples, thanks to the RDF/RDFS/OWL language structure they use. The triples consist of an arrangement called a subject-predicate-object. With these triple structures, both site-specific rules and restrictions can be defined, and area-specific instances selected from the

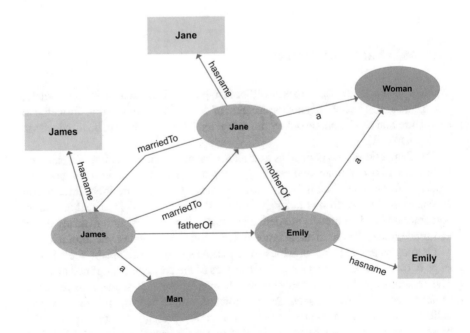

Fig. 6.2 An example of a triple view of family relationship ontology

relevant area can be stored. Figure 6.2 presents an example of a triple view of an ontology in which a person's family relationships are defined.

Ontologies can also store different types of data obtained from different sources, though they use the metadata language. The structural and semantic differences of these obtained data make processing these data difficult for information systems. These heterogeneous systems should be able to work together and provide data integration between them. Ontologies can be used to successfully operate this interaction between systems and to eliminate the problem of heterogeneity. For example, for a system using a combination of video, signal, and textual data, etc., converting the collected data into an appropriate format and using this data as input for another system can be achieved with ontologies. In short, an ontology combines schema specifications with data to represent information (Mehla & Jain, 2020).

In addition to the information storage capacity of ontologies, they also store specially defined rules related to the area in which they are defined. Using these rules, inferences can be made on the existing information through special queries. That is, by using the rules and data defined in an ontology, it is possible to obtain information that is not included in the ontology. Information extraction can be achieved by using the inference mechanism of ontologies.

6.2.2   Ontology and Data Analytics

In data analytics, there are sub-steps such as obtaining data, converting the data into a processable form, analyzing the data, and explaining the obtained analysis. Ontologies can be used at each stage of these sub-steps.

Ontology-based architectures have been developed for data analytics. Ontologies in these architectures can be included in any part of data analytics systems. Ontologies can be used in the process of collecting data, preprocessing data, storing data, and enhancing data quality. For example, during the data collection step, data can be retrieved in a formatted manner by using domain-specific constraints provided by the ontologies. Before analyzing the data, by using ontologies, synonyms can be added to the data set to increase the data quality or enrich the data in a preprocessing step. Subcomponents that make up the relevant part of the data obtained can be included in the data set through ontologies, in case of data deficiency.

In the data processing step, ontologies can be used to reduce the search space. Infrastructure can be created for rule-based data mining algorithms through the inference mechanism provided by ontologies. For example, ontologies can be used for the analysis of human resources. The attributes specific to the human resource sought for the job, including the naming of these attributes, can also be stored in an ontology. While screening people who possess these qualities, the qualities that are defined in the ontology and that can replace each other are taken into consideration.

In addition, the inferences obtained from data mining algorithms can also be enriched through ontologies. Different graphics can be obtained by expanding the analysis results through ontologies. A flexible and analytical visualization environment can be provided if the applications that enable the visualization of analysis results are combined with ontology approaches. It is easy to model the ontologies as a graph. Each concept in the ontology can be shown as a vertex, and the relationships between these concepts can be shown as edges between vertices. Therefore, ontologies obtained by modeling the analysis results can be shown as graphs with more understandable visuality for users. Moreover, different display techniques can be operable over these graphs and different perspectives can be developed.

6.3   Different Perspectives on Ontology and Data Analytics

Ontologies present information in a structured form and provide information extraction from existing data through inference mechanisms. For this reason, ontologies provide a very useful infrastructure for data analytics methods. Ontologies have become an unavoidable part of data analytics with their wide usage area. We have examined a few different examples to make the relationship between ontologies and data analytics more understandable in this section.

6.3.1   Business Intelligence

Business intelligence is a set of processes and architectures that examine the status of the methods planned for a business, identify opportunities for the company, and make the existing raw data meaningful to develop these opportunities. Companies find new opportunities thanks to business intelligence and try to gain an advantage in the competitive market environment by determining their effective strategies. The general flow of business intelligence is shown in Fig. 6.3.

Ontologies are prone to natural language interaction, with their strong abstraction features in terms of defining entities, data properties, and relationships between entities for a specific domain. Ontologies can be used to capture patterns in the expected workload and construct them to build a speech system (Quamar et al., 2020).

In addition, ontologies can capture the measures and dimensions defined in the cube for the business intelligence model by using entities, their taxonomy, or hierarchies. These measures refer to categorical or qualitative properties that contain one or more computable values. At the same time, ontologies can represent a higher-level grouping of data on measures/dimensions provided by an expert or converted data from raw data. Thanks to these superior capabilities of the ontologies, ontologies have replaced the expert opinion effect used in the traditional business intelligence model. Domain knowledge obtained from experts can be automatically added to the business intelligence model by using ontologies defined for the domain without the need for these experts. Similarly, the boundaries of the data to be used in the system can be determined by using the constraints in ontologies. Thus, experts can focus their attention on the analysis of data and showing the results of data in the

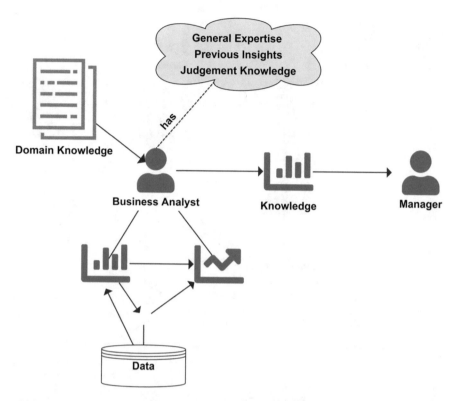

Fig. 6.3 An architecture of traditional business intelligence (Neuböck et al., 2013)

business intelligence systems. The architecture of the use of ontologies in a business intelligence architecture is given in Fig. 6.4.

6.3.2 Healthcare

Data analytics methods can also be used in the field of health, especially for hospitals and clinics, for purposes such as evaluating treatment costs, improving the treatment processes of patients, and preventing patients from having to return to the hospital. A data analytics system that supports doctors can be developed by evaluating various patient information such as MR images, epicrisis notes, patient complaints, and symptoms through the developed ontology-based systems. For example, we assume that an ontology that stores abnormal regions in MR images is integrated into the MR imaging system. For the abnormal region in MR images, these sections can be defined by using properties such as width, length, and diameter in the ontology. Possible abnormal region determinations can be made using defined ontology on an image belonging to the patient. In addition, these data analytics systems can analyze

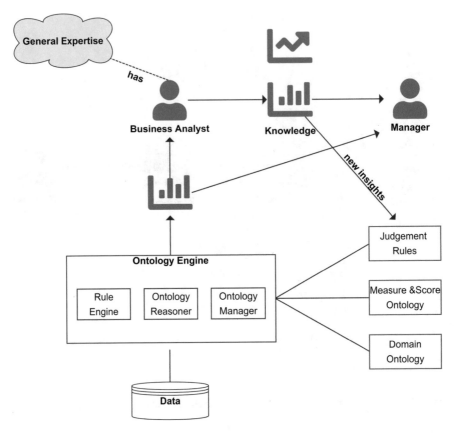

Fig. 6.4 An architecture of integrating ontologies into business intelligence applications (Neuböck et al., 2013)

the complaints for which patients are returning to the hospital, in order to prevent rehospitalization or return of patients to the emergency room. The cost-effectiveness of various procedures and treatments applied in hospitals can also be evaluated with semantic data analysis methods.

Ontologies are also used for biological structures and drug structures. The most comprehensive examples of these are gene ontology and Foundational Model of Anatomy (FMA) ontology. In FMA (Rosse & Mejino, 2003) ontology, there are classes of 75,000 different anatomical terms and 130,000 relationships belonging to these species. In the FMA ontology, it describes all the major parts of the body, starting with the smallest gene structures, especially of humans. Using these definitions, it can be predicted how any drug or treatment developed can cause a reaction without testing on humans.

To give another example, for a newly developed drug it may be possible for the developer company to predict drug interactions that may occur without conducting any human experiments with data analytics. For this process, first the active ingredient of the drug should be checked and it should be determined whether there are similar available drugs. Possible effects can be predicted by assuming that drugs with similar active ingredients will show similar side effects. In addition, knowing the active substances that have a negative effect on each other will enable us to obtain information on whether the patient will interact with any drug or chemical used. It may be possible to use data analytics methods for all these calculations. Data sets required for data analytics steps can be provided by defined drug ontologies such as SNOMED[1] and DRON[2] (the drug ontology).

Considering that the development of gene ontology will continue, in the future, data analytics will contribute to the realization of aims such as developing customized drugs for each person, applying personalized treatment methods, and improving living conditions depending on a person's habits. For example, when an individual's nutritional habits are analyzed, the risk of suffering any disease can be calculated. When this risk factor is combined with the person's gene map, the rate of occurrence of this disease can be calculated. Furthermore, the steps to be taken to prevent the disease can be determined by using this result. Measures can be taken for living conditions and nutritional habits that create individual risk factors. While taking these measures, individuals can create their own conditions with the help of smart Semantic Web applications, instead of being given strict lists. Thus, people can be made aware of alternative nutrition methods or living conditions that can replace existing ones.

6.3.3   Information Retrieval and Ontology

Information retrieval involves obtaining information that includes "query formatting and analyzing," "information and documents indexing," and "projecting the retrieved information" subprocesses to meet an information need in large data collations. Information retrieval is used specifically for the analysis of a document or retrieval of a document. With this information retrieval, specific queries are made on the documents and the appropriate results are obtained for these queries.

Information retrieval, which is widely used in search engines, has four subcomponents: indexing, query processing, searching, and ranking. In the indexing step, generally, extraction of the attributes of the information gathered from various sources, sorting, and storing the descriptive features according to a special format are performed. In the query processing step, the word or phrase to be searched is parsed and converted into suitable objects for searching among the indexed features. In the searching step, the features of searched words are scanned in the previously

---

[1]SNOMED Ontology, https://bioportal.bioontology.org/ontologies/SNOMEDCT, last Accessed: November 30, 2020.

[2]DRON, Drug Ontology, https://bioportal.bioontology.org/ontologies/DRON, last Accessed: November 30, 2020.

indexed attributes. The ranking step calculates the relevance of the word or phrase searched to the information obtained from the search. In other words, the relationship between the documents obtained as a result of the search and the search query is calculated and the documents are displayed to the end-user according to this calculation.

These four-step architectures of search engines can be transformed into smart systems that can carry out intelligence searches by using Semantic Web and ontologies. Search engines can develop data concepts to collect and access similar data from the Internet and the Web. At the same time, ontologies can be used to find semantic similarities of the collected information and to enrich data. While search engines make use of the synonyms stored in the ontologies for indexing steps, they also use a similar feature for query processing. Inference mechanisms and synonymous storage capabilities of ontologies can also be used when transforming the searched words or phrases into the query. In addition to the word or phrase entered by the end-user, similar search expressions can also be added for search by using ontologies. That is, the synonyms of the word entered by the end-user are found by using ontologies, and these found synonyms can be searched together with the originally entered word or words. Thus, a correct and widened flow of information can be provided to the end-user. In addition, ontology matching approaches can be used to establish the links between the query and the search result at this stage. Moreover, during the ranking process, similar data concepts, using the data model generated to store the data, can be shown to users.

6.3.4 Social Network Analysis

Nowadays, most people can share their feelings and thoughts through social media applications. With the widespread use of social media, people's likes, positive or negative comments about a film or product, and their interactions with each other have become important. Recently, feedback shared on social media applications has also attracted the attention of companies. For example, in the past, when there was no use of social media, it took a certain amount of time for a company to collect user reviews for a new product. Now, people are using the company's product and then sharing their positive or negative opinions instantly on social media. The company can see these posts seconds later. This information shared by users via social media on their own has become a fast source of data for companies.

Comments and feedback given by users are among the features that companies can use in their decision-making structures. Many companies include customer feedback in their business intelligence applications. For example, a phone company may consider negative customer comments for the previous model for a new model phone it is about to release. Thus, they can decide which of the parts, such as screen, battery, camera, or processor, will be highlighted for the new model they are developing. Companies can obtain these customer comments from the complaint logs or fault records they receive, as well as from comments made on social networks. They can handle both the comments they collect from social media and the user comments coming to the company and then apply data analytics methods to these comments. Thus, the company can identify the deficiencies related to that product and make improvements for the new product they are releasing.

In addition, specific surveys can be conducted on social media to learn about the general structure of societies. Social networks are applications that people from throughout society can easily access. With its widespread use, any information can spread to the public in a short time. This information can be a survey or news. For example, companies that want to use the speed of social media carry out marketing activities for their newly developed products through social networks. Furthermore, companies benefit from the power of social media to determine their potential customers and to ensure the continuity of their customers.

Some of the methods used in the analysis of social network data are data analytics methods. Especially for applications where user comments are analyzed, using data analytics methods together with ontologies will provide more accurate results. For example, although the abbreviations used in the user comments can be different according to society, this reveals the necessity to evaluate these abbreviations used semantically. Language-based differences and restrictions can be supported through ontologies, and thus it may be possible to evaluate user comments semantically. In addition, this will ensure that the existing language support provided for ontologies and the user comments in different languages are included in the analysis.

Companies can advertise their own products through social media. Searches made via social media applications are evaluated to get an idea about a product, and products produced by other companies similar to the searched product are shown in the application as an advertisement. In this way, companies get the opportunity to market their own products. Similarly, information such as pages, products, and links that comes to us as suggestions is also produced using data analytics methods. Every word we have shared is included in the data analytics process. Social media applications extract attributes of their own users and find similar users using these attributes. These applications offer us pages and products liked by users with similar profiles to ours in the form of advertisements. In this profile extraction process, ontologies can be used to store instances and to calculate similarities of the profiles by interoperating with data analytics methods. Thanks to the instance storage potential of ontologies, instances in ontologies can be used as sample data in analysis processes.

6.4   The Present and Future of Semantic Data Analytics

Rapidly increasing data size and increasing commercial competition have led many companies to use data analytics methods. Data analytics techniques can determine the methods to be followed in order to increase the market percentage of the companies, and can also be a guide for the decisions that companies should take in their internal processes. Data analytics techniques can be used not only by companies but also for banking, healthcare, bioinformatics calculations, chemical interaction estimation, personalization of a product, and even social interactions in a society.

The use of data analytics techniques in many areas has led to numerous problems. The most significant of these problems is obtaining the data required for data analytics. In particular, there is a need for the interaction of nonuniform data obtained from different sources and the development of a system that works in harmony with this data. Ontologies are used together with data analytics techniques in order to ensure cooperation between pieces of data. The use of ontologies together with data analytics techniques has several advantages over other systems, as listed below:

- The data to be analyzed for data analysis is complete and noiseless, which will also increase the accuracy of the results obtained. Ontologies can be used to complete data and to eliminate noises in the data.
- For data analytics, data obtained from different sources can interact with other sources through ontologies. Ontologies are capable of storing any type of data due to their nature. Moreover, for the entities defined in the ontology, different qualifications can be defined, such as what the data type will be, in which value range the data can be found, and the relationship of data with another entity.
- Similarity properties called synonyms can be defined for an entity in the ontology. For example, the words "dictionary" and "glossary" in English can be defined as synonyms. Especially for data analytics where text processing is performed, the integration of this ability of the ontologies with the data analytics architecture will lead to more accurate results. Using data analytics methods and ontologies together will allow the determination of the semantic similarities of the processed data. In addition, adding synonyms for data analytics will enrich the data set.
- Ontologies have the ability to support different languages with their flexible structures. The equivalent of a term in a different language can be defined and stored in the ontology. This feature allows data in different languages to be a source for data analysis and for the processing of this data within the data analytics system.
- Inferences can be made by applying specific rules to ontologies. With this inference mechanism, business rules can be created or association rules of the data can be defined. This inference mechanism can create the infrastructure of rule-based data analytics methods.
- Ontologies are metadata that describe entities, properties of these entities, sample data, and relationships between these properties for a specific field. The sample data, rules, and limitations related to the domain are ready to use for the systems, thanks to the domain information contained in the ontologies. Using data analytics methods and ontologies together facilitates the work of domain experts who take part in the data analysis process.

It is true that ontologies contribute positively to data analytics methods. However, there are situations that need attention and that have disadvantages. These situations and disadvantages are listed below:

- Although the use of ontologies together with data analytics or data acquisition, or during data integration, seems to have positive results, it may cause extra workload in some conditions. For example, in a data analytics architecture where only numerical data is obtained and processed, adding ontologies to the preprocessing step may cause extra controls and decrease the performance of the architecture. Therefore, deciding whether to use ontologies is an important issue.
- In addition to deciding whether ontologies should be included in data analytics or not, it is also important to determine at what stage of data analysis (data collection, data preprocessing, data analysis, or result) these should be included. Incorrect determination of the step in which the ontology will be used may prevent the system from working properly, or using ontology with data analytics may not contribute to the results obtained.
- When companies or experts decide to use ontologies, calibrations should be made on the data analytics techniques that they currently use. There will be a need for expert personnel in the field who know the properties of ontologies well and can use the advantages of the ontologies for making calibrations of these techniques. To overcome this problem, either an expert in ontologies should be hired or existing personnel should be trained, which takes time.
- The inclusion of synonyms and foreign language support in data analytics architecture through ontologies can lead to longer analysis times.
- In addition, data security at every stage of data analytics is also an important problem. If it fails to provide data security, the company could lose the trust of its customers, or this may result in financial loss for the company.

The combined use of data analytics and ontologies will create new opportunities in data management, storage, and processing (Konys, 2016). There will be more architecture for the combined use of ontologies and data analytics techniques in the near future. For example, it will be possible to obtain information about our health status through our mobile phones and to direct first aid personnel automatically in case of any emergency situation. With the applications that will enter our lives, people's behavior, social media shares, and phone messages will be analyzed and people's emotional status can be analyzed. Many products, which are standardized today, will be transformed into a personalized form in the future through ontologies that continue to be defined, such as gene ontologies or ontologies that will be newly defined.

6.5 Conclusion

Nowadays, with the development of technology, data size has increased rapidly, and data storing, data processing and extract information from data have become important. Data analytics architectures are one of the methods used to develop a structure that works in harmony with each of these processes. Data analytics architectures are used in the decision-making processes of companies, as well as in many different areas such as anomaly detection in a network, social network analysis, and health systems.

Data analytics is used to find solutions to questions about the process of changing data in a specific time period, as well as to seek an answer to the question "Why is this problem occurring?" In addition, data analytics can be used to predict future conditions for a decision or process. Data analytics can also improve the way a process is run or solve a problem by using different techniques. Methods used for data analytics vary according to the area of application or the problems identified by the companies.

Obtaining data is one of the most important processes for data analytics. In this step, data should be complete, faultless, and high quality even if it is collected from different sources, in order to get correct results from data analytics. One of the methods to achieve this is using ontologies with data analytics. For data analytics, ontologies can be used to facilitate data collection, improve the quality of the data used, analyze the data, show the results obtained, and ensure the reusability of the designed system. In this study, we provided different examples of how data analytics systems can be used with ontologies. We aimed to show the diversity of the applications developed by showing examples from different fields. We also explained the pros and cons of using data analytics and ontologies together. In summary, we emphasized the importance of using ontologies with data analytics for today's and future technologies.

Review Questions
1. What is data analytics? Why do we need data analytics applications?
2. What are the types of data analytics? Explain the uses of each type.
3. Indicate the steps of data analytics processes and briefly describe the operations performed in each step.
4. What is an ontology? What are the facilities provided by ontologies?
5. Explain the relationship between data analytics and ontologies.

Discussion Questions
1. How can the Semantic Web be included in the stages of data analytics?
2. Which types of problems can you encounter while developing data analytics applications? How can you eliminate these problems by taking advantage of the Semantic Web?
3. How can we integrate user experiences or comments into companies' business intelligence applications? How does this integration process contribute to business intelligence application?
4. Discuss whether search engines can retrieve personalized results by using ontology-based data analytics architectures.

Problem Statements for Young Researchers
1. What kinds of applications come to mind when you think of ontology-based data analytics architectures? Can these applications be smarter than classic data analytics methods?

2. Might the obtained results of ontology-based data analytics methods be different from the results of obtained classic data analytics methods? If you want to change results, how do you integrate ontologies in your data analytics architecture?
3. What are the difficulties in developing ontology-based data analytics applications? How can these difficulties be overcome?
4. Can ontology-based data analytics applications be used for security? If such an application is designed, in which step/steps can ontologies be utilized?

References

Berners-Lee, T., & Fischetti, M. (2001). *Weaving the web: The original design and ultimate destiny of the World Wide Web by its inventor.* DIANE Publishing Company.

Fayyad, U. M., Piatetsky-Shapiro, G., & Smyth, P. (1996). From data mining to knowledge discovery in databases. *AI Magazine, 17*(3), 37–54.

Kolli, R. (2008). *Scalable matching of ontology graphs using partitioning.* Doctoral dissertation, University of Georgia.

Konys, A. (2016, October). Ontology-based approaches to big data analytics. In *International Multi-conference on Advanced Computer Systems* (pp. 355–365). Cham: Springer.

Malik, S., & Jain, S. (2021, February). Semantic ontology-based approach to enhance text classification. In *International Semantic Intelligence Conference, Delhi, India. 25–27 Feb 2021. CEUR Workshop Proceedings* (Vol. 2786, pp. 85–98). Retrieved from http://ceur-ws.org/Vol-2786/Paper16.pdf

Mehla, S., & Jain, S. (2020). An ontology supported hybrid approach for recommendation in emergency situations. *Annals of Telecommunications, 75*(7), 421–435.

Neuböck, T., Neumayr, B., Schrefl, M., & Schütz, C. (2014). Ontology-driven business intelligence for comparative data analysis. In E. Zimányi (Eds.), *Business intelligence. eBISS 2013. Lecture Notes in Business Information Processing* (Vol. 172). Cham: Springer. https://doi.org/10.1007/978-3-319-05461-2_3

Rosse, C., & Mejino, J. L., Jr. (2003). A reference ontology for biomedical informatics: The foundational model of anatomy. *Journal of Biomedical Informatics, 36*(6), 478–500.

Quamar, A., Özcan, F., Miller, D., Moore, R. J., Niehus, R., & Kreulen, J. (2020). Conversational BI: An ontology-driven conversation system for business intelligence applications. *Proceedings of the VLDB Endowment, 13*(12), 3369–3381.

Tsai, C. W., Lai, C. F., Chao, H. C., & Vasilakos, A. V. (2015). Big data analytics: A survey. *Journal of Big Data, 2*(1), 1–32.

Fatmana Şentürk, received the Ph.D. degree in computer science from the Department of Computer Engineering, Ege University, 2019 and the MS and BS degree in computer science from the Department of Computer Engineering, Pamukkale University, 2012 and 2008. She is currently a research assistant at Pamukkale University in Turkey. Her research interests include data science, ontology matching, graph and graph algorithms.

Chapter 7
Multilingual Semantic Representation of Smart Connected World Data

Abhisek Sharma and Sarika Jain

Abstract IoT devices now come in all shapes and forms. IoT is everywhere, from our mobile devices to cars. These devices help to perform various tasks from providing locations for navigation purposes, to detecting a heartbeat inside a locked car to notify parents or pet owners that they have left their child or pet inside the car and need attention. The latter example is not possible only with IoT devices; they need algorithms and systems to detect these heartbeats, and this is facilitated by Artificial Intelligence (AI). We will be working with Artificial Intelligence of Things (AIoT), a combination of Artificial Intelligence and IoT.

We can't ignore the fact that our world is multilingual, with a wide variety of cultures and ethnic and racial groups. One of the AIoT system tasks is hearing a sentence from a user, interpreting what it means, and performing tasks accordingly. But this task is not so easy because of all the existing languages and cultural variations. Understanding cultural variations is crucial because it affects how a language is formed and used. This chapter covers just that, from the use and working of AIoT to how a computer can store and understand language-specific information and work with it.

Keywords Ontology engineering · Artificial Intelligence of Things · Multilingual ontology · Linguistic linked open data · Internet of Things

Key Points
- Provides an overview of AIoT and its effects on our lives
- Discusses various ways in which a multilingual ontology can be developed
- Provides a brief overview of the knowledge bases and systems available to support in the development of multilingual ontology

A. Sharma (✉) · S. Jain
National Institute of Technology Kurukshetra, Kurukshetra, India
e-mail: jasarika@nitkkr.ac.in

© The Author(s), under exclusive license to Springer Nature Switzerland AG 2021   125
S. Jain, S. Murugesan (eds.), *Smart Connected World*,
https://doi.org/10.1007/978-3-030-76387-9_7

7.1   Introduction

Internet of Things (IoT) technologies are allowing us to do/perform specific actions/
tasks that most of the time are not overly important but are distracting and something
that has to be done (such as controlling the thermostat and lights in a house).
Sometimes these technologies also help perform tasks prone to human error that
can lead to a catastrophic failure, which can be a deciding factor between life or
death (such as diagnosis of the correct state of health, or detection of obstacles in
self-driving vehicles). But the real driving force behind all of these services is
Artificial Intelligence (AI), which helps reach IoT's full potential. We call this
amalgamation and marriage Artificial Intelligence of Things (AIoT).

IoT devices use communication technologies (such as the Internet) to collect and
exchange information. IoT relies on AI, high-speed networks with near zero latency
for real-time data processing, and big data as background knowledge for AI algorithms to use for better analysis and predictions.

For background knowledge, understanding semantics, and supporting AI, the use
of vocabularies is preferred, which will be better accommodated in the form of an
ontology. Ontologies allow us to keep the semantics of the data intact, and for AI, the
more meaning we have available with us the better. By semantics here we mean how
the different data elements and concepts are related to each other and define various
properties of these concepts.

There is a lot of work that has been already done to accommodate information in
the form of an ontology, but this is mostly in English, which does not fulfill the needs
of billions of users, as only a small number of individuals globally have English as
their mother tongue. A large percentage of users may understand English as a part of
the curriculum at school or college, and may use it to communicate outside their
communities. But, as also stated by Beka (2016) and Malone and Paraide (2011) and
in,[1] when people use their mother tongue to interact with each other, the effectiveness of communication is higher (more on this in the second part of this chapter).

To support the management of multilingual information and allow applications
(such as the Semantic Web) to accommodate multilingual information and provide
services that are language-independent, first we have to work toward familiarizing
ourselves with data models which support multilingualism and can accommodate
semantics to facilitate developers in developing systems which can provide semantically rich services without fixating on a single language. This chapter motivates the
reader to use semantic technologies and highlights the need to make ontologies
multilingual.

The rest of this chapter is organized as follows. In Sect. 7.2 we discuss the
motivation behind multilinguality; in Sect. 7.3 we present semantic technologies
that allow the creation and management of ontologies and their services; in Sect. 7.4
we cover the steps of creating an ontology and different ways in which multilingual

---

[1] ie-today.co.uk/people-policy-politics/the-importance-of-mother-tongue-in-education/.

information can be added to this ontology; in Sect. 7.5 we discuss some of the applications of AIoT; and lastly we conclude the chapter.

7.2   Motivation

Semantic technologies are working toward the goal of making data machine-understandable. Unlike other data technologies (such as relational databases) which work on the data structure, semantic technologies work with the meaning of data. But semantic technologies contain different formats to formalize ontologies and other supporting technologies that perform various operations such as filtering information from the ontology.

Sir Tim Berners-Lee stated in an interview with Bloomberg: "Semantic Technology isn't inherently complex. The Semantic Technology language, at its heart, is very, very simple. It's just about the relationships between things."

The Resource Description Framework (RDF), SPARQL Protocol, RDF Query Language (SPARQL)* and Web Ontology Language (OWL) are the primary standards on which the semantic technologies are built.

- *RDF* is a format that is used by semantic technologies to store/represent data in a semantic graph database or on the Semantic Web.
- *OWL* is complementary to RDF. It facilitates the creation of ontology/schema, i.e., it can represent complex and rich knowledge about hierarchies of entities/ things. It can also define how they relate to each other.
- *SPARQL* is the semantic query language developed to query databases and data from various systems. Specifically, it is advantageous when working with the RDF format to retrieve and process data (Prud'hommeaux, 2008).

Today's taxonomies and ontology tools are useful, but are meant for trained experts only. There is considerable potential for cross-lingual data analysis, but this is mostly unaddressed. The existing taxonomies achieve structure and hierarchy well but ignore the pragmatics and thereby fail to manage multilingual data. The repository of knowledge is multidimensional (multimodal—textual, image, audio, video—taxonomical, synonymy, and multilingual).

Multilinguality in ontologies is demanded by institutions and organizations worldwide due to the availability of many resources in different languages. The way societies work, communicate, interact* and spend free time has been transformed by the Web. Now is the time to tackle the challenges in achieving multilinguality in the Web of Data. First, we need to make the supporting technologies capable enough to handle multilingual information, which will enable the systems created around these technologies to support multilinguality.

When multilingual information can be handled and used effectively by the Web of Data, the user can query in his/her native language and will also get the relevant result in his/her native language since the Linguistic Linked Open Data (LLOD) cloud will be capable of providing cross-lingual querying and delivery of the result in the same language in which the query has been posed. Ultimately, all of the individual silos containing descriptions related to a specific language will be mapped together to work as a part of one of many multilingual systems to provide seamless accessibility of information present on the Web of Data or any other place without the need to learn the language in which the original data is represented.

Smart applications should be built for global deployment. In essence, AIoT is about intelligently connecting machines, devices, and sensors distributed geographically across multiple organizations, industries, and borders, hence improving data exchange, real-time connectivity, and decision making. This brings up the biggest challenge for the widespread adoption of the Artificial Intelligence of Things to achieve interoperability, which would unlock additional value.

There are three levels of interoperability. Technical interoperability is defined as the fundamental ability to exchange raw data (bits, frames, packets, messages), and is highly standardized today. Syntactic interoperability is the ability to exchange structured data, and is supported by standard data formats such as XML and JSON. Semantic interoperability requires that the meaning (context) of exchanged data is automatically and accurately interpreted. The crux of the matter is that the IoT devices must understand and speak to each other, i.e., they must interoperate. But while the technical and syntactic interoperability has mostly been achieved, little has been available so far to ensure that devices understand each other.

A solution to semantic interoperability could be storing abstract metadata from devices. The controlled vocabularies and ontologies can provide this metadata abstraction by representing knowledge in a machine-readable and machine-understandable form. Today's unstructured haystack of concepts needs to be converted into knowledge to introduce control. Cross-border interoperability is more than a mere translation of concepts and strings. Semantic interoperability also incorporates cultural conventions.

7.3 Ontology Engineering Methodology

We have explained the process of development of multilingual ontology in two parts. The first contains the process describing the steps to be followed to create an ontology to serve various purposes. Second, we discuss how to make any ontology, both those created for specific applications and those that are publicly available pertaining to the general description of a domain.

Let us first go through the process of developing an ontology as described in various publications (such as Jones et al., 1998; Noy & McGuinness, 2001; Li et al., 2016). Some of the methodologies are TOVE (Toronto Virtual Enterprise) (Gruninger & Fox, 1994, 1995; Uschold & Gruninger, 1996a, b) and the Enterprise Model Approach (Uschold, 1996a, b).

From all of the above methodologies, we have found that Noy and McGuinness (2001) have summarized the steps in the best way. They have also stated that there is no one correct way to develop an ontology. The steps are as follows:

1. *Determine domain and scope of ontology*: To develop an ontology, Noy and McGuinness (2001) suggest defining the domain and scope for the ontology. To determine these, the following questions need to be answered:

   What domain does the ontology cover?
   For what purpose is the ontology being created?
   What type of questions should the ontology answer?
   Who will use and maintain the ontology?

   Answers to the above questions may change during the development process, but they work as a reference to limit the scope.

2. *Consider reusing existing ontologies*: It is always advisable to use existing works by either refining or extending them to meet the current requirements. This will also make it possible to connect with other applications that are using the same ontologies and vocabularies.

3. *Enumerate essential terms in the ontology*: It is suggested to make a list of terms that we want to define/explain to the user. This includes the terms along with their properties and details of how they connect with other terms. After this we should move toward defining the class hierarchy (more on this in the next point).

4. *Define the classes and the class hierarchy*: There are various ways to define the class hierarchy (Uschold & Gruninger, 1996a, b):

   - *Top-Down*: This development process starts with the most general concepts and then moves down the hierarchy to specific/specialized concepts.
   - *Bottom-Up*: This development starts from the most specific/specialized concepts, and then these concepts are grouped to move to more general concepts (moving up the concept hierarchy).
   - *Combination of Top-Down and Bottom-Up*: This development is a combination of the top-down and bottom-up processes. Initially, an important concept (dependent on use case) is defined and then they are generalized and specialized based on the requirement (like need of clustering requires parent concepts, so more generalized concepts will be introduced).

5. *Define the properties of classes—slots*: To answer all the questions posed in a particular domain, we must define properties and classes to define a concept wholly. Properties are of two types. The first is object properties that define a relationship between different concepts. Second, data properties have a value associated with them in any of the various data types (i.e., int, string).

6. *Define the domain and range of properties*: Domain means that for which class/concept a property should/can hold value of and range means the data type of value of a property (when working with data properties). In the case of object properties, range will define the relationship two concepts hold with each other.

7. *Create instances*: The final step while creating an ontology is to create instances of classes.

7.4   Making Ontologies Multilingual

As discussed in the motivation, making already available ontologies multilingual will increase the reach of systems that have been developed using those ontologies. In case of ontology is not present, we can create new ones keeping multilinguality in mind. Multiple authors (such as Espinoza et al., 2008, 2009; Cimiano et al., 2010; McCrae et al., 2016) have presented ways to make an ontology multilingual, out of which the most widely used (Espinoza et al., 2009) has provided three core ways which have been extended by multiple authors. The three methods are (1) Inclusion of multilingual information in the ontology, (2) One conceptualization per Linguistic Anthropology, and (3) Association of External Multilingual Information. The ability to incorporate multilingual information allows the developers to create language-independent systems and facilitate users in obtaining results using their native languages. A detailed description of the above-stated ways of making multilingual ontologies is presented below:

7.4.1   Inclusion of Multilingual Information in the Ontology

In this approach, multilingual information is included in the ontology by using rdfs: comment and rdfs:label properties. We generally don't have to make more effort to make information interoperable because multilingual information is present within the ontology. This method is shown in Fig. 7.1, which contains an ontology in which General English greetings are written (as a class in ontology) along with their equivalent representation in Hindi and Germany using rdfs:comment.

But the major problem with this approach is Redundant efforts—meaning "ontology engineers have to rewrite the details that are already available on the web," where the efficient way can be simply linking the information with the concept in the ontology.

7.4.2   One Conceptualization per Linguistic Anthropology

An ontology is created per cultural and language context, and then their matching is performed. Here, ontologies are in different languages containing language-specific details and variations influenced by cultural differences (still more work is needed to incorporate cultural variation in ontologies).

Some systems are working on this task and have tested their system on the Ontology Alignment Evaluation Initiative's website.

Some of the systems working toward matching conceptualization of different culture and language are as follows:

```xml
<rdf:Description rdf:about="https://archive.org/download/English.owl#hello">
    <rdfs:comment xml:lang="hi">नमस्ते</rdfs:comment>
    <rdf:type rdf:resource="http://www.w3.org/2002/07/owl#Class"/>
    <rdfs:subClassOf rdf:resource="https://archive.org/download/English.owl#Greetings"/>
    <rdfs:comment xml:lang="de">Hallo</rdfs:comment>
</rdf:Description>
<rdf:Description rdf:about="https://archive.org/download/English.owl#see_you">
    <rdfs:subClassOf rdf:resource="https://archive.org/download/English.owl#Statements">:
    <rdfs:comment xml:lang="hi">फिर मिलते हैं</rdfs:comment>
    <rdf:type rdf:resource="http://www.w3.org/2002/07/owl#Class"/>
    <rdfs:comment xml:lang="de">wir sehen uns</rdfs:comment>
</rdf:Description>
<rdf:Description rdf:about="https://archive.org/download/English.owl#good_afternoon">
    <rdf:type rdf:resource="http://www.w3.org/2002/07/owl#Class"/>
    <rdfs:comment xml:lang="de">guten Tag</rdfs:comment>
    <rdfs:comment xml:lang="hi">नमस्कार</rdfs:comment>
    <rdfs:subClassOf rdf:resource="https://archive.org/download/English.owl#Greetings"/>
</rdf:Description>
<rdf:Description rdf:about="https://archive.org/download/English.owl#have_a_good_day">
    <rdfs:comment xml:lang="hi">आपका दिन शुभ हो</rdfs:comment>
    <rdfs:comment xml:lang="de">haben Sie einen guten Tag</rdfs:comment>
    <rdf:type rdf:resource="http://www.w3.org/2002/07/owl#Class"/>
    <rdfs:subClassOf rdf:resource="https://archive.org/download/English.owl#Greetings"/>
</rdf:Description>
<rdf:Description rdf:about="https://archive.org/download/English.owl#how_are_you">
    <rdf:type rdf:resource="http://www.w3.org/2002/07/owl#Class"/>
    <rdfs:comment xml:lang="de">wie geht es dir</rdfs:comment>
    <rdfs:comment xml:lang="hi">क्या हाल है</rdfs:comment>
    <rdfs:subClassOf rdf:resource="https://archive.org/download/English.owl#Questions"/>
</rdf:Description>
```

Fig. 7.1 Ontology of general conversation in three languages (English, German, and Hindi)

- *AML*: AgreementMakerLight (Faria et al., 2013) is built on top of the AgreementMaker framework; while keeping core functionalities along with extensibility and flexibility of the AgreementMaker framework, it focuses on handling very large-scale ontologies and providing computational efficiency.

  As stated by the authors (Faria et al., 2013), the efficiency of AgreementMakerLight has been evaluated in two OAEI tracks: Anatomy and Large Biomedical Ontologies. It achieved an excellent run time result. Considering the Anatomy track, AgreementMakerLight is the best system measured in terms of F-measure.

- *KEPLER*: KEPLER uses a translator to handle multilingualism. KEPLER also makes use of the wealth of the used ontologies as a part of the alignment strategy. It inherited the power of Information Retrieval (IR). KEPLER also utilizes a partitioning module for scaling. KEPLER has received competitive results in multilingual scenarios by using a well-defined strategy based on the translator.

- *LogMap*: LogMap (Jiménez-Ruiz & Grau, 2011) is an ontology matching system with reasoning and diagnosis capabilities that is highly scalable. LogMap is one of the matching systems that can work with semantically rich ontologies with many classes. "On the fly" LogMap can detect and repair. The experiments confirm that LogMap is efficient when matching the large ontologies (NCI, FMA, and SNOMEDCT) in the bio-medical track of OAEI. In addition, LogMap was able to produce high-quality mappings in many cases. When checking the obtained ontology by integrating input ontology and output mappings from LogMap, the results were consistent and didn't contain unsatisfiable classes.

- *XMap*: XMap (Djeddi & Khadir, 2010) is an ontology alignment algorithm for OWL-Full ontologies. XMap allows search for the best match through using their OWL-Graph during ontology alignment operation. Along with part-Of and Is-A (taxonomic) relations, it also distinguishes semantic relations (such as Same-as) and features (attributes, functions, and parts) for OWL-Full. The sigmoid function is used along with a weighted sum to handle the problem of heterogeneity depending on the entity's context.

  This approach was applied to domain ontologies of the steam turbine. The alignment was performed on two ontologies as candidates. As reported by the author, XMap provided performance improvements and is easy to use, but the tradeoff was the computational time, which was slightly high compared to other methods.

7.4.3 Association of External Multilingual Information

While dealing with multilingual information, it has been identified that it is necessary to conduct the Ontology Localization Activity, which consists of adapting an ontology to a specific cultural community and language, as defined in Suárez-Figueroa and Gómez-Pérez (2008).

This concept is associated with the pool of concepts available on the LOD cloud to prevent redundant efforts in creating conceptualizations as they are being built on standardized concepts available on the LOD cloud.

1. *Linguistic Information Repository (LIR)* (Montiel-Ponsoda et al., 2011): LIR is specifically designed to account for linguistic and cultural differences among languages. LIR aims toward localizing the terminological layer (names of ontology classes) of ontologies instead of modifying the conceptualization, which generates multilingual ontologies as a result. LIR uses an ontology meta-model for the localization of the terminological layer. The authors have proposed to link ontologies with a linguistic model termed Linguistic Information Repository (LIR). LIR's main feature is that it (1) facilitates localization of ontology concepts to a particular cultural and linguistic universe by providing complete and complementary linguistic information, and (2) also offers seamless access to the aggregated multilingual information.

   The Linguistic Information incorporated in the LIR is organized as LexicalEntry class. A LexicalEntry is defined as "a unit of form and meaning in a certain language" (Saloni et al., 1990). Hence, it is associated with the class's Sense, Lexicalization, and Language. A set of lexicalization/term variants shares the same definition within a particular cultural and linguistic universe concerned with a specific context. With the use of properties such as Same-As, we can relate these multiple variants of the same things to represent all the variations and provide richer information. At the LexicalEntry level, language classes allow for searching based on a particular natural language based on language selection.

2. *Lemon model:* Toward the goal of connecting the world of lexical resources, this is the world of ontologies and semantic data as present on the Semantic Web. McCrae et al. (2012) have proposed a model that the authors have termed lemon (Lexicon Model for Ontologies), which can represent lexical information related to the terms and words concerning an ontology present on the Web. The authors have termed ontology-lexicon "lemon," in which it expresses how elements such as class, properties, and individuals of an ontology are achieved linguistically. In this model, the authors have followed a principle which they term "semantics by reference." Here, the meaning of entities in the lexicon is exclusively expressed in the ontology itself, and the lexicon barely refers to the relevant concept. This differs from other lexical resources because it doesn't include lexico-semantic relations (i.e., hypernym, synonym) as part of the lexicon. Lemon is not developed to provide a collection of resources; rather, it was intended to support the exchange of ontology-lexicas available on the Semantic Web. Lemon has provided domain terminologies that are not domain-specific and can be used with any domain or task. Lemon has been developed with the influence of previous research work such as LIR (Montiel-Ponsoda et al., 2011), Lexinfo (Buitelaar et al., 2009), and Lexical Markup Framework (Francopoulo et al., 2006). The authors have also used the work related to the OLiA project (Chiarcos, 2010) and the ISOcat meta-model registry (Kemps-Snijders et al., 2008).

There are certain systems listed below which are using the lemon model to incorporate the power of Linked Open Data into their systems:

- *DBnary*: DBnary (Sérasset, 2015) focuses on Wiktionary, the dictionary part of the resources sponsored by the Wikimedia Foundation. The authors have presented multilingual lexical data extracted from different Wiktionary language editions, and made a Multilingual Lexical Linked Open Data (MLLOD) available to the community. This work is beneficial for many users who can make use of this data in their NLP systems. Other than this, the extracted information is in Resource Description Framework (RDF) standard and uses the lemon model, which makes this dataset directly useful for researchers working in the field of the Semantic Web, where multiple ontologies of the same domain in different languages can be aligned together and can collectively describe the domain more coherently.

  DBnary contains a significant number of entries, especially in English and French, through which it becomes comparable to Wordnet. It is also comparable to Open Multilingual Wordnet (an aggregation of several existing multilingual Wordnets) because it contains various translations in a particular language pair.

- *lemonUby*: lemonUby (Eckle-Kohler et al., 2015) is a lexical resource created after the conversion of data extracted from UBY, which is an existing large-scale linked lexical resource, into a lemon lexicon model. UBY contains data from VerbNet, FrameNet, WordNet, OmegaWiki (German and English entries), a set of pairs of lexicons at word sense level (links between FrameNet and VerbNet, WordNet and VerbNet, FrameNet and WordNet, Wiktionary and WordNet, German OmegaWiki and WordNet), and the English and German Wiktionaries. The authors have also linked lemonUBY with other linguistic terminological repositories and lexical resources in the Linguistic Linked Open Data (LLOD) cloud.

  The information provided through lemonUby not only provides rich information related to lexical entries in these two languages, but also links at the word sense level within both lemonUby and other resources on the Semantic Web.

- *DBLexiPedia* (Walter et al., 2015): A plethora of datasets are linked to a few datahubs on the Semantic Web; the most prominent one is DBpedia. It is challenging to incorporate data from DBpedia for Natural Language Processing (NLP) applications. To provide the knowledge for NLP applications, the authors they have constructed a lexicon for DBpedia ontology 2014 using existing automatic methods for lexicon induction. For 574 different properties, it contains 11,998 lexical entries in three languages, i.e., German, English, and Spanish. It is the same as DBpedia, which includes a collection of Semantic Web datasets that can facilitate the construction of a hub of lexical Semantic Web, the term for an ecosystem that allows ontology lexica to be published, linked, and reused across applications.

  Datasets can be found at http://dblexipedia.org.

3. *Extended Hierarchical Censored Production Rules (EHCPR) Systems*: The EHCPRs (Jain et al., 2011; Jain & Jain, 2013, 2014; Mishra et al., 2015) system provides a methodology for reasoning, representation, learning, etc. for multilingual thinking machines. EHCPR is also referred to by the authors as a unit of represented knowledge in the globally distributed knowledge. Specifications of EHCPR are close to the entity representations in the real world. EHCPR's ontology's representational units are mapped to the realist framework on a one-on-one basis. A realist approach in ontology engineering talks about the representation of concepts in reality.

7.5 Smart Devices (Applications Using AIoT)

As defined on Wikipedia,[2] "A *smart device* is an electronic device, generally connected to other devices or networks via different wireless protocols such as Bluetooth, Zigbee, NFC, Wi-Fi, LiFi, 5G, etc., that can operate to some extent interactively and autonomously." These smart applications should be built for global deployments. Smart devices include smartphones, smart cars, smart locks, smartwatches, smart bands, and smart thermostats.

Examples of some renowned smart devices are Nest devices (by Google), Alexa (by Amazon), and Mac mini (by Apple). Let's talk about some of the widely adopted applications of AIoT.

7.5.1 Self-Driving Vehicles

Many multinational companies and car manufacturers are working toward an autonomous vehicle future. Companies such as Tesla, Google, BMW, and Mercedes Benz have presented some prototypes and demonstrations of their autonomous vehicles performing tasks such as detecting obstacles and predicting the next move of other vehicles on the road, along with the main functions of driving the vehicle with little to no input from humans.

7.5.2 Smart Cameras

Smart cameras are now being used for various applications such as providing security solutions for homes and monitoring customers at provisional stores. Google Nest uses these smart cameras to offer services such as detecting and alerting

---

[2]https://en.wikipedia.org/wiki/Smart_device.

homeowners if someone is trying to break into their house when they are not at home. Walmart uses thousands of these smart cameras to monitor people who are not scanning products at their numerous self-checkout stores.

It is clear that there are numerous possibilities for these systems and how they can enrich the lives of millions of humans. If these systems can obtain information in multiple languages and provide services in all these different languages, their reach will be unprecedented. These systems will also expand their reach and support to speakers from all over the world. We can see that this has started to happen in products such as Alexa from Amazon, which now supports communication in Hindi, for example.

7.6 Conclusion

In this chapter we have talked about multilingual ontologies, how to work with them, and how AIoT and ontologies can be used together to develop various services offered by smart devices. This chapter's section on multilinguality states that this can make these services available to a wide non-English-speaking audience/customers/ users. Hence, in the end, we want to ask all of you to be a part of this change. We can start by bringing our native language into this loop and making these services more accessible to our community of people who may not have the opportunity to learn English but can benefit from technology. This can also be considered as a starting point where truly each and everyone has an equal opportunity provided by the technologies we have access to in this information age.

Review Questions
- How have different languages evolved over time?
- How is AIoT different from IoT?
- Why is multilinguality important?
- Why and how are semantic technologies helpful in making data machine-understandable?

Discussion Questions
- What improvements can multilinguality bring in various computer systems?
- Discuss how evolution of languages has made them different from each other.
- How can understanding of different languages by computers make all the fields that make use of them more effective?

Problem Statements for Researchers
- Can you think of any better way to incorporate multilingual information to make it machine-understandable?
- What field do you think can benefit from AIoT and semantic technologies that has yet to use these technologies? And how will this be beneficial?

References

Beka, M. B. (2016). Mother tongue as a medium of instruction: Benefits and challenges. *International Journal of Language Literature & Art Studies, 4*(1), 16–26.

Buitelaar, P., Cimiano, P., Haase, P., & Sintek, M. (2009, May). Towards linguistically grounded ontologies. In *European Semantic Web Conference* (pp. 111–125). Berlin: Springer.

Chiarcos, C. (2010, May). Grounding an ontology of linguistic annotations in the data category registry. In *LREC 2010 Workshop on Language Resource and Language Technology Standards (LT&LTS)*, Valetta, Malta (pp. 37–40).

Cimiano, P., Montiel-Ponsoda, E., Buitelaar, P., Espinoza, M., & Gómez-Pérez, A. (2010). A note on ontology localization. *Applied Ontology, 5*(2), 127–137.

Djeddi, W. E., & Khadir, M. T. (2010, October). XMAP: A novel structural approach for alignment of OWL-full ontologies. In *2010 International Conference on Machine and Web Intelligence* (pp. 368–373). IEEE.

Eckle-Kohler, J., McCrae, J. P., & Chiarcos, C. (2015). lemonUby–A large, interlinked, syntactically-rich lexical resource for ontologies. *Semantic Web, 6*(4), 371–378.

Espinoza, M., Gómez-Pérez, A., & Mena, E. (2008, June). Enriching an ontology with multilingual information. In *European Semantic Web Conference* (pp. 333–347). Berlin: Springer.

Espinoza, M., Montiel-Ponsoda, E., & Gómez-Pérez, A. (2009, September). Ontology localization. In *Proceedings of the Fifth International Conference on Knowledge Capture* (pp. 33–40).

Faria, D., Pesquita, C., Santos, E., Palmonari, M., Cruz, I. F., & Couto, F. M. (2013, September). The agreementmakerlight ontology matching system. In *OTM Confederated International Conferences on the Move to Meaningful Internet Systems* (pp. 527–541). Berlin: Springer.

Francopoulo, G., George, M., Calzolari, N., Monachini, M., Bel, N., Pet, M., & Soria, C. (2006). *Lexical markup framework (LMF)*.

Gruninger, M., & Fox, M. S. (1994). The design and evaluation of ontologies for enterprise engineering. In *Workshop on Implemented Ontologies, European Conference on Artificial Intelligence (ECAI)*.

Grüninger, M., & Fox, M. S. (1995). *Methodology for the design and evaluation of ontologies*.

Jain, N. K., & Jain, S. (2013). Live multilingual thinking machine. *Journal of Experimental & Theoretical Artificial Intelligence, 25*(4), 575–587.

Jain, S., & Jain, N. K. (2014, March). A globalized intelligent system. In *2014 International Conference on Computing for Sustainable Global Development (INDIACom)* (pp. 425–431). IEEE.

Jain, S., Chaudhary, D., & Jain, N. K. (2011, March). Localization of EHCPRs system in the multilingual domain: An implementation. In *International Conference on Information Systems for Indian Languages* (pp. 314–316). Berlin: Springer.

Jiménez-Ruiz, E., & Grau, B. C. (2011, October). Logmap: Logic-based and scalable ontology matching. In *International Semantic Web Conference* (pp. 273–288). Berlin: Springer.

Jones, D., Bench-Capon, T., & Visser, P. (1998). *Methodologies for ontology development*.

Kemps-Snijders, M., Windhouwer, M., Wittenburg, P., & Wright, S. E. (2008). ISOcat: Corralling data categories in the wild. In *6th International Conference on Language Resources and Evaluation (LREC 2008)*.

Li, X., Martínez, J. F., & Rubio, G. (2016). A new fuzzy ontology development methodology (FODM) proposal. *IEEE Access, 4*, 7111–7124.

Malone, S., & Paraide, P. (2011). Mother tongue-based bilingual education in Papua New Guinea. *International Review of Education, 57*(5–6), 705–720.

McCrae, J., Aguado-de-Cea, G., Buitelaar, P., Cimiano, P., Declerck, T., Gómez-Pérez, A., Gracia, J., Hollink, L., Montiel-Ponsoda, E., Spohr, D., & Wunner, T. (2012). Interchanging lexical resources on the semantic web. *Language Resources and Evaluation, 46*(4), 701–719.

McCrae, J. P., Arcan, M., Asooja, K., Gracia, J., Buitelaar, P., & Cimiano, P. (2016). Domain adaptation for ontology localization. *Journal of Web Semantics, 36*, 23–31.

Mishra, S., Malik, S., Jain, N. K., & Jain, S. (2015). A realist framework for ontologies and the semantic web. *Procedia Computer Science, 70*, 483–490.

Montiel-Ponsoda, E., Aguado de Cea, G., Gómez-Pérez, A., & Peters, W. (2011). Enriching ontologies with multilingual information. *Natural Language Engineering, 17*(3), 283.

Noy, N. F., & McGuinness, D. L. (2001). *Ontology development 101: A guide to creating your first ontology.*

Prud'hommeaux, E. (2008). *SPARQL query language for RDF, W3C recommendation.* Retrieved from http://www.w3.org/TR/rdf-sparql-query/

Saloni, Z., Szpakowicz, S., & Świdziński, M. (1990). The design of a universal basic dictionary of contemporary polish. *International Journal of Lexicography, 3*(1), 1–22.

Sérasset, G. (2015). DBnary: Wiktionary as a Lemon-based multilingual lexical resource in RDF. *Semantic Web, 6*(4), 355–361.

Suárez-Figueroa, M. C., & Gómez-Pérez, A. (2008). *Towards a glossary of activities in the ontology engineering field.*

Uschold, M. (1996a). *Converting an informal ontology into ontolingua: Some experiences.* Technical Report-University of Edinburgh Artificial Intelligence Applications Institute AIAI TR.

Uschold, M. (1996b, September). Building ontologies: Towards a uni ed methodology. In *Proceedings of 16th Annual Conference of the British Computer Society Specialists Group on Expert Systems.* Citeseer.

Uschold, M., & Gruninger, M. (1996a). Ontologies: Principles, methods and applications. *Knowledge Engineering Review, 11*(2).

Uschold, M., & Gruninger, M. (1996b). *Ontologies: Principles, methods and applications.* Technical Report-University of Edinburgh Artificial Intelligence Applications Institute AIAI TR.

Walter, S., Unger, C., & Cimiano, P. (2015). Dblexipedia: A nucleus for a multilingual lexical semantic web. In *Proceedings of 3th International Workshop on NLP and DBpedia, co-located with the 14th International Semantic Web Conference (ISWC 2015)*, October 11–15.

Abhisek Sharma, currently working as a Research Scholar since 2019 in the National Institute of Technology, Kurukshetra, under the supervision of Dr. Sarika Jain, Assistant Professor, Department of Computer Applications. His Ph.D. is in the field of Knowledge Representation and Engineering. He has completed his Master's in Computer Applications in 2018. He has also worked on project funded by DRDO, India. In general, he is driven towards finding solutions for humans' problems when trying to get Multilingual and Multicultural semantically rich results from computers and the issues currently making the processing of semantics by the computers difficult.

Sarika Jain graduated from Jawaharlal Nehru University (India) in 2001. Her doctorate, awarded in 2011, is in the field of knowledge representation in Artificial Intelligence. She has served in the field of education for over 19 years and is currently in service at the National Institute of Technology, Kurukshetra (Institute of National Importance), India. Dr. Jain has authored or co-authored over 150 publications including books. Her current research interests are knowledge management and analytics, the semantic web, ontological engineering, and intelligent systems. She is a senior member of the IEEE, member of ACM, and a Life Member of the CSI.

Part II
Applications and Case Studies

Chapter 8
Smart Manufacturing

Paul D. Clough and Jon Stammers

Abstract The ability to connect a growing range of technologies, such as sensors, Internet of (Industrial) Things, cloud computing, Big Data analytics, AI, mobile devices, and augmented/virtual reality, is helping to take manufacturing to new levels of "smartness." Such technologies have the opportunity to transform, automate, and bring intelligence to manufacturing processes and support the next manufacturing era. In this chapter, we describe the manufacturing context; emerging concepts, such as Industry 4.0; and technologies that are driving change and innovation within the manufacturing industry.

Keywords Industry 4.0 · Smart manufacturing · IoT · Industrial IoT · AI

Key Points
- Review of the key technologies being used to support smart manufacturing, such as AI, Industrial IoT, cloud computing, and augmented/virtual reality
- Content broken down into the following sections: from sensors and connectivity (e.g., Industrial IoT), through developing business value with data (e.g., Big Data analytics and AI), to applications beyond the physical world (e.g., simulation and digital twins)
- Inclusion of several real-life examples and use cases showing how smart manufacturing can be used to transform the manufacturing process
- Discussion of manufacturing applications that go beyond the physical world, including simulation, digital twins, and extending reality
- Summary of the benefits and challenges of smart technology in manufacturing, including change management, integration, security, and lack of skills

P. D. Clough (✉)
Peak Indicators, University of Sheffield Information School, Sheffield, UK
e-mail: paul.clough@peakindicators.com

J. Stammers
Advanced Manufacturing Research Centre (AMRC), University of Sheffield, Sheffield, UK
e-mail: j.stammers@amrc.co.uk

8.1 Introduction to Smart Manufacturing

New technologies, such as AI and Industrial Internet of Things, and the ability to connect them, the availability of vast amounts of data, the maturity of analytics and intelligent systems, and advanced manufacturing techniques are bringing about "smart" manufacturing systems (SMSs) and a new data-driven era for manufacturing (Li et al., 2017; Zheng et al., 2018; Qu et al., 2019). In fact, access to new forms of data and technologies is enabling a convergence between the physical and cyber/digital worlds (Tao et al., 2018). This has manifest itself in the manufacturing strategy of countries with the introduction of new notions of manufacturing, such as Manufacturing Innovation 3.0 in Korea, Made in China 2025, Industry 4.0 in Germany, and Smart Manufacturing in the USA.

8.1.1 The Manufacturing Process

Manufacturing is a well-established industry that turns raw materials into products through a series of processes and activities, such as product design, acquiring of raw materials, and the processing of materials (Dahotre & Harimkar, 2008). Many manufacturing processes exist; however, the industry is facing continuous changes—new technologies, new processes, and new consumer demands—making manufacturing increasingly more complex and dynamic. Figure 8.1 illustrates a typical manufacturing process—multistage manufacture of a high-value component (e.g., the fabrication of metal components and assembling them into parts), covering the journey from raw material from the supplier, through design, to the shipping of an assembly (Bralla, 2007).

In the example in Fig. 8.1, the component undergoes multiple machining processes using computer numerical control (CNC) machinery where pre-programmed software and code control the movement of production equipment. In addition, various inspection and testing stages are undergone using coordinate measuring machine (CMM), a device that measures geometry of physical objects by sensing discrete points on the surface of an object with a probe, as well as final assembly. These stages—4 through to 16—can be considered the *core* manufacturing processes where smart technology could have an impact. However, the stages outside of this can also play a role in enabling smart manufacturing, such as product design and supply chain management, and offer data capture opportunities which can influence the manufacturing processes itself. In the remainder of this chapter, we summarize technologies involved in smart manufacturing that could transform stages of the process in Fig. 8.1.

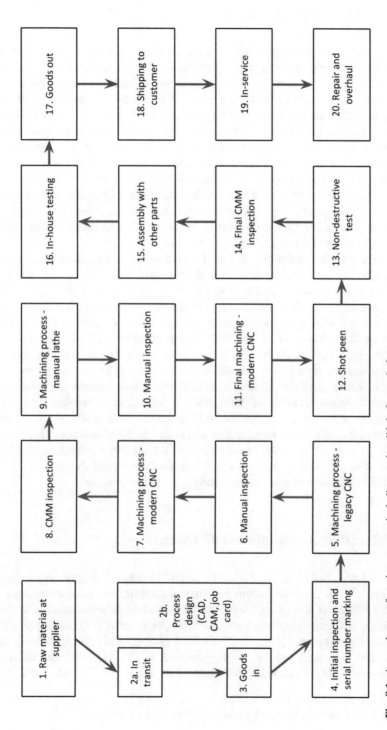

Fig. 8.1 A sample manufacturing process, including product life before and after

8.1.2 Making Manufacturing Smarter

In many ways, manufacturers have often been "smart" by developing or applying new technologies and methods or creating efficient and effective processes to turn raw materials into products, thereby adding value. Indeed, the terms "smart" and "intelligent" were used in earlier industrial eras (Industry 3.0) to describe automation and collaborative manufacturing systems that respond in real time to changing demands and needs. However, the move now is toward data-driven smart manufacturing, whereby wide-scale collection and analysis of vast amounts of (real-time) data at all stages of the manufacturing process is enabling companies to reach new levels of intelligence: "Smart manufacturing, also known as Industry 4.0, refers to the next generation manufacturing paradigm that makes use of smart sensors, cloud computing infrastructures, AI, machine learning, additive manufacturing, and/or advanced robotics to improve manufacturing productivity and cost efficiency" (Wu et al., 2018:1).

In addition to the availability of data, the evolution of smart manufacturing is a combination of technical innovation and emerging technologies, advances in manufacturing, and new manufacturing paradigms (e.g., agile, lean and additive) and automation. This has gone from computer-integrated manufacturing in the 1970s, through intelligent manufacturing in the 1990s, to smart manufacturing systems or SMSs today (Qu et al., 2019; Tao et al., 2018). This is also linked to the fourth industrial revolution and Industry 4.0[1]—the digital transformation of manufacturing/production and related industries and value creation processes (Xu et al., 2018; Alcácer & Cruz-Machado, 2019), which captures the use of data in a connected manufacturing infrastructure (e.g., factory, supply chains, etc.). In the next section, we discuss some of the building blocks for Industry 4.0 and smart manufacturing, including data generation and connectivity using sensors and Industrial IoT (Sect. 8.2), data management and analysis using cloud computing, Big Data and AI (Sect. 8.3), and technologies that take the user beyond the physical world such as simulation, augmented reality, and digital twins (Sect. 8.4).

8.2 The (Industrial) Internet of Things

The term "Internet of Things" (IoT) is now commonplace, referring to devices found in homes, offices, and other environments that contain embedded technology to allow them to sense and interact with their surroundings. When connected to other technology, either directly using local networking or via Internet connectivity, it can lead to intelligent systems (Chu, 2016). Depending on the use of the technology and the intended user, there are three main categories of IoT: (1) *consumer IoT* (e.g., smartphones), (2) *commercial IoT* (e.g., connected medical devices), and

---

[1]Industry 4.0 itself is also often synonymous with the term "smart industry."

(3) *Industrial IoT*. When applied in industrial systems, IoT technology brings the opportunity to optimize monitoring and control of industrial systems, capturing large amounts of data about those systems, exposing insight previously hidden.

Industrial IoT (IIoT) is a "network of intelligent and highly connected industrial components that are deployed to achieve high production rate with reduced operational costs through real-time monitoring, efficient management and controlling of industrial processes, assets and operational time" (Khan et al., 2020:1). Further enabling technologies include edge computing and analytics, cyber security, cloud computing, wide area networks (4G, 5G, long-range WAN, etc.), wireless networks (WiFi), and data science techniques, such as artificial intelligence and Big Data analytics. Bringing some, or all, of these technologies along with the smart "things" to a production environment can enable smart manufacturing.

A typical IIoT system is illustrated in Fig. 8.2 and highlights a number of typical components found in IIoT scenarios: sensing devices broadcast their measurement results, control devices provide actions as a result of measured data, and devices capture images, either still or video. Importantly, there are multiple assets being monitored, and data from all of these is communicated to the central control center for analysis, insight, and action.

8.2.1   Sensing Technology

A sensor is a device that measures something about its surroundings and sends a signal to an acquisition system. Sensors are a fundamental element of any IoT system (Zheng et al., 2018) and are usually a primary source of data for developing understanding and insight into how a system, or individual asset, is performing. In particular, smart assessment of asset health requires one or more sensing devices. In any sensor application in manufacturing, the typical sequence of events and data flow is the following: process variables → sensorial perception → data processing and analysis → cognitive decision → action. Not covered is data transfer from sensor to the system processing the data and feature extraction. These data acquisition (DAQ) devices and data transfer protocols are fundamental to any sensor system, ranging from reading a simple voltage output signal to a more sophisticated (bidirectional) protocol, e.g., IO-Link.[2]

Figure 8.3 illustrates an approach that has been adopted at the University of Sheffield Advanced Manufacturing Research Centre (Dominguez-Caballero et al., 2019). Rather than storing all raw data in long-term storage, which incurs storage and networking costs, a short-term buffer is used for raw data, providing storage for a number of weeks, and then overwrites the earliest data. Edge-processed *summary* data is sent to a central database, either on-premise or cloud-based, for long-term

---

[2]https://www.io-link.com/en/Technology/what_is_IO-Link.php.

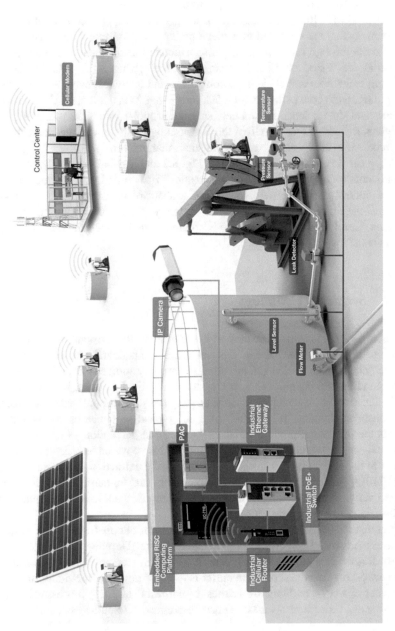

Fig. 8.2 An example of an IIoT system (Alcácer & Cruz-Machado, 2019)

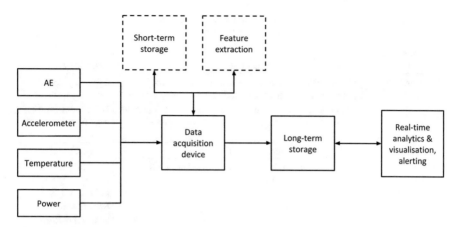

Fig. 8.3 Data flow from sensors to storage and beyond

storage and analytics. The edge processing of the raw data typically includes extraction of features in the time-, frequency-, and time-frequency domains.

Table 8.1 presents a summary of sensors or measurement types, their potential applications in manufacturing, and typical frequencies of data capture. The choice of which sensor to use is entirely dependent on the intended use case (e.g., predictive maintenance, environmental monitoring, process health, etc.), with some sensors being useful across multiple tasks. Fujishima et al. (2016), for example, use 24 sensing devices to monitor a machine tool and its processes for applications, including energy saving, predictive maintenance, and safety. Further example uses of sensing in smart manufacturing include the following.

8.2.1.1 Tool Condition Monitoring

Monitoring tool condition is an important, yet time-consuming, task in many machining scenarios. This is because the tool condition has a direct impact on the achieved surface quality and geometrical properties of a workpiece. Checking on tool condition usually involves a manual visual inspection by an operator or using a tool measurement system within the machine tool itself. Either way, the machining process must be stopped to perform these tasks. Therefore, there is a desire to automate the process, and the use of sensors provides a potential solution to this. Different sensing can be used to monitor tool condition. Prior literature has shown that cutting tool surface temperature is a key indicator of cutting process quality. Heeley et al. (2018) propose the use of temperature measurement to capture thermal data from as close to the cutting tool surface as possible. Another approach to measuring tool condition in situ is presented by Maier et al. (2018) who designed an Industry 4.0 tool holder, which incorporated strain gauges, to measure cutting forces during machining operations. An increase in the cutting force can be a

Table 8.1 Sensors and measurement types and their applications in manufacturing environments

Sensor/ measurement type	Applications in manufacturing	Frequency
Temperature	Factory environmental conditions, machine tool structure monitoring (potential deformation), cutting tool condition, motor and drive condition, component temperature (growth, shrinkage), additive process assessment	Typically, low (<1 Hz) High for cutting tool condition (>1 kHz)
Humidity	Factory environmental conditions	Low (<1 Hz)
Power	Machine tool motor and drive monitoring, building management systems	Low for general energy usage calculations (<1 Hz) Medium for asset health monitoring (<1 kHz)
Accelerometer	Machining vibration, spindles and bearings, floor vibration	High (1 kHz–20 kHz)
Force and torque	Machine tool structure and fixture monitoring, conveyor system monitoring, spindle and bearing monitoring	Low to medium (1 Hz–1 kHz)
Encoders, proximity	Position of guideways, rotary systems, robot arms, conveyor belt tension, etc.	Medium (<1 kHz)
Acoustic emission	Cutting tool condition	Very high (>50 kHz)
pH, composition, particulates	Fluids condition monitoring (e.g., metal working fluids for machining, fluid components in pharma and food)	Low (1 Hz or less)
Vision systems	Part identification, quality monitoring, asset identification and location, asset attendance	N/A

predictor of tool wear. Duro et al. (2016) propose a cost-saving approach to monitoring tool wear by using acoustic emissions (AE) data.

8.2.1.2 Machine Tool Health Monitoring

Machine tools are a core component of many manufacturing systems. If a machine tool fails, it can cause both irreparable damage to any component currently in process and significant delays. Therefore, monitoring the health of machine tools is a key activity of any smart manufacturing system, both for ongoing monitoring and proactive maintenance activities (Lee et al. 2018). There are many types of sensor that play an important role in machine tool health monitoring, and the choice of sensor depends on which element of the machine is to be monitored. For example, bearings can be monitored using vibration, force, and deformation sensing. Spindle health can likewise be monitored with vibration, as well as temperature and data from a machine tool controller. Determining which elements of a machine to monitor, and consequently choosing sensing devices, can be achieved using a Failure Modes and Effects Analysis (FMEA)—identifying where failures might occur and what these may be.

8.2.1.3 Additive Process Performance

Additive manufacturing (AM) is gaining popularity in all sectors as it has the potential to reduce material use, as only the required material is added to gain a near-net shape, as opposed to surplus material being subtracted. Furthermore, additive methods offer new ways for designing both the external and the internal structure of components, allowing increasingly complex designs to improve component quality, previously unattainable using traditional subtractive methods. Sensing plays a key role in ensuring that an additive process is performing as expected. Xia et al. (2020) provide a comprehensive overview of how sensing technologies can be used to monitor, and ultimately control, AM processes. They include details on how vision systems, spectroscopy, acoustic emission, and thermal data can assist in detecting various AM defects, such as cracks, porosity, voids, and surface defects.

8.2.1.4 Sub-surface Material Quality

In the high-value manufacturing sector, metallic components are typically machined from billets or forgings of raw materials. Understanding the material properties of the raw stock is paramount to ensuring the quality and longevity of the final product and often forms part of the final acceptance "sign off" for a component. The tests employed for capturing these material properties, either destructive on sample parts or nondestructive on almost all parts, are time-consuming and costly and in some cases rely heavily on chemicals with significant environmental footprints. One such test is chemical etching for grain size analysis, typically in titanium billets (a length of metal), which only captures a selection of billets due to the time and resources involved. Recent research has shown that force dynamometry data (measurement of force expended) contains enough information to accurately predict grain size during a machining process (Fernández et al., 2020), and embedding such techniques in machining processes would allow sub-surface quality to be captured in situ rather than as an additional manufacturing activity.

8.2.1.5 Legacy Devices and Low-Cost Sensing

Enabling Industry 4.0 and IoT technologies is expensive; therefore, these technologies are often not being adopted by small-to-medium enterprises (SMEs) because of

Fig. 8.4 Colchester Bantam lathe with a low-cost Industry 4.0 solution (Lockwood et al., 2018)

cost and a lack of expertise within those companies.[3] Many of these SMEs can see the value in digital technology in their business, in particular when many of the assets being used in daily production are considered *legacy* devices—usually translated to "old," but can actually refer to devices that are 10 years old or less. What is common across legacy devices is a lack of connectivity and data capture capability. This makes Industry 4.0 adoption challenging for those SMEs that predominantly use legacy devices.

In 2018, a project was undertaken at the University of Sheffield Advanced Manufacturing Research Centre (AMRC) to digitize legacy devices, thus demonstrating that it was possible and did not need to be prohibitively expensive (Lockwood et al., 2018). The project took two legacy machine tools, a Colchester Bantam lathe (c. 1956) and a Bridgeport Turret Mill (c. 1980), and installed both low-cost (<£500) and high-cost (<£5000) sensing systems. The data captured was used to populate a web-based dashboard that informed on overall equipment effectiveness (OEE), operating cost, machine condition, and process condition. The lathe with the dashboard is shown in Fig. 8.4, along with an operator viewing critical data on a mobile device.

---

[3] https://www.gov.uk/government/publications/made-smarter-review.

8.2.2   Smart Hand Tools

Modern manufacturing environments are implementing more automation and making use of robotics to assist and speed up processes; however, manually operated hand tools are still commonplace. Use of hand tools can range from setting parts in a machine tool fixture to assembly of components, or for maintenance operations. It is unlikely that robots will completely replace the use of hand tools, and therefore manual operations using them can be part of the smart manufacturing paradigm. Indeed, these operations offer perhaps the greatest opportunity to move from processes in which no data is captured, or is simply verified, to processes where accurate measurements and records are made and stored. "Smart" hand tools are tools that have some element of sensing and connectivity built-in, allowing necessary parameters to be captured. For example, a smart torque wrench when combined with digital work instructions are "aware" of current operations, allowing appropriate torque limits to be set remotely.[4] Sequences of operations can also be programmed to allow a series of torque values to be worked with. Communication is two-way: not only can torque values be set, but the torque values actually achieved can be stored, thus avoiding manual recording of results where errors can creep in.

There are immediate benefits in using smart hand tools in manufacturing. The reduction in recording data manually, either check boxes for correctly set torques or measurement results, leads to more reliable data capture. Furthermore, the event data is digitized immediately, allowing it to be combined with other process data, providing a digital paper trail. For workers, reducing administrative tasks in measurement data capture means that skilled operators can get on with the tasks that actually require their skills.

8.2.3   Location Tracking Technologies

Knowing the location of an object in a manufacturing environment can save significant time and cost. This applies to both knowing the location of a component or part and other assets that are essential to the manufacturing process. There are a number of technologies that can assist with locating objects, allowing tracking to take place at the local through to the global level. For example, printed codes that are read by a scanner, such as QR codes and barcodes, are common in many manufacturing facilities.

The ability to quickly scan a code to log the location of an object allows production to be tracked with high fidelity. Printed codes also allow users to quickly retrieve electronic information about an asset, or to input data to an object's data store. A challenge with scanning printed codes for location tracking is the reliance on busy operators to perform the manual scanning process, often in the midst of busy

---

[4]https://www.facom.com/uk/products/Smart-Torque-Description.html.

production environments. Better is the use of automated location tracking technologies. Radio-based technologies, including RFID, WiFi, and Bluetooth, can be used for passively tracking the location of almost any manufacturing asset. Not only is this useful for updating a manufacturing execution system (MES) on the progress of a part in real time (Yang et al., 2016), but such technology can also be used to find the approximate location of tools, fixtures, lifting equipment, etc. This would mean that engineers are not spending their time looking for missing objects in busy workshops.

As well as tracking items at the local level, location technologies can be used for tracking across multiple buildings at a site (e.g., using LoRaWAN), or for tracking on a much wider scale using GPS. The latter, combined with 2G and 3G wireless networks, could be particularly useful for providing near-real-time updates on the location of parts from suppliers headed toward a manufacturing facility. The same applies for keeping customers updated on the location of shipped finished products. Location technologies can also play a significant role in the health and safety of the workers, e.g., stopping a robot in a cell if a person enters that cell.

8.2.4 Industrial Machinery Connectivity

All smart manufacturing scenarios include machinery that is connected to the overall architecture and has data captured from it. Such machinery is typically controlled by a PLC (Programmable Logic Controller), and may be connected to other systems and machines using, for example, SCADA (Supervisory Control And Data Acquisition) technology. Where a manufacturing plant contains machinery from many different equipment manufacturers who may all have their own proprietary protocol for capturing data, there will be challenges in retrieving data from machine controllers.

There have been efforts to overcome the incompatibility challenge by developing standards and protocols that can be applied across any control system. For example, the MTConnect standard[5] proposes a method of communicating data from controllers and sensors that is based on eXtensible Markup Language (XML), a data format that is easily interpretable and follows a clearly defined structure. Another standard that is widely used to facilitate equipment connectivity is OPC-UA.[6] Described as a "platform independent service-oriented architecture," OPC-UA is natively available on equipment from many industries including oil and gas, pharmaceutical, and building systems, as well as manufacturing. The openness of OPC-UA makes it a very flexible standard that allows it to handle most equipment data transfer needs.

Lu et al. (2020) provide an excellent overview of the many connection standards that currently exist in manufacturing, ranging from what the authors refer to as the

---

[5]https://www.mtconnect.org.

[6]https://opcfoundation.org/about/opc-technologies/opc-ua/.

field (i.e., shop floor connectivity) through to enterprise resource planning (ERP) systems. With regard to IIoT, Lu et al. provide the landscape as illustrated in Fig. 8.5. The authors highlight that the "…wide variety of connection options can be applied to meet various requirements of smart manufacturing applications…" but also point out that carefully structuring the data and information being shared is critical to the success of Industry 4.0. Additional shop floor connectivity is now offered by a new breed of industrial PCs coming into the realm of asset data capture. These PCs have capability for both acquisition, processing, forwarding to persistent storage, and even triggering an action on the asset. Such PCs are referred to as edge devices or gateways and vary in capability, size, operating system, connectivity options, and so on. However, one thing that all edge devices have in common is the desire to bring actionable insight to the shop floor as quickly as possible. Such edge devices are aligned with the desire to move to cloud-based services (see Sect. 8.3).

8.2.5 *Moving to Wireless Connectivity*

Connectivity in many manufacturing environments still relies heavily on a physical connection between devices. Therefore, infrastructure must be in place to provide cabling, connectivity management, and security. Wireless technologies can ease this challenge by removing the need for physical connection. However, simply moving to a wireless network using WiFi will still require considerable management and could introduce conflicts between Information Technology (IT) and Operational Technology (OT) system bandwidth. Furthermore, a standard WiFi network is range-limited and only able to function where devices are in reach of a router and so cannot be used for communication beyond the factory. As such, technologies such as Low-Power Wide Area (LPWA) networks, LTE-A, and 5th Generation mobile networks (5G) offer a number of advantages over standard wireless networking solutions. Of these, 5G is most commonly associated with being the solution of choice as it is a modern, future-looking option.

The benefits of 5G for manufacturing are emphasized on Ericsson's Insights pages.[7] 5G communication also features heavily in many scholarly articles discussing Industry 4.0, the Fourth Industrial Revolution, and IIoT. Its uses range from time-critical process control and health monitoring across many assets and sites, combining with AI to enable a "learning factory" (Zhang et al., 2020). As such, it is inevitable that any smart factory of the future will rely on 5G communication. This is further illustrated by the "5G Factory of the Future" research project[8] funded by the UK5G Innovation Network, launched in August 2020. With a value of £9.5 million (sterling), the project aims to address some of the key challenges in

---

[7]https://www.ericsson.com/en/networks/trending/insights-and-reports/5g-for-manufacturing.
[8]https://uk5g.org/discover/testbeds-and-trials/5g-factory-future/.

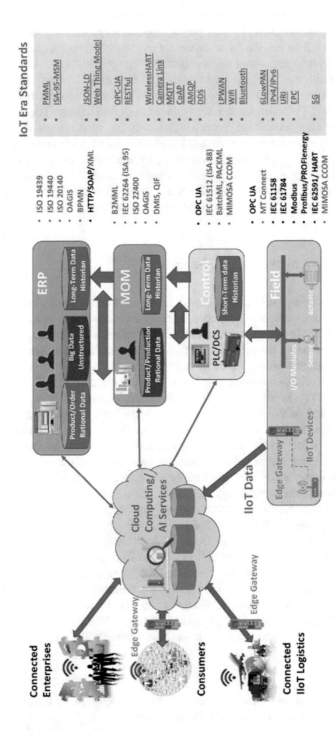

Fig. 8.5 The IIoT era integration standards landscape (Lu et al., 2020)

deploying 5G in manufacturing, testing use cases such as robotic assembly, reconfigurable assembly lines, and distributed augmented and virtual reality.

8.3 From Sensors to Business Value

An important attribute of manufacturing is captured by the notion of *value chain—* the interlinked resources and processes that go from raw materials to value-added products. In smart manufacturing, data is key to transformation and, therefore, must be managed as an asset. The generation of data, its storage and governance, and subsequent analysis and use are captured by the *data value chain*. In this section, we discuss core technologies that support data management, data analysis, insight, and automation in smart manufacturing.

8.3.1 Cloud Computing

Increasingly in business, cloud-based technologies are being adopted to provide scalable and flexible solutions. The infrastructure must also provide appropriate networking, connectivity, gateways, and standardized interfaces along which the data can flow. In manufacturing, the use of cloud-based solutions (provision of computing resources over the Internet) enables businesses to outsource their IT resources and offers a scalable, integrated, and centralized store for manufacturing data, such as multiple IIoT devices, where data can be ingested, transformed, and analyzed in real time and at Big Data scale. Cloud manufacturing (CMfg) has been proposed as a concept that uses cloud computing technology (computing and service-oriented technology) to improve current manufacturing systems (Alcácer & Cruz-Machado, 2019). There are many benefits of utilizing cloud-based solutions and for smart manufacturing, including (1) cost-effective and dynamic access to large amounts of computing power, (2) almost immediate access to hardware resources without upfront capital investments, (3) lower barriers to innovation, (4) easy dynamic scaling of enterprise services, and (5) enabling of new classes of applications and services (Schmitt et al., 2020).

However, despite the benefits, cloud computing also offers several disadvantages, such as network latency and bandwidth issues, performance issues with multiple customers and applications running on the same infrastructure, and issues around security, such as regulatory compliance and governance through the use of external third-party providers. The use of edge computing is often used to reduce the potential bottleneck arising from large volumes of data and use of cloud computing by performing computations at the data source. These devices can consume and produce data; handle computing tasks, such as processing, storage, caching, and load balancing and exchange data with the cloud; as well as incorporate AI capabilities to perform predictions locally (rather than having to interact with the cloud).

8.3.2 Big Data Analytics

To support smart manufacturing requires substantial compute power and networking infrastructure to handle data being generated in real time by sensors and actuators. However, data have not just grown in terms of *volume* and rate of production (*velocity*); data have also changed in terms of *variety* (range and types of data sources) and reliability (*veracity*). Being able to process multiple forms of data in real time and offer real-time decision support requires (Big Data) computational systems to gather, store, manipulate, and analyze data, for example, distributed data storage and advanced analytical methods (Oussous et al. 2018; Gao et al., 2020). Other attributes of Big Data that have emerged within Industry 4.0 include *validity* (correctness of data), *volatility* (tendency to change in time), and *vulnerability* (to breach or attacks).

The use of techniques from across disciplines is common (e.g., Computer Science), including methods for various types of data analysis, e.g., descriptive, diagnostic, predictive, and prescriptive. Although existing statistical methods can often be used, the characteristics of Big Data also call for alternative methods. For example, dealing with *uncertainty* is a situation which involves unknown or imperfect information (e.g., noise in sensors), and methods, such as Bayesian theory or probability or belief function theory, are often used (Hariri et al., 2019). The process of extracting insights from Big Data can be broken down into stages for data management and analytics (Gandomi & Haider, 2015).

Being able to process large volumes of data in real time has led to advances in data management and processing, e.g., the use of distributed files systems, parallel processing technologies, and ingestion of streaming data (Oussous et al. 2018). In many scenarios, Apache Hadoop has become the de facto open-source standard for sharing and accessing data. Figure 8.6 summarizes a generic Big Data architecture, whereby data sources (batch and real time) are ingested into centralized storage (e.g., a data lake). Real-time data is handled separately from data loaded in batch and using stream processing. Machine learning is often used for tasks, such as predictive analytics, and results stored in an analytical data store (e.g., data warehouse or SQL database), which can be used for analytics and reporting.

The architecture in Fig. 8.6 can often be seen in manufacturing examples. For example, Fig. 8.7 shows the use of Microsoft Azure for IoT and Big Data analytics[9] with a number of core Azure components. Data is ingested in batch (e.g., maintenance logs) using *Azure Data Factory*, an Azure component for orchestrating data ingest and transfer, or as streaming data (e.g., IoT or sensor data) using *Azure IoT* or *Event Hubs*—these enable a security-enhanced bidirectional communication between IoT applications and devices. Real-time streaming data will typically be stored in the *Azure Data Lake,* a massively scalable data store that includes security and auditing functionality. As the data is pre-processed and transformed (in this case using *Azure Databricks*), refinements of data will be stored back in the data lake in

---

[9]Example of Azure architectures: https://docs.microsoft.com/en-us/azure/architecture/browse/.

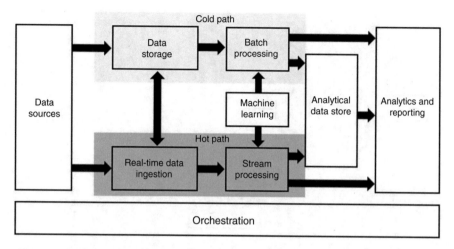

Cold path

Fig. 8.6 Generic Big Data analytics infrastructure (Based on: https://docs.microsoft.com/en-us/azure/architecture/data-guide/big-data/)

separate zones (raw, enriched, and aggregated). Non-streaming data can be ingested in batch using *Azure Data Factory* and also stored in the data lake. *Azure Databricks* and *Azure Machine Learning* can be used for tasks, such as predictive analytics. In Fig. 8.8, *Azure Synapse* provides a data warehouse and analytical functionalities. Real-time analytics is provided using *Azure Data Explorer*. Finally, reporting and dashboards are provided with *Power BI*.

8.3.3 Artificial Intelligence

Perhaps one of the biggest drivers of disruptive innovation has been the rise in artificial intelligence (AI) technologies, especially machine learning (ML). In manufacturing, coupling AI with data generated more widely across the manufacturing process and the evolution of robotics and autonomous systems and agents is enabling the *automation* of data-driven decision-making in production and service delivery. AI uses computational methods to encapsulate and mirror human intelligence, allowing a nonhuman system to learn from experience and imitate human intelligent behavior, typically using machine learning. The combination of AI techniques, especially *deep learning*, with developments in other areas, such as semantic computing, robotics, and computer vision, is enabling Industry 4.0. For example, AI and the Internet of Things, Web of Things, and Semantic Web are enabling the vision of Industry 4.0, e.g., the Semantic Web of Things for Industry 4.0 (SWeTI) platform proposed by Patel et al. (2018).

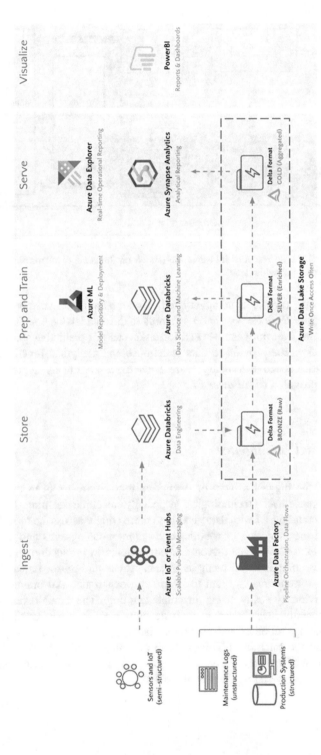

Fig. 8.7 An example of a Microsoft Azure architecture for IoT and Big Data analytics (source: Databricks, https://databricks.com/blog/2020/08/03/modern-industrial-iot-analytics-on-azure-part-1.html)

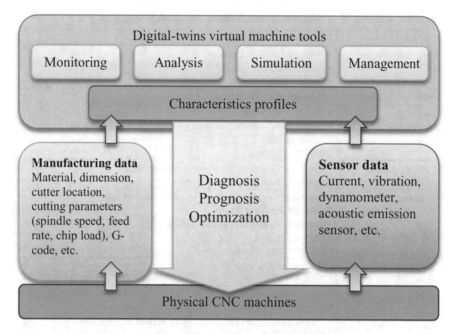

Fig. 8.8 Digital twin sensor and data fusion concept (Cai et al., 2017)

In manufacturing, the use of AI is considered critical to future success. For example, in a 2018 survey on AI by Forbes Insights,[10] 44% of respondents (from the manufacturing and automotive sectors) considered AI as "highly important" to the manufacturing function in the upcoming 5 years. A further 49% deemed it as "absolutely critical to success." Common uses include (a) predictive maintenance, (b) collaborative and context-aware robots, (c) yield enhancement in manufacturing, and (d) automated quality testing. The 2020 Capgemini report "Scaling AI in manufacturing operations: a practitioners' perspective"[11] goes further and identifies even more use cases (Table 8.2). The Capgemini report states that machine maintenance and quality control are the leading transformative AI projects in manufacturing operations, along with increasing use of robotics.

8.3.3.1   Predictive Maintenance

Predictive maintenance (PdM) is seen as one of the top manufacturing use cases for AI as "the impact of maintenance represents a total of 15 to 60% of the total costs of operating all manufacturing" (Zonta et al., 2020:2). PdM is the application of

---

[10]http://forbes.com/sites/insights-intelai/2018/07/17/how-ai-builds-a-better-manufacturing-process/#7aa455621e84.

[11]https://www.capgemini.com/research/scaling-ai-in-manufacturing-operations/

Table 8.2 Example of AI use cases in manufacturing operations (Capgemini[11])

Function	Use cases
Product development/ R&D	• New product development • Product validation in R&D • Product enhancement
Demand planning	• Demand planning/forecasting
Inventory management	• Order optimization • Standardized communications with suppliers using Natural Language Processing (NLP) Inventory planning
Process control	• Real-time optimization of process parameters • Optimize equipment changeover
Production	• Optimizing overall productivity in production line • Reduction in Takt time • Computer vision for product identification • Layout planning • Collaborative robots (cobots)
Quality control	• Product quality inspection • Predicting final product quality
Maintenance	• Intelligent maintenance • Energy management • Spotting anomalies in communication network • Worker safety • Scrap/wastage reduction • Increasing equipment efficiency

predictive analytics that can assist many industries, not just manufacturing, to utilize assets (e.g., manufacturing and computing equipment, aircraft engines, turbines, etc.) in the most efficient way and thereby reduce costs associated with downtime and defective products. AI, in particular machine learning, can be used for common maintenance tasks, such as fault diagnosis, predicting mechanical failures and Remaining Useful Life (RUL), and maintenance scheduling to support planned equipment downtime. Using predictive analytics offers a more *proactive* rather than *reactive* approach to maintenance: *corrective maintenance* replaces parts when they fail, *preventative maintenance* determines useful lifespan for a part and replaces it before a failure, and *predictive maintenance* enables just-in-time replacement of components.

Machine learning methods, especially neural networks and deep learning approaches, are commonly used in predictive maintenance applications to examine relationships between data points and the labelled output (e.g., failures) and build models to predict such outcomes (Zonta et al., 2020). Historic data can therefore be used to recognize patterns from past events and enable manufacturers to predict future failures or prevent them based on learning from the root causes of the breakdown events. Predictive models can be used to predict machine breakdowns, and historic training data could include sound to detect anomalies in device operations, sensors to detect changes in operational conditions (e.g., temperature, vibrations, etc.), or IoT divided integrated into manufacturing equipment or processes.

Additional data sources may also be used and input to machine learning, such as maintenance logs, quality measurement of machine outputs, and external data sources (e.g., weather).

8.3.3.2 Identifying Defects and Quality Control

The demand for consistently high quality within manufacturing processes and products has driven the use of innovative methods, including AI, to enable reliable quality inspection. Common approaches to quality improvement include *visual inspection methods*, e.g., monitoring parts or mechanical processes, such as welding or soldering, on a production line. Traditionally, quality control is time-consuming if performed manually where specialists must test products for defects. The introduction of image recognition technologies enabled manufacturers to identify potential flaws based on sets of predefined conditions or rules.

Automated visual inspection approaches typically compare (pixel by pixel) a reference image of a product with a selected image for inspection. However, such methods can suffer from issues with imperfect lighting conditions or variations in product mounting during inspection that cause differences between the selected image and reference version. The use of computer vision and AI can overcome these issues as models become invariant to differences in testing conditions and can focus on the patterns within the image which represent quality issues, such as defects. This has enabled algorithms to learn the features of a "good" product and, after training, to recognize different types of defects automatically, e.g., identifying defects in surfaces, typically in combination with existing quality checking processes (human and automated). For example, Schmitt et al. (2020) describe a quality assurance approach for a printed circuit board (PCB) whereby a predictive model is used to determine which PCBs to test with an existing automatic optical inspection (AOI) system (i.e., an X-ray inspection system). The rationale is that due to the high volumes of production, it has become a bottleneck in the process. The predictive model, trained on data gathered from PCB examples and an outcome of OK or Not OK (NOK), classifies the PCBs, and any that are categorized as NOK are then sent to the X-ray inspection unit. This reduces the bottleneck and improves product quality as only suspected faulty boards require further verification.

8.3.3.3 Robots and Automation

Advances in mechatronics, computing, and communication technologies are driving the field of modern robotics and autonomous systems. Stand-alone industrial robots have been central to automation in industries, such as aerospace and automotive, in transforming production by replacing or assisting humans in performing various manufacturing tasks, since first appearing in the 1960s. Recent advances have seen the development of collaborative robots (or "cobots")—robots designed and built to collaborate with humans and work alongside them (Hentout et al., 2019). Another class is mobile robots or automated guided vehicles (AGVs), commonly seen in warehouses and distribution centers and used to move objects between machinery or machinery. The use of advanced sensor, location, and camera technologies is being coupled with AI to provide robots with the intelligence to be able to navigate and work unaided by humans.

8.4 Beyond the Physical World

In Sect. 8.2, the discussion focused on connectivity and monitoring of physical assets and processes within manufacturing systems. It was highlighted that the data from such activities can yield new actionable insights that were previously unknown, and this is especially true when the data is fed into AI systems (Sect. 8.3). An additional use for such data is to feed into systems that take the user beyond the physical world and into the realm of digital twins, extended reality, and manufacturing process simulation.

8.4.1 Digital Twin

A recent report published by the University of Sheffield Advanced Manufacturing Research Centre (Eyre et al., 2020) defines a digital twin as: "A live digital coupling of the state of a physical asset or process to a virtual representation with a functional output." The report breaks down the key elements of this statement, namely, that:

- The data is *live*, or as close as is acceptable to live
- There is a *digital coupling* to transmit data over a digital carrier medium
- The *state* of the system is the condition of the system or process at a given time
- There is a *physical asset or process* that the digital representation is linked to, as opposed to a simulation or a reply of an event
- The *virtual representation* is analogous to the physical thing
- There is a *functional output* from the digital twin, such as information transmitted to a system or human that can take action on the output, to deliver some value

The above definition implies that the digital twin has a purpose and will deliver value to a manufacturing asset or process, rather than simply acting as marketing material or a dumb simulation. This definition is in contrast to the idea of a digital twin as proposed by Cai et al. (2017) and illustrated in Fig. 8.8. The authors discuss how sensors and other data streams can be used to feed a "digital twin" as a model of a virtual machine tool. There is no proposal that the data is live, but rather the data can be used for prognosis and diagnosis of machine or process faults. Gao et al. (2020) also define the digital twin as "...an emerging concept that leverages data and information collected from a physical system to create a digital representation of that system that may be used to generate some desired control action." The authors discuss how data can be fed into a digital twin to optimize performance, predict maintenance-related faults, and virtually verify or validate equipment.

There is no mention of the digital twin being a live representation; when a digital representation is fed data in a unidirectional way, this is sometimes referred to as a *digital shadow* (Kritzinger et al., 2018). Maier et al. (2018) provide an example of a digital twin that provides real-time feedback based on sensor data. The authors developed a system for monitoring the wear of a cutting tool to be used in a machining process. Importantly, for our initial definition of a digital twin, the data is presented live to the machine tool operator with some indication of what the data means. As such, the operator can take action as needed. This example highlights that a digital twin can be of almost anything, such as a tool, single process, a complex machine tool, a production line, or even numerous global facilities.

8.4.2   Extended Reality

Technologies that extend reality, either fully through virtual reality (VR) or partially through augmented reality (AR), are commonplace in the consumer market and are starting to gain traction for what they can offer in industrial settings. In a 2018 report, Gartner predicts that 70% of businesses will be experimenting with immersive technologies, but it is likely that only 15% will have deployed them into production.[12] Virtual reality provides a fully immersive digital environment; augmented reality is the use of digital overlays of information on the physical world, but with very little interaction with the virtual objects. Mixed reality is a true blend of the virtual and physical worlds, allowing users to interact with both real and virtual objects. Such technologies are not new. For example, Caudell and Mizell (1992) proposed an augmented reality heads-up display (HUD) to assist manual manufacturing processes (e.g., guide operators to correct drilling locations). Modern AR use cases in manufacturing still include guiding shop floor operators in assembly, maintenance, or quality control tasks, as well as enhancing training experiences (Syberfeldt et al., 2017). The key difference now is that AR is available on many more devices, such as smartphones or tablets, as well as more advanced and lightweight AR glasses.

Another key reason for increasing interest in the use of AR is the amount of data being captured in manufacturing environments and how this data can be presented through AR technology. For example, a modern maintenance engineer can use AR technology to guide them to the source of an issue, as a result of sensor readings within a machine tool. The AR technology can also guide the maintenance engineer to complete the task more quickly. Another use case based on volume of data could be providing shop floor supervisors an overview of current production activity and

---

[12]https://www.gartner.com/en/documents/3881066/virtual-reality-and-augmented-reality-using-immersive-te.

Fig. 8.9 Example of an AR overlay for identifying service and maintenance items on a train chassis

capacity by donning a pair of AR glasses and looking around their shop floor to identify any challenges. Through a connection to a central data store, the glasses could present the supervisor with real-time information on equipment status and product locations. Virtual reality completely immerses uses in a virtual world, with no visibility of the real world around them. Instead, the user is presented with a 3D virtual world in which they can explore and interact with objects, usually through handheld controllers.

The example shown in Fig. 8.9 demonstrates how AR has been applied at the AMRC for identifying and instructing maintenance tasks on a train chassis. This same technology can be applied in a manufacturing setting for both maintenance and assembly. There are a number of uses for VR in manufacturing, including training and practicing procedures which can be costly in the real world, or visualizing component or even factory designs before they are first created in the real world and more clearly than using 2D drawings.

8.4.3 Simulating Manufacturing

Simulation in manufacturing can mean many different things—simulating stresses on a part design, simulating a machining process, simulating an assembly, simulating how the tooth of a tool interacts with a material it is cutting, simulating complete production flow in a factory, or all the way through to simulating supply chain and logistics (Mourtzis, 2020). Simulation that relies on a model of a system (where the model is based on analytical, numerical, or mechanistic methods) can be improved through observation of experimental results, with the model updated based on findings. However, with the increase in data capture through IIoT technologies, simulations can now more easily be compared and contrasted against real-world results, and ultimately simulations can be improved by incorporating actual process data into the simulation design. This data-driven manufacturing paradigm can update manufacturing simulations using the data sources and capture methods discussed in Sect. 8.2, and either update a model automatically or omit the modelling altogether, using the result of AI algorithms to influence the manufacturing system.

Simulation can be coupled with many other technologies discussed in this chapter. An example of combining simulation with real-time data can be seen at the Boeing factory in Sheffield, UK (Hughes, 2018). Before the layout of this facility was finalized, a complete model of the factory was developed as a simulation (specifically discrete-event simulation—DES) to model a number of production scenarios and "what-if" situations. The model was also viewable as a 3D representation through a virtual reality system, so Boeing manufacturing engineers could test the layout of the production environment.

8.5 Summary

Manufacturing is an important and well-established industry and for decades has been implementing the latest methods and technologies. Recent developments in connected devices, the generation of vast quantities of data, and advanced manufacturing techniques are accelerating progress in manufacturing (Tao et al., 2018; Kusiak, 2018; Zheng et al., 2018), providing new opportunities for transforming manufacturing processes and improving products and services. However, despite the many benefits, there are also significant challenges to tackle (Al-Abassi et al. 2020). For example, in manufacturing in general, the adoption and implementation of new technologies and methods, developing sustainable processes, and adapting to new innovations are challenging. Besides these, smart manufacturing may also present the following challenges:

- *Acceptance and change*—data-driven transformation may require significant changes to existing manufacturing processes, job roles, technologies, and ways of working that have to be managed appropriately.
- *Integration*—implementing new technologies, such as cloud computing and AI, and integrating them into existing legacy business infrastructure and processes is challenging and costly, maybe requiring new skills and staff.
- *Security*—the importance placed on data means that security is a key concern in manufacturing where espionage, unwanted data access, or cyberattacks are potential issues with using the Industrial Internet and cloud-based digital systems.

- *Big Data*—the volume of real-time data produced by IIoT typically surpasses the capabilities of existing infrastructure, and therefore, new data processing and management systems are required. This can mean in practice significant financial investment.
- *Re-skilling*—existing job roles may be changed with the introduction of smart manufacturing, and there may be overall a lack of skills within manufacturing organizations to manage and take advantage of smart technologies. There is a shortage of qualified people to recruit with the right digital skills that can support data-driven projects.

Review Questions
- How would you define smart manufacturing (or Industry 4.0)?
- How can technologies, such as AI and augmented/virtual reality, be used to make manufacturing smarter?
- Within a factory, what kinds of data might be generated and collected for smart manufacturing?
- How can data collected within manufacturing be used to generate business insights?

Discussion Questions
- Manufacturing is a long-established practice and has often used new technologies and methods in innovative and smart ways. What then is different, or unique, about the new Industry 4.0 era?
- How can smart technologies be integrated into a factory? What are some of the challenges of doing this?
- What skills and knowledge might the engineers and technicians working in manufacturing in the future require?

Problem Statements for Young Researchers
- What are the benefits that smart manufacturing could bring to a company, to workers involved in the manufacturing process, to consumers of the products created, and more widely to society? What are the potential barriers faced in implementing Industry 4.0 and making manufacturing smart? Are there any short-term and long-term negative consequences or disadvantages of smart manufacturing on businesses, workers, national economies, or the environment?
- In what ways can you effectively and efficiently model real-time factory environments, and what are the opportunities afforded?
- Smart manufacturing allows organizations to gather and utilize data from the entire lifecycle of the product (the so-called digital passport). How can this be achieved in practice, and what are the likely challenges in doing this?

References

Al-Abassi, A., Karimipour, H., HaddadPajouh, H., Dehghantanha, A., & Parizi, R. M. (2020). Industrial big data analytics: Challenges and opportunities. In K. K. Choo & A. Dehghantanha (Eds.), *Handbook of big data privacy*. Cham: Springer.

Alcácer, V., & Cruz-Machado, V. (2019). Scanning the Industry 4.0: A literature review on technologies for manufacturing systems. *Engineering Science and Technology, an International Journal, 22*(3), 899–919.

Bralla, J. G. (2007). *Handbook of manufacturing processes – How products, components and materials are made*. New York: Industrial Press.

Cai, Y., Starly, B., Cohen, P., & Lee, Y. S. (2017). Sensor data and information fusion to construct digital-twins virtual machine tools for cyber-physical manufacturing. *Procedia Manufacturing, 10*, 1031–1042.

Caudell, T. P., & Mizell, D. W. (1992). Augmented reality: An application of heads-up display technology to manual manufacturing processes. In *Hawaii International Conference on System Sciences* (pp. 659–669).

Chu, L. P. (2016). *Data science for modern manufacturing: Global trends: Big data analytics for the industrial Internet of Things*. O'Reilly Media. ISBN: 1491958960.

Dahotre, N. B., & Harimkar, S. P. (2008). Manufacturing processes: An overview. *Laser Fabrication and Machining of Materials*, 69–96.

Dominguez-Caballero, J., Stammers, J., & Moore, J. (2019). Development and testing of a combined machine and process health monitoring system. *Procedia CIRP, 86*, 20–25.

Duro, J. A., Padget, J. A., Bowen, C. R., Kim, H. A., & Nassehi, A. (2016). Multi-sensor data fusion framework for CNC machining monitoring. *Mechanical Systems and Signal Processing, 66*, 505–520.

Eyre, J., Hyde, S., Walker, D., Ojo, S., Hayes, O., Hartley, R., Scott, R., & Bray, J. (2020). *Untangling the requirements of a Digital Twin*. Advanced Manufacturing Research Centre. Technical Report. Available online: https://www.amrc.co.uk/files/document/406/1605271035_1604658922_AMRC_Digital_Twin_AW.pdf

Fernández, D. S., Jackson, M., Crawforth, P., Fox, K., & Wynne, B. P. (2020). Using machining force feedback to quantify grain size in beta titanium. *Materialia, 13*, 100856.

Fujishima, M., Ohno, K., Nishikawa, S., Nishimura, K., Sakamoto, M., & Kawai, K. (2016). Study of sensing technologies for machine tools. *CIRP Journal of Manufacturing Science and Technology, 14*, 71–75.

Gandomi, A., & Haider, M. (2015). Beyond the hype: Big data concepts, methods, and analytics. *International Journal of Information Management, 35*(2), 137–144.

Gao, R. X., Wang, L., Helu, M., & Teti, R. (2020). Big data analytics for smart factories of the future. *CIRP Annals, 69*(2), 668–692.

Hariri, R. H., Fredericks, E. M., & Bowers, K. M. (2019). Uncertainty in big data analytics: Survey, opportunities, and challenges. *Journal of Big Data, 6*, 44.

Heeley, A. D., Hobbs, M. J., Laalej, H., & Willmott, J. R. (2018). Miniature uncooled and unchopped fiber optic infrared thermometer for application to cutting tool temperature measurement. *Sensors, 18*(10), 3188.

Hentout, A., Aouache, M., Maoudj, A., & Akli, I. (2019). Human–robot interaction in industrial collaborative robotics: A literature review of the decade 2008–2017. *Advanced Robotics, 33* (15–16), 764–799.

Hughes, R. (2018). *Virtual simulation of new Boeing facility based in Sheffield*. Advanced Manufacturing Research Centre. Technical Report. Available online: https://www.amrc.co.uk/files/document/241/1542814525_AMRC_BOEING_case_study.pdf

Khan, W. Z., Rehman, M. H., Zangoti, H. M., Afzal, M. K., Armi, N., & Salah, K. (2020). Industrial Internet of things: Recent advances, enabling technologies and open challenges. *Computers & Electrical Engineering, 81*, 106522.

Kritzinger, W., Karner, M., Traar, G., Henjes, J., & Sihn, W. (2018). Digital twin in manufacturing: A categorical literature review and classification. *IFAC-PapersOnLine, 51*(11), 1016–1022.

Kusiak, A. (2018). Smart manufacturing. *International Journal of Production Research, 56*(1–2), 508–517.

Lee, G., Kim, M., Quan, Y., Kim, M., Kim, T. J. Y., Yoon, H., Min, S., Kim, D., Mun, J., Oh, J. W., Choi, I. G., Kim, C., Chu, W., Yang, J., Bhandari, B., Lee, C., Ihn, J., & Ahn, S. (2018). Machine health management in smart factory: A review. *Journal of Mechanical Science and Technology, 32*(3), 987–1009.

Li, B. H., Hou, B. C., Yu, W. T., Lu, X. B., & Yang, C. W. (2017). *Applications of artificial intelligence in intelligent manufacturing: A review.* Frontiers of Information Technology and Electronic Engineering. Zhejiang University.

Lockwood, A. J., Hill, G., Moldoveanu, M., Coles, R., & Scott, R. (2018). *Digitalisation of legacy machine tools.* AMRC Technical Report. Available online: https://www.amrc.co.uk/files/document/239/1542365809_WHITE_PAPER_LEGACY_AW.pdf

Lu, Y., Witherell, P., & Jones, A. (2020). Standard connections for IIoT empowered smart manufacturing. *Manufacturing Letters, 26*, 17–20.

Maier, W., Möhring, H. C., & Werkle, K. (2018). Tools 4.0–Intelligence starts on the cutting edge. *Procedia Manufacturing, 24*, 299–304.

Mourtzis, D. (2020). Simulation in the design and operation of manufacturing systems: State of the art and new trends. *International Journal of Production Research, 58*(7), 1927–1949.

Oussous, A., Benjelloun, F. Z., Lahcen, A. A., & Belfkih, S. (2018). Big data technologies: A survey. *Journal of King Saud University-Computer and Information Sciences, 30*(4), 431–448.

Patel, P., Ali, M. I., & Sheth, A. (2018). From raw data to smart manufacturing: AI and semantic web of things for industry 4.0. *IEEE Intelligent Systems, 33*(4), 79–86.

Qu, Y. J., Ming, X. G., Liu, Z. W., Zhang, X. Y., & Hou, Z. T. (2019). Smart manufacturing systems: State of the art and future trends. *The International Journal of Advanced Manufacturing Technology, 103*(9–12), 3751–3768.

Schmitt, J., Bönig, J., Borggräfe, T., Beitinger, G., & Deuse, J. (2020). Predictive model-based quality inspection using machine learning and edge cloud computing. *Advanced Engineering Informatics, 45*, 101101.

Syberfeldt, A., Danielsson, O., & Gustavsson, P. (2017). Augmented reality smart glasses in the smart factory: Product evaluation guidelines and review of available products. *IEEE Access, 5*, 9118–9130.

Tao, F., Qi, Q., Liu, A., & Kusiak, A. (2018). Data-driven smart manufacturing. *Journal of Manufacturing Systems, 48*, 157–169.

Wu, D., Weiss, B. A., Kurfess, T., Wang, L., & Davis, J. (2018). Introduction to the special issue on smart manufacturing. *Journal of Manufacturing Systems, 48*, 1–2.

Xia, C., Pan, Z., Polden, J., Li, H., Xu, Y., Chen, S., & Zhang, Y. (2020). A review on wire arc additive manufacturing: Monitoring, control and a framework of automated system. *Journal of Manufacturing Systems, 57*, 31–45.

Xu, L. D., Xu, E. L., & Li, L. (2018). Industry 4.0: State of the art and future trends. *International Journal of Production Research, 56*(8), 2941–2962.

Yang, Z., Zhang, P., & Chen, L. (2016). RFID-enabled indoor positioning method for a real-time manufacturing execution system using OS-ELM. *Neurocomputing, 174*, 121–133.

Zhang, W., Cai, W., Min, J., Fleischer, J., Ehrmann, C., Prinz, C., & Kreimeier, D. (2020). 5G and AI technology application in the AMTC learning factory. *Procedia Manufacturing, 45*, 66–71.

Zheng, P., Sang, Z., Zhong, R. Y., Liu, Y., Liu, C., Mubarok, K., Xu, X., et al. (2018). Smart manufacturing systems for Industry 4.0: Conceptual framework, scenarios, and future perspectives. *Frontiers of Mechanical Engineering, 13*(2), 137–150.

Zonta, T., da Costa, C. A., da Rosa Righi, R., de Lima, M. J., da Trindade, E. S., & Li, G. P. (2020). Predictive maintenance in the Industry 4.0: A systematic literature review. *Computers & Industrial Engineering*, 106889.

Paul D. Clough is Professor of Search and Analytics at the Information School, University of Sheffield. His research interests include AI and Data Science, Information Retrieval, Data Analytics and Natural Language Processing. Paul is also Head of Data Science for Peak Indicators, a UK-based Business Intelligence and Analytics company, where he is helping to develop data products and services, produce educational resources and grow the data science capability within Peak Indicators.

Jon Stammers is a Technical Fellow at the University of Sheffield Advanced Manufacturing Research Centre. There, he leads a team of engineers working on monitoring and control challenges in machining environments, developing new sensor systems and data analysis methods to garner production insight. His research interests include the application of machine learning and AI to large datasets, appropriate visualisation of data for a given audience, and holistic data capture and analysis in manufacturing environments.

Chapter 9
Role of Semantics in Smart City Applications

Neama Abdulaziz Dahan (iD) and Fadl Ba-Alwi

Abstract Technology is being used to provide solutions for daily life problems that are usually related to people, the environment, the economy, or society. Using technology, sustainable solutions to environmental issues have been provided to maximize quality of life. This way of thinking was the first step to develop a new version of our traditional cities—specifically, smarter ones—in which everything can give us information about its status and also provide us with a pre-defined set of reactions as a response to environmental changes. Smart cities are cities that provide smart solutions for different life issues, either for citizens or the environment itself, by collecting information based on ontologies. This type of information should be gathered considering the semantics of both the issues and the devices used to deal with them, which are in many cases sensors. Ontologies were the first unit for implementing semantics, followed by sensors with the Internet of Things (IoT) to apply the technology that helps us to communicate with almost everything. This communication is based on interoperability standardizations, networking, and semantics to explain the contexts of the received information. There are also many other applications that cities can adopt to be considered a smart city, such as healthcare, energy saving, and traffic management.

To understand the roles of semantics in smart city applications, we must start from the terms and their origins as well as efforts toward standardization. Hence, in Sect. 9.1 of this chapter we present a definition of the smart city, the factors to consider it smart, and the efforts published to issue standards for smart cities. In Sect. 9.2, we provide brief principles of the semantic applications in smart cities, in ontology, data, energy-saving, security, traffic, and healthcare. Section 9.3 describes some roles of semantics in smart cities and the relations among semantics and IoT and sustainable development. Section 9.4 discusses challenges and Sect. 9.5 illustrates the criteria to compare the ontologies of smart cities and IoT. Section 9.6 summarizes the chapter.

N. A. Dahan (✉) · F. Ba-Alwi
Computer Sciences Department, FCIT, Sana'a University, Sana'a, Yemen

© The Author(s), under exclusive license to Springer Nature Switzerland AG 2021
S. Jain, S. Murugesan (eds.), *Smart Connected World*,
https://doi.org/10.1007/978-3-030-76387-9_9

Keywords Smart cities · Semantics IoT · Ontology · Interoperability · Sustainable development · Semantic applications

Key Points
- This chapter defines the term "smart" as it is used with "smart cities," thereby listing certain available standards.
- We underpin the relationship between smartness and semantics, while mentioning some important aspects such as data, security, health, and traffic.
- The chapter discusses some of the available ontologies for smart city applications in an effort to look for potential challenges involved and criteria to compare the different ontologies.

9.1 Introduction

Smart city is a term that describes a city that manages, in a smart manner, all its linked resources and properties to enhance the quality of the services introduced to residents and to improve the quality of their lives. Several enterprises and initiatives in this field have emerged, which signify the efforts and investments that industries, countries, regions, and governments are making to manage the resources of the city in a better manner (Espinoza-Arias et al., 2019). This can inspire other cities which have been working on long-term strategies to also become smart cities (Ramaprasad et al., 2017). "Smart Cities focus on, as shown in Fig. 9.1, (Smart Cities, Ranking of European Medium-Sized Cities, 2007; Caragliu et al., 2011): governance, environment, living, energy, mobility, and economy." The essential goal of a smart city is to support inclusive and sustainable development applications that should serve the burgeoning population and the need for the materials of comparatively populated and large cities, according to experts in the smart cities field (Sivrikaya et al., 2019). The accelerated growth of cities and their populations is a major driver of smart cities (Okai et al., 2018).

There are many efforts to provide a set of standards and factors for the different characteristics of smart cities (Okai et al., 2018). The British Standards Institution standard is divided into three layers, as shown in Fig. 9.2: the criteria in the top layer denote those who help the administration to adopt a complete approach for a smart city, comprising its assessment and auditing. The middle layer efficacies aim to cover the functional insurance and administration of the projects of the smart cities. The lowest one take the applicable criteria of technical specifications for the lively implementation of harmonious determinations of smart cities (Okai et al., 2018). The International Organization for Standardization has also covered all of the facets of smart city standards. The Smart and Sustainable Cities and Communities Coordination Group (CEN-CENELEC-ETSI) incorporates multiple European standards and is a matching point for the criteria's operations regarding smart cities in Europe (L.1601, 2015). An additional standard by ISO/IEC (Smart City Concept Model

Fig. 9.1 The six smart
factors of the smart city

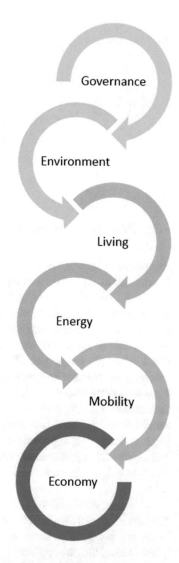

(L.1601, 2015)) principally focuses on data interoperability, to provide a high-level
structure to specify notions and relations by collecting the ontologies from different
sectors. However, there are still many other enterprises and groups that are promot-
ing the improvement of the standards for smart cities.

Ontologies are important for smart and ongoing commissioning (SOCx) because
they make reasoning and data readability for machines easier. A clearer ontology is
always needed to improve and integrate them in SOCx (Gilani et al., 2020).

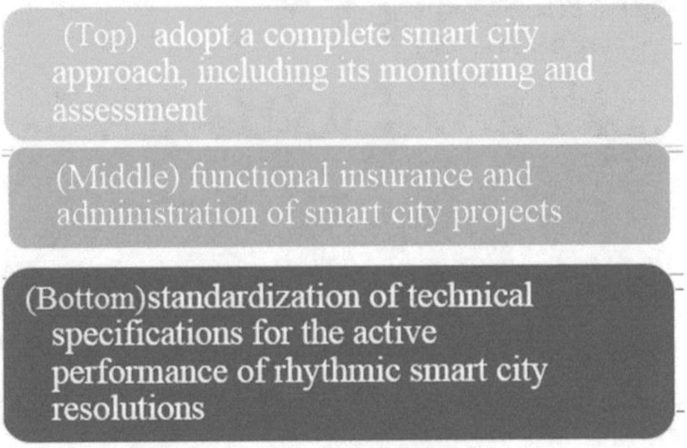

Fig. 9.2 The British
Standards Institution layers

(Top) adopt a complete smart city
approach, including its monitoring and
assessment

(Middle) functional insurance and
administration of smart city projects

(Bottom)standardization of technical
specifications for the active
performance of rhythmic smart city
resolutions

9.2 Principles of Semantic Applications of Smart Cities

Komninos et al. described the steps of using ontologies in smart cities development (Komninos et al., 2019). To begin a smart city application, one must start by making a general smart city ontology. Next, characterize the structure classes of this ontology regarding the most referred to meanings of vanguard urban areas. Then, organize this ontology with an editor such as Protégé 5.0, declaring the instances, class relations and branches, object properties, and datatype properties. To verify that the sample ontologies of smart city applications are suitable for the general ontology of smart cities, possible factors can be the steadiness of digital areas, knowledge operations, application areas, or the sorts of development that decide their effects. Finally, to outline the connections among originations and ontology, we should determine how to enhance the adequacy of the applications of smart cities, joining master and client-driven ontology structure with the coordination and integration of these applications over the operating systems and bigger city objects, for example neighbors, areas, hierarchies, and zones of city exercises (Komninos et al., 2019).

Gyrard et al. highlighted the most important application areas for smart cities (Gyrard et al., 2018): waste administration, smart lighting, noise checking, traffic blockage, air quality, smart parking, city vitality utilization, and smart building. They showed that the applications of smart cities encompass various areas. Ontology libraries are classified as follows: Reason and scope clarify that the ontologies can be restricted to a specific area and change in estimate and kinds of ontologies. The collection of instances depicts the way that modern ontologies are embedded inside this library and the measures of quality control that were utilized before including the new ontology. Ontology metadata gives ontology title, area, owners, date of creation and adjustment, version, license, etc. (Gyrard et al., 2018).

The components that might delineate a smart city include a connected framework to extend political and financial efficiency and allow urban and social improvement; essential affirmation on business-led metropolitan advancement; a solid condensation of the target of accomplishing the communal consideration of different urban inhabitants in open administrations; significant consideration of the role of relational and communal maintenance in metropolitan development; and ecological and communal sustainability as a vital element (Caragliu et al., 2011). Albino, Berardi, and Dangelico also specified some general features of the smart cities that comprise communal attachment of several metropolitan citizens and communal principle in metropolitan advancement; a city's interacted structure which permits political, social, efficiency, and public improvement; the ingrained environment as a promising asset for the coming future; and an affirmation on business-led metropolitan enhancement and events for metropolitan evolution. The use of information technology has been considered as a main standard in the smart city as it can communicate, sense, audit, and control most services of the city (Albino et al., 2015).

9.2.1 Ontologies for Smart Cities

Gyrard et al. compiled a list of modern ontologies that are used in smart cities (Gyrard et al., 2018), such as SOFIA, NOW, SCRIBE, KM4City, STAR-CITY, FIESTA-IoT, VITAL, CityPulse, SCO, SOFIA2, PRISMA, and SCOnt. They also described some ontology catalogs that make it easier to edit and improve the ontologies, as well as their usage, for example:

- BioPortal is a catalog of biomedical ontologies that brings numerous functionalities, for example finding an ontology, ontology statistics, and searching for a specific class. It also offers a group of tools:

  - Annotator with specific ontologies to get annotations
  - Browser to browse the ontologies library
  - Searching for a class in multiple ontologies
  - Recommender for the most related ontologies
  - Resource Index to display all of the ontologies
  - Mapping between a selected ontology and all ontologies referenced within BioPortal

- WebProtégé14: a tool to develop collaborative ontologies that indicate the ontologies that were developed using it
- Ontology Design Patterns: ontologies repository
- Ready4SmartCities provides an ontologies catalog of developing smart cities that consists of seven major areas: weather, climate, power, structure, occupancy, environment, and user behavior and characteristics. It also offers five cross-cut areas: governmental, arithmetical, time-based, measurement, and spatial. Ready4SmartCities divides the ontologies using the next standards: (1) open license, (2) online availability (RDF, HTML), (3) name, (4) syntax, (5) language, (6) natural language (e.g., English), and (7) domain. The catalog of Ready4SmartCities designed an ontology to distinguish all of the related ontologies. This ontology uses properties and concepts from the other ontologies (VOAF, OMV, DC, and VANN) to specify the metadata of the ontology.

- The OpenSensingCity: a catalog that aims at fostering real-time open data use in a smart cities context by offering functioning tools for an ontology catalog for smart cities. It also helps application developers to obtain benefits from the streams of open data.
- The Smart City Artifacts (SCA): a web gateway that gathers the smart cities information and visualizes the menu of ontologies, datasets, and current projects. The ontology provided by SCA has been designed to distinguish and specify the projects of smart cities and objects. It reprocesses some of the external ontologies, for example DC, DOAP, Prov-O, FOAF, sc, Muto, Fabio, Dbowl, and OMV.
- Linked Open Vocabularies (LOV): a catalog that denotes more than 648 terms, but a few are denoted as IoT and smart cities terms. The smart cities tag can be related to easily regain the ontologies. If we search for a city keyword within LOV24, only four ontologies can be found: GCI, km4city, iso37120, and Turismo. LOV has an interface to suggest ontologies for contributors.

Finally, ontologies have some Ontology Design Patterns (ODPs) categories: Reengineering, Content, Logical, Alignment, Architecture, Exemplary, and Lexico Syntactic. However, within the catalog, it may be hard to search for an exact word such as "city" or "IoT" to retrieve the denoted ontologies.

9.2.2   Data

The available smart city ontologies permit the introduction of distinctive types of data from cities. These ontologies were created as to diverse ontological obligations. However, they don't participate in the least principal show that might encourage interoperability in the middle of information frameworks of smart cities (Espinoza-Arias et al., 2019). Kettouch et al. stated that linked data provides connections among distinctive information bases to form an individual worldwide data area, "the web of data." The Linked Data concept is another name of the collection of finest performance for the data that is interlinked, distributed, and organized on the web, depicted by Tim Berners-Lee Linked Data, being: the names for things (URI); HTTP URIs to identify those names; to offer valuable data; and to find more things (related data) by including links to other URIs. Data integration is the method of introducing homogeneity to a collection of autonomous and heterogeneous sources. Data interlinking can be considered as an inverted preparation of data integration because it shows the process of finding the partners of the same real objects that can be arranged for the data sources. Smart city data as linked data may extend its accessible information to the linked data cloud, by making new instances and setting up new relations (Kettouch et al., 2017).

9.2.3   Energy-Saving

Komninos et al. stated that there are numerous ontologies-based smart city applications but with low noticed affect, in vitality, and transport, which essentially rely on the ontology, and then on smart technology and programming highlights (Komninos et al., 2019). According to Gilani et al. (Gilani et al., 2020), energy management in smart cities is one of the foremost basic problems arising in sustainability applications. Cities require smart innovations to specify sustainability problems related to the improvement of energy utilization. Researchers focused, as a portion of their work on smart cities, on decreasing energy utilization. Knowing that global energy demand is constantly increasing, new research interest should be directed toward a more effective technique to conserve energy and decrease bills. A few applications were integrated into a real-time process of the energy administration framework. This is helpful to diminish the framework's working expenses and maximize the real-time reaction in the organized equipment testbed for testing the energy building administration framework. The test is to discover the ideal control required, and the fuzzy rationale controller to screen the building gadgets and genetic algorithms to optimize energy utilization in real time with a GIS framework. It also permits the identification of the position of buildings and all of the related data. After that and based on semantics, a few analysts chose an ontological approach to screen vitality utilization, in a smart building, by combining machine-learning methods with semantics modeling and thinking. A directed learning calculation with K-means clustering is coordinated to distinguish and anticipate power utilization in buildings. Another method was to move forward energy efficiency in buildings. That was achieved by considering inhabitant behavior and building environment based on context-awareness to decrease energy utilization and allow inhabitants comfort. The coordinate ontology offers a generic demonstration to permit coherent induction and a calculation of data mining classification, which is utilized to get the rules speaking to ordinary energy utilizations. OWL and SWRL are utilized for knowledge presentation and intelligent thinking to diminish energy utilization in smart cities. The intelligent framework proposed by Gilani supplies a few points which show efficient power-saving factors (Gilani et al., 2020):

1. Decreases energy utilization in each smart domestic unit and thus throughout the smart cities
2. Decreases equipment cost utilized in each building and handles information in less time
3. Guarantees a high level of system availability
4. Offers versatility by taking advantage of the Big Data environment, which can prepare massive data in real-time
5. Provides independence and decreases data stream over the network
6. Observes the energy request in peak time and prevents system crash
7. Offers a viable long-term energy conveyance policy
8. Helps to decrease natural contamination and advances environmental sustainability

9.2.4 Security and Safety

A determination language called 'ACE' utilizes common language, and is understandable by people and also can be made understandable by machines. ACE may change into OWL ontology and discourse representation structures (DRS). The formal method (Event-B) is utilized to empower formal determination and systems advancement. It is a B strategy expansion. There are four fundamental stages to develop reliable, secure, and safe smart city systems:

1. Creating brief, steady, and clear needs via ACE-driven prerequisites conquest process via particular areas ontologies and ACE
2. Developing models based on Event-B from the requirements of ACE to decrease the difference between the loose needs and official determination
3. Organizing the refinements of Event-B according to OntoGraf and applying the traceability among the prerequisites and the models developed previously
4. Generating codes of these models using the supporting tools

The needs conquest process should be performed by:

1. Choosing suitable OWL ontologies of the area
2. Utilizing OWL syntax parser by changing OWL ontologies over to OWL/XML
3. Changing OWL/XML into ACE-driven needs by utilizing OWL verbalizer converter (Alkhammash, 2020)

Zhang et al. divide smart applications from various angles such as industrial, power, ecological, living, and services-based applications. Intelligent ecological solutions ensure a convenient and safer place and observe greenhouse fuel, city noise, waste fuel, etc. Intelligent living solutions bring a convenient home environment and enhance power utilization. Industrial solutions provide robust and industrial generation. Power solutions contribute mechanisms to generate power, enable transition and conveyance, monitor consumption, and avoid error. Intelligent services solutions offer advantages for individuals such as health and transportation applications (Zhang et al., 2017). A paper by Cui et al. identifies the needs that are relevant to making the diversity of the smart system levels secure. These needs include:

1. Privacy and authentication of client data
2. Accessibility and integrity of tools and facilities
3. Lightweight intrusion discovery
4. Privacy assurance

Cui et al. also list several tools that can be utilized to extend the privacy and security of smart applications. One of the specified technologies is the selection of scientific tools, for example the game theory, to resolve certain privacy and security problems. Using these techniques, utilizing the ontology is additionally recorded as a means to show knowledge formally, eliminate irregularities, and solve privacy and security problems such as cyber-attack discovery (Cui et al., 2018).

9.2.5 Traffic

According to Vijayaraghavan et al. (Vijayaraghavan & Leevinson, 2020), smart transport administration systems may be considered an unavoidable necessity to meet the requirements of the tremendous number of vehicles on the road. Routine systems need to be intelligently patched up to process advanced metropolitan transportation cases and to explain occurrences and extraordinary cases. This is relevant in the situation of smart cities improvements where transportation systems should be exceedingly normalized and improved to function at greatest effectiveness. Smart transport administration frameworks are a large-scale assembly of diverse systems, administrations, and gadgets. Such frameworks may comprise millions of single distributed IoT gadgets. Intelligent traffic administration systems gather and handle very secure information connected to people's individual information. It can incorporate pictures, individual information, living area of individuals and their vehicles, individual ID numbers, numbers of vehicle enlistments, etc. Smart transport administration systems control nearly all of the perspectives of street traffic including transportation signals, crisis celerity, fee gathering, and stopping administration. If it wasn't managed very well, malicious instances can stop the system, or they can make fake notices or cautions, accordingly disrupting street traffic or may cause the traffic process to be stopped or terminated nearly within the whole city.

However, this type of system needs high starting speculation costs because such systems generally comprise tremendous sensors, sets, networks, and servers which require establishment, justification, and verification. In addition, the establishment of cameras and sensors on private belongings may require legal authorization and endeavors that might obstruct the execution of such solutions (Vijayaraghavan & Leevinson, 2020). Tangible parts of transportation administration solutions such as cameras and sensors are also types of smart city applications. Drivers can use various sensors such as IoT or GPS sensors to enjoy the different intelligent services such as the roadmap, auto-engine, and auto-conditioner. Cars also can be tracked to discover their locations if they are stolen or used for suspicious activities. A perfect smart transportation management system might be enabled to professionally specify and process the different types of crimes and offenses involving property damage. It could also be used for irregularity recognition and the analysis of entity-based actions. All of these can be applied in the form of integration with cross-vision cameras which protect each other in their area of vision, and tougher vehicle specification solutions with larger penalties for criminals (Vijayaraghavan & Leevinson, 2020). It has also been mentioned that recognition and learning among the community plays an essential role in the realization of smart transportation management systems (Debnath et al., 2014).

9.2.6   Healthcare and Social Applications

According to Quijano-Sánchez et al. (2020), there is a type of smart application that can suggest to you what you should do to monitor your health, such as an application that offers personalized suggestions from media and distinctive alarms for the elderly and those who are differently abled. Another application proposes healthier habits to avoid sedentariness by linking these to a decrease in healthcare system expenses. In addition, there is an application that suggests course of physical exercises that better fit the user's abilities to enhance lifestyle, while reducing chronic illnesses and therapeutic costs. Another application enhances living circumstances by anticipating the user's most likely infections and prescribing treatment, offering wearable devices that can support observance of their health. For disease prevention, a type of application was proposed, for example, that reminds the user to get a health checkup to heighten awareness of chronic diseases in healthcare systems. This could help greatly in preventing long queues of patients in hospitals and in providing healthcare staff with auto-retrieval for patients' medical history and current diagnoses. Another framework involves a recommender which offers personalized diets for diabetes patients including particular types of food and medicine. In addition , there is an application to enhance health electronic assistance by suggesting the best hospital or doctor for a described illness. Moreover, suggesting and recommending systems was dedicated to the establishment of health-related information to prevent wrongly combining two or more drugs or taking them with food which may lead to toxicity or, in the worst case, death (Miah & Vu, 2020).

Moreover, the convenience of data on social media for monitoring illnesses has been proved in a study of hay fever in Australia. The analysis, according to the main features of hay fever noted in a sample of tweets, brought about valuable findings. New knowledge discovery has been facilitated as a result of a visualization tool for pattern surfing, as well as illuminating the advantages of high-quality input data (Pérez-delHoyo et al., 2016).

9.3   Role of Semantics in Smart Cities

The Ontology of Smart Cities should be the main means for organizers to utilize and government authorities to evaluate the smartness level of these cities among numerous viewpoints at diverse layers of complication. Ontologies give a guide for new designs for smart cities, outline the state-of-the-art, and disclose the lively, lite and blind points of cities. Next, this ontology is essential for scientists because it permits them to outline the state-of-the-art of the research area (Ramaprasad et al., 2017).

This planning may uncover the holes within the practice and literature, and the opportunities for research in different refinements included in the ontology. In addition, the combined identification of smart cities as an ontology is in common structured English and may be adjusted as the development advances and to distinctive frameworks, due to its unit structure. It can be extended by including a dimension and diminished by ignoring a dimension. For instance, the Temporality of Outcomes may be an extra dimension; or the components of Outcomes can be gathered within the wide area of a smart city, and the dimension can be disposed of. The specification may be enhanced by compromising subclasses of a component and diminished by adding a few components. To illustrate, governments can be subclassed as Government, Educational Businesses and Institutions, and State and Local Authority; these may be merged together as Governments. The combined identification can be treated like a cornerstone for the advancement of practice and research within the space of smart cities (Ramaprasad et al., 2017).

According to Gyrard, in intelligent and smart cities, market powers and vital arranging are used to construct broadband systems, urban functional frameworks, software and embedded systems, and all of the modifications and processes of a city. Nevertheless, bottom-up activities and the inclusion of people and companies become more than just being domineering drivers ever of city-construction, particularly the creation of smart cities, that depends on the innovation, learning functions, and digital abilities which improve the abilities of the population, especially in developing applications and solutions of smart cities regardless central arranging or case-control. By showing knowledge in official speech with obviously characterized semantics, it is conceivable to induce novel facts from pre-defined knowledge bases and data sets, declare webpages semantics, and permit semantic confirmation, that empowers expansion and evaluating of instances simultaneously. The utilization of ontologies arises from the smart cities' multidimensional nature, as a system of systems, in which data is attained from different registers and frameworks, for example from sensors, authorities, locations, the web, and social media and smartphones. This is a general equation that all of these frameworks have their equipment and software ontologies and structure and are called in to supply interconnection and meaning via the applications and frameworks (Gyrard et al., 2018). Moreover, enhancing citizens' quality of life is an important goal of smart city advancement. The availability of urban public domains specifies the living conditions for individuals. Technology provides modern opportunities for independence for an expanding group of occupants with particular disabilities (Alkhammash, 2020).

Smartphones and web systems for smart cities are becoming progressively crucial for the improvement of smart cities, where applications are made in tremendous numbers by citizens, designers, governments, and companies. Smart city applications are supported by cloud stages, software advancement toolkits, managing content platforms, the reuse and compilation of present solutions, hackathons, widespread digital abilities, and open developers' communities, which have removed obstacles to technology, diminished entrance expenses, and provided smart city applications with accessibility to any city, metropolis, or rural area. The well-known culture that smart city applications highlight may be a development of user-driven technology and wide commerce models via the more extensive scenario of open development, the democratization of advancement, and digital disturbance of advancement and enterprise. The trend of "innovation for all" is a case that empowers people and enables individuals and organizations to create technological ecosystems among virtual connectivity, intelligent cities, and smart environments (Komninos et al., 2019).

Ontologies have catalogs as a part of their meta-data. However, an examination of the ontology catalog of smart cities and IoT catalogs has noted the need for more help with respect to the assignment of learning and reusing ontologies (Gyrard et al., 2018). In addition, there is widespread assertion that smart cities are specified using the prevalent utilization of data and telecommunication technologies, which, in different metropolitan areas, can support cities to make better use of their assets. A few of these technologies incorporate portable applications, open data infrastructures, Internet of Things platforms, open participation devices, etc. The information dealt with or created by these technologies is heterogeneous in terms of groups, structure, and delivery methods, within both the diverse cities and the selected city. A few smart city ontologies have been created to show and keep data related to cities. These ontologies, in contrast, depend on more specified ontological assurances. To achieve its good job, the snippets of the generic and small ontology, with getting key and reusable knowledge, can be utilized. These snippets, in engineering of ontologies, have been utilized since the 2000s and are called Ontology Design Patterns (ODPs). In addition, it is considered that the utilization of the catalogs of ontologies for the smart city spaces and IoT is significant in supplying the designers with a means to discover, select, and reuse these ontologies which suit their requirements. It may be supportive to provide a list of ODPs to bolster center space images for the information on smart cities. To our knowledge, there is no list of ODPs for the smart city space, and the available ODPs within the general ODP catalogs do not cover all of the regular ODPs which will be utilized within the setting of the smart cities (Espinoza-Arias et al., 2019).

Approximately 500 homes, in the Geuzenveld neighborhood of Amsterdam, were provided with intelligent meters, part of which featured a screen to permit users to monitor their power consumption and power-saving activities (Gyrard et al., 2018). Other researchers have collected applications according to their fields of study. For instance, as healthcare Applications, there's a variety of applications, such as MobSpiro for Detecting Chronic obstructive pulmonary disease (Zubaydi et al., 2017), pulmonary rehabilitation chronic obstructive pulmonary disease (Sanghavi, 2019), and eCAALYX to serve elderly people with various chronic diagnosis (Boulos et al., 2011). As for devices, there are some implantable smart systems or chips that can be imbedded surgically inside the human body to monitor the organs, such as "SmartPill" which transfers pressure, temperature data, and intraluminal pH at regular periods to the SmartPill GI Monitoring system (Maqbool et al., 2009), and the Titan implantable hemodynamic monitor (IHM), which can be embedded in a patient's heart to measure critical variables such as temperature and then wirelessly transmit this data to a secure database (N N, 2015). Zaib Ullah et al. provided a classification for the applications according to the techniques used: artificial intelligence (AI), machine learning (ML), and deep reinforcement learning (DRL) (Ullah et al., 2020). In this group of studies, we can see many applications and solutions that can serve the smart cities and their engineers. READY4SmartCities is a system proposal that minimize power consumption and CO_2 production in smart cities with ontologies and linked data. This proposed solution introduces guidelines to help providers to generate power-relevant data as linked data. It proposes the fundamentals of cross-domain data such as climatic, job, pollution, traffic, and practices. It develops a data set with ontologies of 50 areas which are specific to smart homes and smart cities (Raj & Raman, 2017).

9.3.1 The Role of Semantics and IoT

The Internet of Things (IoT) performs an accelerating job in empowering the applications of smart cities. The semantic approach based on the ontologies may support enhancing the interoperability among complementary information required to run the applications and the various IoT generated to improve these applications. As found with different catalogs of ontologies, utilizing them for smart city and IoT applications requires an important set of work (Gyrard et al., 2018).

Jara et al. (2014) noted that IoT gives a semantic explanation that is restricted to a particular range, which can be called the context. The Semantic Web provides the essentials to allow the stream of data gathered based on a particular context, via the World Wide Web. Subsequently, the data may be joined, reused, and shared to create new services. The objective of the Semantic Web of Things (SWoT) is to coordinate data that is semantically valuable and easily available in the tangible world. Accordingly, linking smart objects and computerized instances (Jara et al., 2014) can be done in several applications and areas, simplifying the communication between people from diverse societies or languages, such as NAN (Dahan & Ba-Alwi, 2019). Recently, the IoT helped the worldwide to scale incorporation of the recognition, localization, and information retrieved from everything around us and everywhere. The SWoT idea permits knowledge-based systems that accomplish higher grades of autonomic ability for discovery, information management, and storage, and for allowing clear access to the sources of information in a given space (Jara et al., 2014). The smart city is one of the most impressive and portentous IoT applications (Petrolo et al., 2014). Smart city applications not only need professional processes for large-scale IoT streams but also require professional functions to analyze the data in a dynamic environment by summarizing, aggregating, and abstracting sensor data on demand (Harrison et al., 2010). Lom et al. claimed that the main allowance of the applications of a smart city is potentially the IoT that daily connects objects and devices related to the network technologies (Lom & Pribyl, 2020). Gyrard et al. (2018) stated that "IoT shows an eternally growing responsibilities in permitting the applications of Smart City. The infrastructures of Smart city are luxurious to create, deploy, maintain and design. Also, the data generated by its applications are meant to provide the seven Vs of data standardization, which are: value (meaning), volume (size), variability (able to change), visualization (readability and accessibility), veracity (trustworthiness), variety (different types), and velocity (changing speed)". According to Sivrikaya et al. (2019), interoperability is the most important of the fundamental components of smart city standards. Interoperability is an essential way to reduce cost and is required at different stages, encompassing the system, basic plan, workflow to oversee IoT applications, services and data, and extrapolation of information. A semantic strategy, particularly which supports the utilization of important ontologies, may help to manage the assortment related to IoT and related corresponding data sorts, and help with interoperability, but numerous catalogs of ontologies are related to smart cities and IoT, which also reveals the difficulties in choosing the correct catalogs and their ontologies (Gyrard et al., 2018).

9.3.2 Sustainable Development and Its Impacts

Sustainable urban development is directly related to the smart cities concept, and we can consider it as the first step to develop smart cities because it involves environmental, economic, and equity concerns (Kumar & Dahiya, 2017). The smart city is estimated to enhance the power-saving system from a more sustainable perspective, which requires a comprehensive systems vision and intelligent, ideal approaches to the sketching and development of metropolitan power-saving systems (EERA Joint Programme on Smart Cities, 2013). However, the focus now is on smart city development (Ahvenniemi et al., 2017) because it cannot be merely sustainable; it must also provide a high level of conceptual information and interoperability. The information that can be gathered from the devices and their application all around the smart city can be used to enhance the economy of individuals and companies and the living standards of the population; to provide good interactivity with the environment according to well-prepared standards to conserve the ecology; to provide smart buildings, sensors, homes, and self-driving vehicles; and also to use less power for operations. All of the collected information can be used according to specific objects to make decisions to provide simple, effective, and creative solutions to the interoperability, data analysis, and integration issues.

9.4 Challenges for Semantics in Smart City Applications

Giddens proposed that the process of modernization in cities is directly connected to risks, especially the "manmade risks" that have spread recently due to improvements in scientific knowledge that accompany the intelligence of the city, and the emergence of novel technologies (Giddens, 1999). Komninos et al. (2019) mentioned the low effect of the applications relies on their ontology, hence, the solution will be by making a general smart city's ontology, characterizing the development pieces of that ontology concerning the foremost mentioned specifications of the targeted smart cities, characterizing the classes hierarchy, entities, data type properties, and object properties. The plenty of applications of smart cities, which was made in an awkward bottom-up way, leads to the smart cities' development by the agglomeration. As a result, smart cities have ambiguous structures, which show up as a design arising from chaotic behavior within complex frameworks. Despite this, the areas usually focused on by smart city applications are limited to financial advancement, e-government, e-administration, transportation, vitality, and e-commerce, and the influence of these applications is still restricted since detailed documentation is also scarce. Besides, many researchers within the field of keen vitality and shrewd transportation frameworks have recorded a few advancements of cities through smart and personal applications. Assuming that total impacts are missing, because of lack of organization and the complementarity of applications, the general effect of applications remains restricted, with brief anticipations of an essential change for cities via computerized systems. Amsterdam Smart City (ASC) is a well-known smart city example for its applications, and universal arrangements, but its measured effect is low. The general Climate Program of the City, in which ASC could be an essential part, points to form every civil organizations' climate affect neutrally before 2015 and diminish CO2 emanations by 40% concerning the 1990 baseline by 2015. ASC points to be engaged to such goals by decreasing power usage by about 14% and diminishing CO2 outflows by an equal sum. These effects' evaluations of the solutions record and applications of smart cities pick up less than 10% on the minimum circumstance to save the power, CO_2 and mote decrease, and transportation enhancement. Financial profits and the improvement of the information economy in the smart cities in Europe change significantly, and in numerous instances are equivalent to or under the EU-27 rate. At this level of enhancement, it still not good enough if we compare it with the anticipations and ambitious targets all around the applications of smart cities, multi-billion estimates concerning the rising smart city global market, and real challenges emerging from actual rates of urbanization and climate change (Komninos et al., 2019).

No solution has emphasized a complete transformation in a city's sustainability, competitiveness, or considerations. However, the development and utilization of applications remains the most common technique for the improvement of this type of city. It is expected that the reasons for this constrained adequacy should be discovered within the ontologies of the applications utilized, and the way in which the applications are applied to the issues and needs of cities, instead of the programming aspects utilized or exact smart technology. The issue is connected to the urban functionalities and solutions' fundamentals, instead of shortcomings in computer energy, data sources and analytics, modeling, programming abilities, or any other angles of the technology stack included in smart city solutions. Smart city applications focus on changing the traditional methods and providing more viable and creative techniques for doing things. Connecting smart cities' applications to generic cities' schedules raised two essential issues based on the effectiveness of these applications: city locations and the data that is represented by the solution. To further the applications' influence and effectiveness, their design needs must be extended to the design of their ontologies, the method of connecting to the most general ontology, and the classes and properties included within the application. An arrangement of techniques can be a part of more effective and more influential applications, such as the design of pieces of applications rather than independent arrangements, working among large-scale metropolitan examples such as the city locale or societies of clients, focusing on arrangements that support improving the skills of human assets, and prioritizing applications that influence the advancement framework of the city instead of the daily working of the city. In sum, the designers of smart city applications might seek the guidelines and counsel of innovation and metropolitan experts, client inclusion, crowdsourcing, and design of experience, to increase the likelihood of finding ideas and visions for development (Gyrard et al., 2018).

9.5   Factors to Compare the Ontologies of Smart Cities and IoT

A group of factors can be characterized to classify smart city ontologies that can be connected to IoT ontologies. These factors are primarily concentrated on the ontologies' reusability. The following factors, also shown in Fig. 9.3, are listed in Gyrard et al. (2018), and Zimmermann (2010), as the standards to compare the ontologies of smart cities and IoT:

- The goal of the ontology to be clearly specified
- Ontology size
- Ontology documentation to decrease the learning curve
- Ontology accessibility to support the interoperability
- Ontology acceptance to establish the influence of the ontology
- Periodic ontology maintenance needs to be achieved
- Ontology metadata is required for building automatic mechanisms

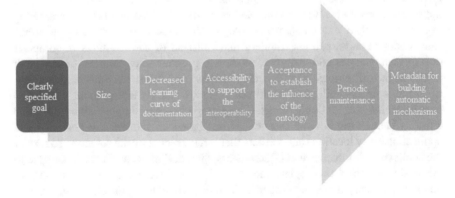

Fig. 9.3 The factors to compare smart city ontologies

9.6 Summary

Smart cities are cities that provide high-quality standardization for living and making decisions according to daily challenges. Semantic computing in smart city applications provides us the ability to analyze the data and enhance life and decision making. There are many studies that talk about smart cities based on which we wrote this chapter. Interoperability and sustainability are issues that are being revived. In future work, researchers can conduct comparative studies to show which solution is better and why and can thus enhance sustainable smart city frameworks. Semantics in IoT should be studied comprehensively to apply it widely and to take advantage of this promising technology.

Review Questions
1. What are the six factors to consider a city a smart city?
2. What are the British Standards Institution layers? And what does each layer indicate?
3. What are the most important application areas for smart cities?
4. List some of the ontologies for smart cities.
5. What is BioPortal? Write down the tools it offers.
6. According to which standards did Ready4SmartCities divide the ontologies?
7. How do smart cities manage data?
8. The intelligent framework proposed by Gilani supplied a few opportunities to invest funds; list them.
9. What is Event-B?
10. What are the fundamental stages to develop reliable, secure, and safe smart city systems?
11. What are the needs that are relevant to making the diversity of the smart system levels secure?
12. Smart transport administration systems control nearly every aspect of street traffic; write some examples.
13. How can smart cities use their smart traffic systems to decrease the crime rate?
14. Describe the role of semantics in smart cities.
15. What is the relationship between semantics and IoT? And how is this advantageous for smart cities?
16. How can smart cities be sustainable?
17. Describe the challenges that face the semantics in smart city applications, and then suggest how to solve these.
18. What are the factors to compare the ontologies of smart cities?

Discussion Questions
1. The main problem that faces every computer-based system is the lack of electricity or the threat of shutdowns. In your opinion, what are the alternatives to keeping your city always on even in times of crisis such as war or natural catastrophe.

2. We all know that smart cities data should be collected in data centers. Even with the highest secure systems we cannot ensure the data will be always safe. Describe the protocol that you will apply to your data always safe.

Problem Statements for Young Researchers

1. For cities that are still very far from being smart cities, where should the city start? And what will be the criteria to accelerate this process?

2. Ontology levels, catalogs, and mapping are still under study because the uppermost ontology will be abstract and all of the ontologies should inherit it. It is still hard to collect all the available ontologies and to make them all extended from one upper-level ontology.

References

Ahvenniemi, H., et al. (2017). What are the differences between sustainable and smart cities? *Cities, 60*, 234–245.

Albino, V., Berardi, U., & Dangelico, R. M. (2015). Smart cities: Definitions, dimensions, performance, and initiatives. *Journal of Urban Technology, 22*, 3–21.

Alkhammash, E. (2020). Formal modelling of OWL ontologies-based requirements for the development of safe and secure smart city systems. *Soft Computing, Springer, 24*, 1–14.

Boulos, B., et al. (2011). How smartphones are changing the face of mobile and participatory healthcare: An overview, with example from eCAALYX. *Bio Medical Engineering Online open access, 10*(24).

Caragliu, A., Bo, C. D., & Nijkamp, P. (2011). Smart cities in Europe. *Journal of Urban Technology, 18*(2), 65–82.

Cui, L., et al. (2018). *Security and privacy in smart cities: Challenges and opportunities*. Access. IEEE.

Dahan, N. A., & Ba-Alwi, F. M. (2019). Extending a model for ontology-based Arabic-English machine translation. *International Journal of Artificial Intelligence and Applications (IJAIA), 10*(1), 13.

Debnath, A. K., et al. (2014). A methodological framework for benchmarking smart transport cities. *Cities, 37*, 47–56.

EERA Joint Programme on Smart Cities. (2013). [11/07/2020]. Retrieved from http://www.eera-sc.eu/sites/eera-sc.eu/files/attachments/smartcitiesbrosch_lowres_single_pages.pdf

Espinoza-Arias, P., et al. (2019). Ontological representation of smart city data: From devices to cities. *Applied Sciences, 9*(1), 1–23.

Giddens, A. (1999). *Runaway world: Reith lectures*.

Gilani, S., Quinn, C., & McArthur J. J. (2020). *A review of ontologies within the domain of smart and ongoing commissioning* (p. 182). Building and Environment, Elsevier.

Gyrard, A., Zimmermann, A., & Sheth, A. (2018). Building IoT-based applications for smart cities: How can ontology catalogs help? *Internet of Things Journal IEEE, 5*(5), 3978–3990.

Harrison, C., et al. (2010). Foundations for smarter cities. *IBM Journal of Research and Development, 54*(4), 1–16.

Jara, A. J., et al. (2014). Semantic web of things: An analysis of the application semantics for the IoT moving towards the IoT convergence. *International Journal of Web and Grid Services, 2*(3), 244–272.

Kettouch, M., et al. (2017). Semantic data management in smart cities. In *International Conference on Optimization of Electrical and Electronic Equipment (OPTIM) & Intl Aegean Conference on Electrical Machines and Power Electronics (ACEMP)* (pp. 1126–1131). IEEE.

Komninos, N., et al. (2019). Smart city ontologies: Improving the effectiveness of smart city applications. *Journal of Smart Cities, 1*(1), 31–46.

Kumar, T. V., & Dahiya, B. (2017). Smart economy in smart cities. In *Smart economy in smart cities* (pp. 3–76). Springer.

L.1601. (2015). *Key performance indicators related to the use of information and communication technology in smart sustainable cities*. ITU Smart Sustainable Cities.

Lom, M., & Pribyl, O. (2020). Smart city model based on systems theory. *International Journal of Information Management*, 102092.

Maqbool, S., Parkman, H. P., & Friedenberg, F. K. (2009). Wireless capsule motility: Comparison of the SmartPill® GI monitoring system with scintigraphy for measuring whole gut transit. *Digestive Diseases and Sciences, 54*(10), 2167–2174.

Miah, S. J., & Vu, H. Q. (2020). Towards developing a healthcare situation monitoring method for smart city initiatives. *Australasian Journal of Information Systems, 24*.

N N. (2015). *Left heart wireless implantable hemodynamics monitor*. [12/07/2020]. Retrieved from http://mems-iss.com/left-heart-wireless-implantable-hemodynamic-monitor/

Okai, E., Feng, X., & Sant, P. (2018). Smart cities survey. In *2018 IEEE 20th International Conference on High Performance Computing and Communications; IEEE 16th International Conference on Smart City; IEEE 4th International Conference on Data Science and Systems (HPCC/SmartCity/DSS)*. IEEE.

Pérez-delHoyo, R., et al. (2016). Making smart and accessible cities: An urban model based on the design of intelligent environments. In *International Conference on Smart Cities and Green ICT Systems (SMARTGREENS)* (pp. 1–8). IEEE.

Petrolo, R., Loscri, V., & Mitton, N. (2014). Towards a smart city based on cloud of things. In *Proceedings of the 2014 ACM International Workshop on Wireless and Mobile Technologies for Smart Cities*.

Quijano-Sánchez, L., et al. (2020). Recommender systems for smart cities. *Information Systems*.

Raj, P., & Raman, A. C. (2017). *The Internet of Things: Enabling technologies, platforms, and use cases*. New York: CRC Press.

Ramaprasad, A., Sánchez-Ortiz, A., & Syn, T. (2017). A unified definition of a smart city. In *International Conference on Electronic Government* (pp. 13–24). Cham: Springer.

Sanghavi, J. (2019). *Review of smart healthcare systems and applications for smart cities* (pp. 325–331). ICCCE, Springer.

Sivrikaya, F., et al. (2019). Internet of smart city objects: A distributed framework for service discovery and composition. *IEEE Access, 7*, 14434–14454.

Smart Cities, Ranking of European Medium-Sized Cities. (2007). Available from http://www.smart-cities.eu/

Ullah, Z., et al. (2020). Applications of artificial intelligence and machine learning in smart cities. *Computer Communications, 154*, 1–564.

Vijayaraghavan, V., & Leevinson, J. R. (2020). Intelligent traffic management systems for next generation IoV in smart city scenario. In *Connected vehicles in the Internet of Things* (pp. 123–141). Cham: Springer.

Zhang, K., et al. (2017). Security and privacy in smart city applications: Challenges and solutions. *Communications Magazine, IEEE, 55*(1), 122–129.

Zimmermann, A. (2010). Ontology recommendations for the data publishers. In *Workshop on Ontology Repositories (ORES) at ESWC*. CEUR Workshop Proceedings.

Zubaydi, F., et al. (2017). MobSpiro: Mobile based spirometry for detecting COPD. In *Proceedings of IEEE 7th Annual Computing and Communication Workshop and Conference (CCWC)*.

Neama Abdulaziz Dahan, Master of Computer Science in Ontology-Based Machine-Translation from Sana'a University, 2019. Bachelor of Information Systems from Sana'a University, 2011. A teacher in Sana'a University since 2012. Interested in Artificial Intelligence, Machine Learning and Data Science. https://scholar.google.com/citations?user=G1EThN0AAAAJ&hl=en&oi=ao

Fadl Ba-Alwi, Professor in Artificial Intelligence (AI), presently working as a Vice President of the Council for Accreditation and Quality Assurance-Ministry of higher Education and Scientific Research, Yemen. In addition, he is working as a professor in Faculty of Computer and Information Technology at Sana'a University. He held a Ph.D. in Artificial Intelligence (AI) Data Mining field Computer Science–JNU-New Delhi-India. He completed his master's degree in computer Application, Jawaharlal Nehru University, also has master degree in Technology (M-Tech). https://scholar.google.com/citations?user¼G1EThN0AAAAJ&hl¼en&oi¼ao

Chapter 10
Detection of Depression Signals from Social Media Data

Tameem Ahmad, Sayyed Usman Ahmed, and Nesar Ahmad

Abstract In recent years, social media use has increased significantly, spanning a range of applications from expression sharing, to networking, advertising, and branding to stay up-to-date. The use of social media has become ingrained in our daily life, and people share information, photos, and videos, expressing themselves through the comments on these social media. Medical healthcare specialists are now able to infer people's state of mind by analyzing their activities on social network services. An early indication of depression can help to initiate a remedial action to avoid devastating results. To get a complete picture and truthful information about the state of a person's mental health, more congenial and interoperable methods are needed to gather insights from several social media sites, as one social network website depicts only one aspect of a human being. Semantic Web technology is suitable for this purpose and ideally overcomes the limitations of analyzing information from various social media sites. This chapter will address some of the issues surrounding Semantic Web technologies and ways to analyze users' interaction patterns to depict the personality and hence the depression state.

Keywords Semantic Web · Emotion analysis · Sentiment analysis · Depression detection · Microblogging · Social network analysis · Text analysis · Mental illness · Natural language processing

Key Points

The readers of the chapter will surely learn about the following topics by the end of the chapter:

- Social web and its challenges
- Semantic Web technologies

T. Ahmad (✉) · S. U. Ahmed · N. Ahmad
Faculty of Engineering and Technology, Department of Computer Engineering, Zakir Husain College of Engineering and Technology, Aligarh Muslim University, Aligarh, Uttar Pradesh, India
e-mail: tameemahmad@zhcet.ac.in; syedusmanahmed@zhcet.ac.in; n.ahmad.ce@amu.ac.in

- Sentiment analysis and emotion analysis
- Microblogging platforms and their features
- Depression detection and recognition

10.1   Introduction

The use of social media and especially microblogs has increased in the past decade. As per a recent survey (Pew Research Center Survey, 2019), 72% of the public uses some type of social media to communicate their feelings, and 38% of users of the Internet who are between 18 and 29 years of age use the microblog Twitter as a social media platform (Pew Research Center, 2019). Such microblogs have fewer restrictions and privacy settings than other platforms. Thus, users feel free to openly communicate with other users about any topic, including public interests, such as films, politics, and games. This behavior and the content of the activities on the social network platform can suggest many attributes of a personality including mental illness such as major depressive disorder (MDD) (Cavazos-Rehg et al., 2016; Giuntini et al., 2020; Küçük & Can, 2020).

According to the World Health Organization, depression is a common illness worldwide, affecting over 264 million people of all ages. Most depressed people also suffer from insomnia. Several studies have been carried out to examine this mental state of depression, self-harm, and suicidality using social media (Wang et al., 2007; James et al., 2018). To detect a person with depression using by his/her social media activities, it is important to identify the underlying indications of major depressive disorder. According to the Diagnostic and Statistical Manual of Mental Disorder Fifth Edition (DSM-5), the symptoms of MDD include "...depressed mood or irritable most of the day, nearly every day, decreased interest or pleasure in most activities, significant weight change or change in appetite, change in sleep...*fatigue*... worthlessness [and] self-harm/suicidality" (Cavazos-Rehg et al., 2016).

To understand the state of mind of a depressed person, some inputs from the field of psychology can be very helpful and reliable to obtain his/her background information (Aalbers et al., 2019). For data analysis, support from a technical perspective alone is not enough. More sophisticated methods need to be designed to study the depression patterns on social media platforms to help youth if one or more of the symptoms mentioned above are observed.

Emotion analysis (detection and recognition) from social media data (only text is considered for this study) is gaining popularity and attracting researchers. Emotion analysis aims to determine a person's mood by analyzing their posts (text) and classifying these into one of the possible categories such as anger, disgust, fear, happiness, sadness, or surprise (Raghib et al., 2017). Emotion analysis is correlated with sentiment analysis (Wang et al., 2013), which aims to indicate positive, neutral, or negative feelings from the post (text).

Social media is a lifeline in today's world, and data is the second most expensive commodity after oil. This chapter is an attempt to briefly describe the vital role played by social media in this current time. Thus, the following sub-sections will elaborate on some of the methods by which data can be fetched and retrieved on social media sites. Next, we will look at some of the most popular social network platforms and analyze the state-of-the-art methods and techniques for emotion analysis. This study of sentiments will finally lead to the identification of depression disorders.

We have also tried to explain how sentiment analysis can help recognize depression in a microblogging system, using a sample case study at the end of the chapter.

10.2   Background Study

The need for active communication led to the development of various web technologies, starting from the web of context (Web 1.0) to the web of thoughts (Web 5.0). The earlier web, before 1999, was called "Read-only" web (or Web 1.0) as users were restricted to just reading the information which was displayed to him/her via a web interface. The need for active interaction led to the advancement of "Read-Write-Publish" web technologies, also known as Web 2.0. Users were empowered with applications such as blogging, social media, and streaming. The shift from Web 2.0 to Web 3.0 came with the notion of formatting data by software agents using simple web services. With web services, Web 3.0 applications can now talk to each other with simpler interfaces.

The web has now expanded far beyond Web 3.0. Table 10.1 summarizes this transformation of web technologies:

Social networking sites (SNSs) have now become part of daily life. SNS users are not only using them for personal or professional interaction but for every aspect of their lives to share information on achievements, thoughts, news and updates, emotions, views, reviews, business, and other areas, and SNSs have been generating a huge amount of data since they began to be popular around 2002. Since then SNSs have been growing rapidly, except for the rise and fall in the popularity of particular social networking websites based on time and location. For example, Orkut (Google's SNS) was most popular in Brazil and India around 2008 and was shut down in 2014. Other popular SNSs include Facebook, Instagram, Twitter, and LinkedIn. In addition, content-sharing websites with social networking features including YouTube (video sharing), Flicker (image sharing), Slideshare (presentation sharing), and ResearchGate (academic article Sharing and discussion) are gaining popularity among users for their specific purposes. The common property of these social networking sites is collaboration and sharing, whereby each user contributes a small subset and gains more than he/she could ever gain individually.

For example, the Mendeley Reference Manager Tool (Mendeley) by Elsevier for managing and sharing research articles provides a bibliography for academic researchers where each user can contribute a small subset of the bibliography, generally for newly published articles, and gains a great deal from their huge indexed database.

Table 10.1 Transformation of web technologies

Categories	Web of content (Web 1.0) (Earliest, 1993)	Web of communication (Web 2.0)	Web of context (Web 3.0)	Web of things (Web 4.0)	Web of thoughts (Web 5.0) (latest, 2020)
Business	Catalog forms	eCommerce, social commerce	Smart search, smart advertising	AI robots, voice processing, smart personal assistant, location-based intelligence	Artificial brain, collective intelligence
Communication	Mail, search, forms	Blogs, wikis, social networks, Instant Messenger	Semantic Web, smart interface, Crowdsourcing	Connected spaces, geospatial web, wearable technology	Brain drain link, digital aura, brain wave control
Entertainment	Picture, text	P2P audio, video, widgets	In media search, Virtual worlds, MMORPG	Augmented reality, gesture technology, cinematic games, blurring boundaries	Five sense immersion, AV implant, active contact lens

Efficient Human-Computer Interaction (HCI) requires a piece of well-organized information. The Semantic Web, which is a simple enhancement of the current web, provides the capabilities for these types of interactions (Berners-Lee et al., 2001). *Semantic technology*, which began with the web of context (Web 3.0), uses formal semantic techniques that augment Artificial Intelligence systems to understand natural language and basic processes as human beings do. Using the Semantic Web supports interoperability and the exchange of data (personal, commercial, scientific, or cultural) in cases where data sources are of a heterogeneous nature.

This technology has attracted researchers in the last two decades. Figure 10.1 presents research articles published on the Semantic Web indexed at Elsevier's Scopus. The graph depicts the increase of work on the Semantic Web (Source: Scopus® Elsevier) (Elsevier B.V., 2004). The publications include articles from journals (including IEEE Access), symposiums, conference proceedings (ACM, Springer, Elsevier, IEEE), and workshops. The number of publications was highest in 2010. The decline in the research on semantic technology is appearing in recent years e.g. 2020. This requires adaptation of semantic technology-based formats and standards for the web by W3C (World Wide Web Consortium, an international standards organization for the World Wide Web) to reinvigorate the research in this area.

Knowledge representation plays a vital role in the implementation of the Semantic Web, and ontologies are the key to this knowledge representation. The Resource

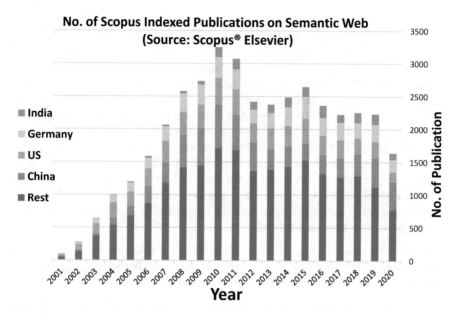

Fig. 10.1   Year-wise publication projection

Description Framework (RDF), Resource Description Schema (RDS), and Web Ontology Language (OWL) are the leading standards for implementation of these ontologies. Ontologies are used in various Semantic Web-based applications for the following reasons:

1. To analyze the domain and operational knowledge and differentiate between them
2. To reuse domain-based knowledge
3. To explicitly define the basic assumption related to each domain

Entities play a vital role in describing and implementing ontologies. The following properties should adhere to the successful implementation of ontologies:

1. A clear and unambiguous definition of an entity should be provided.
2. It should have a well-defined identification number, a meaningful label, and, if possible, a set of synonyms.
3. The diverse interrelated semantic relationship must be explicitly established between entities.

At a glance, three leading standards that use semantic technologies for the exchange of data are briefly described:

1. Resource Description Framework (RDF): This is a standard format that is used by semantic technologies to store data and information on the Semantic Web or in a semantic database. It is a standard for data exchange on the World Wide Web. It is a popular data exchange model as it has features that help to merge data even if

the schema is different. The central part of an RDF document is a Uniform Resource Identifier, generally written as URI. In Semantic Web-based applications, such as RSS and FOAF, the resource is represented by URIs. However, the motive of RDF-based ontologies on the web is often to establish the meaning of the resource identifiers used to represent the data in RDF.

2. SPARQL: This is a combination of *SPARQL Protocol And RDF Query Language*. It is a semantic query language to help users write sophisticated queries across various databases and retrieve data in RDF format.

3. Web Ontology Language: This is about naming parts and their relationships, and provides similar hierarchal forms. It provides computational logic-based language that shows the structure of the data (schema) to represent a complex hierarchy of knowledge for entities and their relationship. It works hand in hand with RDF to formalize the structure of the data in a given domain without doing anything with the data itself.

These standards thus help semantic technology-based systems to better understand, share, and process data like we humans do. There are various industries that use this semantic technology to better manage their content:

- Organizations such as the BBC and Springer Nature use this technology for media and publishing. Using semantic technology, they implement data integration and knowledge discovery more efficiently.
- Medical and other healthcare companies use this semantic technology for analysis of Electronic Health Records (EHR), and monitoring and prediction of adverse health reactions, etc.
- Automobile, e-Commerce, financial, and insurance companies use semantic technology to extract extensive data from the vast sea of data from various datasets.

10.3   Challenges of Social Web

There are many SNSs that are popular among users and provide collaboration, interaction, and sharing among users. Every SNS's backbone is networks of connection or networks of friends, with additional features such as commenting on private chats and ratings and reviews, etc. They are commonly used for specific purposes (e.g., LinkedIn is used for professional connections). These SNSs depict one part of a personality as the user projects this based on that SNS's orientation only. The complete picture of a personality is actually distributed among different SNSs where these SNSs are not interoperable (De Choudhury et al., 2013; Hussain et al., 2019). For example, a person's education or professional details can be found on LinkedIn, personal photos and likes and dislikes are available on Facebook, comments, thoughts, views, and expressions can be presented on Twitter, photos can be displayed on Instagram, and videos and lectures can be uploaded to YouTube. Parts are distributed and one cannot have a complete view in one location. The sea of information pertaining to an entity spans social networking websites in a way that collectively constitutes vast information.

There are many reasons for this non-availability of interoperability among SNSs. Each social network wants to keep its users on its website only. Another important reason is that there are no common standards for these SNSs. Furthermore, the interlinking of these SNSs will give more in total but the big giants (like Facebook) will have negligible gains. As the new SNSs emerge, interoperability will decrease.

Therefore, Semantic Web technologies are most suitable and can act to overcome this interoperability problem by providing the bridge between social networks and social data, and can enhance the overall value.

Online shopping sites, blogs, and wikis are other forms of social networking websites and contain lots of information, and, again, they are not interlinked and it is complicated to reuse their data. For example, at Amazon there is much information about the product (i.e., reviews, rating,, photos, and customer profile) but this information is not accessible from outside. Flipkart, another online shopping giant, has details for the same product but the real challenge is to club them to have all details (reviews from Amazon, details from Flipkart) at one view (Akhtar et al., 2019; Bansal et al., 2019).

A single person with profiles on different social networking websites projects himself/herself and presents feelings, thoughts, interests, and behavior patterns differently on different websites. The information existing on these websites belongs to the same person but is actually distributed and disconnected. Often these data may appear completely different and project different personalities (Varshney et al., 2018). The reasons are (1) people share and project themselves depending on the orientation and purpose of that site and (2) for privacy, people project themselves as they wish to show to their network connections (Somya & Ahmad, 2016; Ahmad et al., 2020b). Joining and connecting all related data is a challenging task in the absence of common standards. Moreover, often the user does not wish to mix his/her personal and professional lives (distributed on different networks).

10.4   Microblogging (e.g., Twitter)

Microblogging has emerged as an important and prompt form of communication and interaction in the last decade or so. It is used for expressing feelings and views and giving updates in short text (limited number of characters). Other features of microblogging such as tagging and sharing of other media data add a great deal of useful information to it. This short-expression (text post) is commonly known as "tweets" after the most popular microblogging website, Twitter. It often works as the fastest channel for sharing information (news updates) (Ahmad et al., 2020a) and raising complaints. Another feature of its trend of tags (#Trending Hashtags) has attracted attention for depicting a particular topic's popularity. These features have attracted people to repost updates and news on microblogs. Social media has thus emerged as a powerful tool for grassroots journalism.

Microblogging provides updates on what is going on around you in your community and area of interest. It allows to you to comfortably view your connections' status updates from one location.

The above scenario is the case for one microblogging platform. A single person might have accounts/profiles on several microblogging platforms and express himself/herself on these SNSs on different occasions. Thus, the owner/creator of these posts is actually one person. However, due to the non-availability of interoperability among different websites, the data are distributed (disconnected) and finally not reusable, and it is challenging to connect them. Semantic Web technologies can act as a bridge to connect these data and can provide computer-readable data and metadata for structure and reusability. Semantic Web technologies are considered an essential part of collecting, merging, and aggregating data from heterogeneous sources on social media networks. However, it is difficult for researchers and data scientists to analyze a large volume of data. Therefore, new frameworks and approaches are needed to merge Semantic Web technologies with Big Data to utilize its potential to the fullest (Kulcu et al., 2016). Furthermore, semantic technologies can provide an open and interoperable environment for microblogging.

10.5   Semantics Microblogging

As Semantic Web technologies can provide interoperability among microblogging platforms, the two ontology bases' commonly used formats are FOAF and SIOC.

FOAF: *Friend of a Friend* is used to describe people, their connections, and their relationships. Furthermore, it makes web pages machine-understandable. foaf:Person class identifies person, foaf:Document identifies the content created, and foaf: knows creates relationship. These are the most commonly used FOAF properties that provide the backbone of this semantic web page. A user can articulate their network through this tool and can have a higher level of view. Another advantage of FOAF is its integration with any other Semantic Web technology, such as SIOC. Aggregation of data from many different websites has become possible using FOAF. The third-party exporter is working for major websites such as Flicker, Twitter, Myspace, and Facebook.

SIOC: *Semantically Interlinked Online Communities* provides a way to interlink correlated community content from different platforms by providing the structure of the activity in the community. SIOC is further suitable for other types of content-sharing such as audio and video by providing metadata on these multimedia data and tags. In combination with other semantic ontologies such as FOAF, SIOC also provides a way to link posts and content to other related posts and people. This is possible by linking user accounts/profiles to topics using tags and concept representation.

The Semantic MicrOBlogging (SMOB) (DERI) platform has been developed as an *example* that leverages the strength of Semantic Web technologies to provide the decentralized content of microblogs. This has revealed the control and ownership of the content for reusability by giving the ownership of data to whoever has created them. This ownership and control has provided the reusability of the content (the owner can reuse the same data in different places and on different platforms). SMOB predominantly explores the above-discussed FOAF and SIOC ontologies. FOAF and SIOC are used to model users, their relationships, account information, services, and content. Furthermore, they provide tagging on microblogs which is semantic itself, i.e., semantic tags. A geographical tag is an example of a semantic tag that can add meaning to the content with a new meaningful visualization. Similar to SMOB, there are many other attempts to make microblogging more powerful and interoperable with semantics, including smasher (Smesher), StatusNet (Status.net). Microturtle (Microturtle), Star Priority Notation (StarPriorityNotation), and microsyntax (Microsyntax).

10.6 Semantic Technologies and Their Importance for Social Media and Depression Signals

There is much information available online, but unfortunately such information is hard to retrieve by a machine on its own. Artificial Intelligence-based technologies can act as a bridge to minimize this knowledge gap. Similarly, social media services are also creating a vast amount of data every day with a large amount of information. Semantic technologies can act as an intelligent link to fill this knowledge gap and make the machine more like a human. That is, semantic technologies can provide a way for a computer to become capable of processing the knowledge available on web pages and social media services. Hence, semantics of social network data can play a crucial role in information extraction and interoperability. Further semantic representation promotes the facility to exchange data (Jain & Patel, 2019, 2020; Patel & Jain, 2019).

In principle, the state-of-the-art social network data are represented in the form of graphs G (V, E) where vertices are the individual users' profiles and edges represent the relationship between them in the web-based social network. Unfortunately, this representation of vertices and edges for social networks loses important information such as individuals' identity and characteristics. Thus it will not be able to figure out the same profiles to support aggregation (for interoperability) in the case of multiple data sources.

Certainly, the SNSs posts are the source of rich information. Moreover there is lot of information available about the users i.e. user's profile. Interests, location, and network connections are some of the basic pieces of information associated with each profile of the SNS user. This information is necessary for the aggregation and reuse of data from multiple sources as well (interoperability). Semantics-based representation of profiles can help to infer a great deal. Furthermore, searching for other profiles with similar interests and goals, etc. is also possible. Therefore, the

(a)   (b)

Fig. 10.2 Word cloud of negative words. (**a**) Selected negative keywords and (**b**) extracted words from sample tweets

Social Semantic Web can provide an extra edge of information over a traditional web-based social network of people.

Depression affect a person's entire life, and the consequences can be multiple disorders. Loss due to depression could be financial, physical, or mental. The most disastrous form of this loss could be loss of life by suicide. Early detection of depression (or any other mental health disorder) is critical to safeguard from these problems. It can be identified by analyzing the pattern of personal activities. People are free to share and express themselves on SNSs and can speak from the heart. These expressions and feelings revealed in posts on SNSs are good data sources for analyzing people's mental health as their mood and cognitivism are enclosed in their language and expressions (Hussain et al., 2019; Dalal et al., 2020). Analysis of the pattern of activities on SNSs can help in effectively identifying depression disorder.

The high number of young people who commit suicide is strongly correlated with depression at the time of their death (Cash & Bridge, 2009). Depression can also lead to a reduction in productivity, which in turn has a considerable negative effect on the economy of a country. Hence, it is now of prime importance when studying depression signals that represent various levels of depression to note that social media networks are widely responsible for engaging a large section of these young people. Figure 10.1 shows the word cloud of negative keywords. These keywords are points of attraction for detecting depression. The extraction of these words from the expression (post) can suggest negativity. Such posts can further require analysis for detecting depression. Part (a) of Fig. 10.2 is the word cloud generated with the selected 140 negative keywords along with their frequency representation, and part (b) of this figure is the cloud generated with the sample of the selected 400 negative tweets from our dataset (explained in Sect. 10.7.1).

Depression analysis through people's various negative emotions and moods can be done using ontologies. Emotion ontology (EO) and metal disease ontology (MDO) can be used to study people's emotions and mental states (Larsen &

Hastings, 2018). Once we can capture these, depression detection can be carried out effectively and proactive steps can be taken.

10.6.1 Emotion Ontology

In the simplest terms, emotion ontology can be defined as an ontology concerned with a person's emotions, moods, and feelings. This type of ontology clearly distinguishes emotions such as anger and fear from praise and other subjective feelings. We can use machine learning techniques such as regression analysis, Naïve Bayes, and SVM to capture these emotions from social media content, for example on Twitter or Facebook.

10.6.2 Mental Disease Ontology

This type of ontology identifies parameters related to a person's mental state. Some of the emotions after a certain threshold can be categorized as depression rather than just simply feeling down. The results of these depressed emotions are mental trauma and other health-related issues. We have used a machine learning algorithm, Naïve Bayes, to study various emotions in microblog data and have captured some of the key terms (e.g., kill, anger, disgust, frustrated, and fear) related to these depression moods from the tweets (Fig. 10.3).

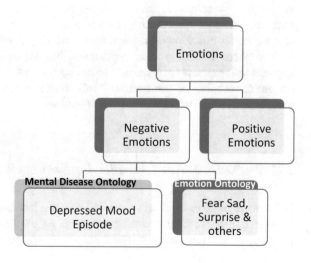

Fig. 10.3 Ontology overview for depression detection

10.7 Sample Case Study: Depression Detection from Twitter Dataset Using Naïve Bayes Classifier for Sentiment Analysis

Sentiment Analysis Understanding and studying depression in humans requires some inputs from the field of psychology to provide reliable background information (Aalbers et al., 2019). The first step in depression detection is sentiment analysis (Wang et al., 2013; Chakraborty et al., 2020). And building a corpus is the initial part of this process. We can build a corpus manually or use an inbuilt tweet corpus such as *twitter_samples* or *sentiment140*. NLTK's Twitter corpus has a sample of about 20,000 tweets (called twitter_samples). These have been retrieved through the Twitter Streaming API, together with another set of 10,000 tags which is divided into positive and negative sentiments. Another corpus is Sentiment140, which can be used for sentiment analysis of brands and their products, or topics available on Twitter.

10.7.1 Data Pre-processing

Once we have selected the corpus for our work, we need to pre-process the Twitter data for *file conversion*, *data cleaning*, and *stop word removal* types of activities. In the *file conversion* stage, we need to process the raw data to remove all special symbols of no use in depression analysis (Injadat et al., 2016). In the *data cleaning* stage, we will have to remove the punctuation symbols, digits, special characters, etc. Along with it we also removed retweets, tweet-handlers, hashtags, etc. which are of no use for sentiment analysis and depression analysis based on tweets. *Stop words* are generally the most common words in a language and they do not add much meaning to the sentence. Even if we ignore these stop words the meaning of the sentence can be interpreted easily by a machine. We can import the NLTK corpus of stop words for this. However, when to remove stop words and when not to remove them depends on the type of application. For example, if you are building an application for review analysis, then removing a stop word such as "not" will change the entire meaning of the review: "This movie is not good" (negative) will be transformed into "This movie is good" (positive).

10.7.2 Naïve Bayes Classifier for Sentiment Analysis

Naïve Bayes is an example of supervised machine learning; it is called naïve because it assumes that all features are independent. As we have to solve a classification problem, we need two corpora (one for positive and one for negative). This classifier

```
In [52]:  result = {}
          tweets = ['i am good', 'i am bad', 'i am sad', 'he is tired', 'i am tricked']
          ys = [1, 0, 0, 0, 0]
          count_tweets(result, tweets, ys)
```

```
Out[52]:  {('good', 1): 1, ('bad', 0): 1, ('sad', 0): 1, ('tire', 0): 1, ('trick', 0): 1}
```

Fig. 10.4 Dictionary mapping with (key, pair) output

uses conditional probabilities to find the sentiment of a tweet (Haand & Shuwang, 2020). To begin processing a tweet we use the following steps:

(a) Count tweets: This method takes a dictionary that will be used to map each pair to its frequency. Pair here stands for a combination of a word in a tweet and its labels. Here label is 0 for negative and 1 for positive. The output is a dictionary mapping for each pair to its respective frequency.

   In Fig. 10.4, we have five hypothetical tweets, an empty dictionary result, and a list of labels ys. The output is again a dictionary with pair, frequency mapping.

(b) Log-prior and log-likelihood: These are just simple logarithms of the probabilities of positive words and negative words in a tweet. To reduce the risk of numerical underflow we use a property of logarithms in which the score of Naïve Bayes is the prior multiplied by its likelihood.

   If the sum of the likelihood for a given tweet is greater than zero (0) then the sentiment of the tweet is positive.

(c) Predicted Values: Based on the prior value and likelihood value we created a predict function that predicts the sentiment of the tweets.

$$p = \text{logprior} + \sum_1^n \text{loglikelihood}$$

If the value of p is >0 the tweet has a positive sentiment; otherwise it has a negative sentiment.

In our case, this log prior $= 0$. Table 10.2 summarizes the output of key terms related to depression sentiments and their predicted class (negative or positive) for several tweets.

10.7.3   Testing the Model Using Naïve Bayes Classifier

For testing the Naïve Bayes Classifier-based model, we used the 1000 tweets from the testing set from the NLTK tweet corpus (twitter_samples). We calculated $y^\wedge$ (actual output) and y (predicted output). Based on these two outputs, the error was computed as:

Table 10.2 Predicted values of key terms related to depression signals

S. No.	Tweet	Depression keyword	Predicted value	Class (positive/ negative)
1.	they killed off a character on one of my favorite shows and now i am upset	Kill	−0.737	Negative
2.	@honeymunchkin My *anger* is getting bigger for every minute that goes by. I got some ugly comments on one of my videos	Anger	0.425	Positive
3.	@Schofe I feel so sorry for the women that lost her husband to those *disgusting* thugs! Hearing her story made me cry	Disgust	−9.772	Negative
4.	@theasiangoddess OUCH! that really looks like it hurts! One of my biggest *fears* is that happening	Fear	−3.365	Negative
5.	That left me with a queesy feeling. So much frusteration and *anger* with this team	Anger, frustration	−1.251	Negative
6.	i didnt wake up early enuff for my work out stupid me...now im gonna be at wrk alll day no workout no energy *saddness*	Sad	−4.202	Negative

Table 10.3 Basic structure of confusion matrix

Actual class	Predicted class		
		Positive	Negative
	Positive	True positive	False negative
	Negative	False positive	True negative

$$\text{error} = \frac{1}{m}(y^- y), \text{ where } m \text{ is total number of tweets}$$

The accuracy of the model can be computed as $1 - \text{error}$.

Accuracy, in turn, depends on the confusion matrix. A *confusion matrix* is represented as a table (Table 10.3) that tells us about the performance of a classification model on a set of data for which the true values are known.

Let us now briefly discuss the parameters of the confusion matrix and how they are used in the computation of the accuracy of any model.

1. *True Positive*: The classification model has two classes – one with predicted values and another with actual values. True positives are the values that are correctly predicted as *positive* by the model, i.e., if the value of the actual class is 1 and the value of the predicted class is also 1 then it will be part of True Positive.
2. *True Negative*: These are the values that are correctly predicted as *negative* by the model, i.e., if the value of the actual class is 0 and the value of the predicted class is also 0 then it will be counted in True Negative.

```
                      Predicted Negative  Predicted Positive
Actual Negative              996                    4
Actual Positive                8                  992
-------------------------------------------------------
```

Fig. 10.5 Actual confusion matrix based on our case study

3. *False Positive*: These are the values for which the actual class value is 1 (true) and predicted class value is 0 (false), i.e., there is a contradiction between actual class and predicted class.
4. *False Negative*: These are the values for which the actual class value is 0 (false) and the predicted class value is 1 (true), which means there is a contradiction between the actual and predicted class.

For our model the confusion matrix has the following values (Fig. 10.5):

Based on these four parameters, i.e., true positive, true negative, false positive, and false negative, we compute the accuracy, precision, and recall values for the model.

10.8   Further Work

As we have seen in the text above, RDF can be used to assemble and depict data from various social platforms, which allows the simple creation of semantic mash-ups and combined views from both branded and community information. We know that Hypertext Markup Language-based content can work with RDF using RDF annotations (RDFa), assisting in efficient semantic search without crawling.

An important future step for the formation of the Semantic Web could be the use of RDFa along with Markup Language Templates. Companies like Monkey have issued sets of suggested terminologies (such as FOAF, hReview, vCard) that issuers can use to create assembled information and thus attract more users to their products.

Query languages such as SPARQL can be used for probing dependencies between entities and objects, along with some keywords in a combined Social Semantic Web dataset. If we combine RDF and SPARQL it will help to incorporate miscellaneous data from various social sites, which in turn will help to improve navigation and skill to query over these data (Woods, 1978; Katz, 1988; Ahmad & Ahmad, 2020).

10.9   Summary of the Chapter

This chapter provides an overview of Semantic Web technologies and analysis of social media data for depression detection. The work has focused on identifying sentiments and depression detection, based on a microblogging social media platform (for our case study we used Twitter). It includes studies of sentiment analysis and determining emotions from the sampled tweets. In depression detection, a trustworthy software model is the most crucial aspect as it helps in the early detection of a person's depressive moods.

The Semantic Web attempts to make the future web as capable as humans for processing text and natural language, by accessing and processing the information available on web pages in the form of text, images, audios, videos, tags, etc. Exploiting such capabilities, computers will be able to answer a more complicated question correctly by utilizing information extraction precisely along with logic to decide for itself how to deal with complexities such as anomalies and ambiguities (Shaukat et al., 2021). All this requires the adoption of Semantic Web formats for this capability generation. As more things will be available in these formats, the system will become more potent in its processing, and hence it will become more exciting and attractive for others to use these formats to publish their websites and services.

The study has presented the latest work in the field of sentiment analysis, keeping our focus on depression detection on microblogging platforms. The following points summarize the work:

(a) We found that the most commonly used social media platforms are Twitter and Facebook, with Twitter leading as the biggest microblogging platform. The resources that help in the identification of depressive mood are generally textual content, which includes emotions. Hence, analyzing images and their associated tags can enhance this work.
(b) We also found that some of the techniques used in Semantic Web implementation are RDF, RDFa, and SPARQL. Techniques that help in the identification and classification of the text include Naïve Bayes, Logistic Regression, and Support Vector Machines.

Review Questions
 1. What are the different types of web technologies discussed in this chapter?
 2. Why does knowledge representation play a vital role in the Semantic Web?
 3. Explain the various standards of semantic technology used for data exchange.
 4. What is microblogging? Explain semantic microblogging: FOAF and SIOC.
 5. What are the popular social network platforms that are common and highly in use?
 6. What is Web Ontology Language? Explain emotion and mental disease ontologies.
 7. How can sentiment analysis help in depression detection and recognition?
 8. Explain the confusion matrix and its parameters.
 9. Why is Naïve Bayesian classification called naïve? Briefly outline the major ideas of Naïve Bayesian classification?
10. What are the attractive features of microblogging that have gained popularity?

Discussion Questions

1. How does the Semantic Web resolve the interoperability issue?
2. What are Electronic Health Records (EHRs)? How do medical and healthcare companies use the Semantic Web for analysis of EHRs?
3. What are the challenges of social network analysis?
4. Discuss the role of semantic technologies for social media data and depression analysis.
5. Why is proactive detection of depression important and what could be the benefits of timely detection of depression in humans?

Problem Statements

1. We have various data formats available in Semantic Web technology, including RDF and SPARQL. Now, we wish to make an efficient system by combining some or all of these standards. Is this possible?
2. How can we use RDFa along with the Markup Language Template to assemble information and attract more users to our products?
3. What are the other state-of-the-art techniques for depression analysis?
4. What are the current challenges for health information interoperability?
5. What are the standards for interoperability? How can these help to draw complete information?

Acknowledgments This work was supported by the Visvesvaraya PhD Scheme for Electronics and the IT fellowship of the Ministry of Electronics and Information Technology (Meity), with awardee number MEITY-PHD-2979, MEITY-PHD-3137, Government of India.

References

Aalbers, G., McNally, R. J., Heeren, A., et al. (2019). Social media and depression symptoms: A network perspective. *Journal of Experimental Psychology. General.* https://doi.org/10.1037/xge0000528

Ahmad, T., & Ahmad, N. (2020). *A simple guide to implement data retrieval through natural language database query interface (NLDQ)* (pp. 37–41).

Ahmad, T., Ahmed, S. U., Ali, S. O., & Khan, R. (2020a). Beginning with exploring the way for rumor free social networks. *Journal of Statistics & Management Systems, 23*, 231–238. https://doi.org/10.1080/09720510.2020.1724623.

Ahmad, T., Anwar, M. A., & Haque, M. (2020b). Machine learning techniques for intrusion detection. In B. B. Gupta (National Institute of Technology, Kurukshetra, India) & Srivathsan Srinivasagopalan (AT&T U) (Eds.), *Handbook of research on intrusion detection systems* (pp. 47–65). IGI Global.

Akhtar, N., Javed, H., & Ahmad, T. (2019). Hierarchical summarization of text documents using topic modeling and formal concept analysis. In *Advances in Intelligent Systems and Computing*.

Bansal, P., Somya, K. N., et al. (2019). Extractive review summarization framework for extracted features. *International Journal of Innovative Technology and Exploring Engineering.* https://doi.org/10.35940/ijitee.i8997.078919

Berners-Lee, T., Hendler, J., & Lassila, O. (2001). The semantic web. *Scientific American.*

Cash, S. J., & Bridge, J. A. (2009). Epidemiology of youth suicide and suicidal behavior. *Current Opinion in Pediatrics.*

Cavazos-Rehg, P. A., Krauss, M. J., & Sowles, S., et al. (2016). A content analysis of depression-related tweets. *Computers in Human Behavior.* https://doi.org/10.1016/j.chb.2015.08.023

Chakraborty, K., Bhattacharyya, S., & Bag, R. (2020). A survey of sentiment analysis from social media data. *IEEE Transactions on Computational Social Systems.* https://doi.org/10.1109/TCSS.2019.2956957

Dalal, S., Jain, S., & Dave, M. (2020). A systematic review of smart mental healthcare. *SSRN Electronic Journal.* https://doi.org/10.2139/ssrn.3511013

De Choudhury, M., Counts, S., & Horvitz, E. (2013). Social media as a measurement tool of depression in populations. In *Proceedings of the 5th Annual ACM Web Science Conference, WebSci'13.*

DERI. Semantic MicrOBlogging Platform Project. Accessed January 1, 2019., from http://smob.sioc-project.org

Elsevier B.V. (2004). Scopus preview – Scopus – Welcome to Scopus. In *Welcome to Scopus Preview.* Accessed December 31, 2020, from https://www.scopus.com/

Facebook. Accessed November 6, 2020., from https://www.facebook.com/facebook

Giuntini, F. T., Cazzolato, M. T., & dos Reis, M. de J. D., et al. (2020) A review on recognizing depression in social networks: Challenges and opportunities. *Journal of Ambient Intelligence and Humanized Computing.* https://doi.org/10.1007/s12652-020-01726-4

Haand, R., & Shuwang, Z. (2020). The relationship between social media addiction and depression: A quantitative study among university students in Khost, Afghanistan. *International Journal of Adolescence and Youth.* https://doi.org/10.1080/02673843.2020.1741407

Hussain, J., Satti, F. A., Afzal, M., et al. (2019). Exploring the dominant features of social media for depression detection. *Journal of Information Science.* https://doi.org/10.1177/0165551519860469

Injadat, M. N., Salo, F., & Nassif, A. B. (2016). Data mining techniques in social media: A survey. *Neurocomputing.* https://doi.org/10.1016/j.neucom.2016.06.045

Instagram. Accessed November 6, 2020., from www.instagram.com/

Jain, S., & Patel, A. (2019). Smart ontology-based event identification. In *Proceedings – 2019 IEEE 13th International Symposium on Embedded Multicore/Many-Core Systems-on-Chip*, MCSoC 2019.

Jain, S., & Patel, A. (2020). Situation-aware decision-support during man-made emergencies. In *Lecture Notes in Electrical Engineering.*

James, S. L., Abate, D., Abate, K. H., et al. (2018). Global, regional, and national incidence, prevalence, and years lived with disability for 354 diseases and injuries for 195 countries and territories, 1990–2017: A systematic analysis for the global burden of disease study 2017. *Lancet.* https://doi.org/10.1016/S0140-6736(18)32279-7

Katz, B. (1988). *Using English for indexing and retrieving.* RIAO.

Küçük, D., & Can, F. (2020). Stance detection. *ACM Computing Surveys, 53*, 1–37. https://doi.org/10.1145/3369026.

Kulcu, S., Dogdu, E., & Ozbayoglu, A. M. (2016). A survey on semantic web and big data technologies for social network analysis. In *Proceedings – 2016 IEEE International Conference on Big Data, Big Data 2016.*

Larsen, R. R., & Hastings, J. (2018). From affective science to psychiatric disorder: Ontology as a semantic bridge. *Frontiers in Psychiatry.* https://doi.org/10.3389/fpsyt.2018.00487

LinkedIn. Accessed November 6, 2020., from https://about.linkedin.com/?trk=homepage-basic_footer-about

Mendeley. Elsevier. Accessed November 6, 2020., from www.mendeley.com/

Microsyntax. Accessed January 1, 2019., from http://www.microsyntax.org

Microturtle. Accessed January 1, 2019., from http://buzzword.org.uk/2009/microturtle/

Monkey YS. Yahoo Search Monkey. Accessed January 1, 2019., from https://developer.yahoo.com/

Orkut. Google. Accessed November 6, 2020., from http://www.orkut.com/index.html

Patel, A., & Jain, S. (2019). Present and future of semantic web technologies: A research statement. *International Journal of Computers and Applications.* https://doi.org/10.1080/1206212X.2019.1570666

Pew Research Center. (2019). *Social media fact sheet.* Accessed November 6, 2020, from https://www.pewresearch.org/internet/fact-sheet/social-media/

Raghib, O., Sharma, E., Ahmad, T., & Alam, F. (2017). Emotion analysis and speech signal processing. In *2017 IEEE International Conference on Power, Control, Signals and Instrumentation Engineering (ICPCSI)* (pp. 2872–2875). IEEE.

Shaukat, M. S., Tanzeem, M., Ahmad, T., & Ahmad, N. (2021). Semantic similarity–based descriptive answer evaluation. In *Web semantics* (pp. 221–231). Academic Press. https://doi.org/10.1016/B978-0-12-822468-7.00014-6. Accessed from https://www.sciencedirect.com/science/article/pii/B9780128224687000146. ISBN 9780128224687.

Smesher. Accessed January 1, 2019., from http://www.smesher.org

Somya, B. P., & Ahmad, T. (2016). *Methods and techniques of intrusion detection: A review.*

Star Priority Notation. Accessed January 1, 2019., from http://civilities.net/Star_Priority_Notation

Status.net. Accessed January 1, 2019., from http://status.net

Twitter. Accessed November 6, 2020., from https://twitter.com/explore

Varshney, V., Varshney, A., Ahmad, T., & Khan, A. M. (2018). Recognising personality traits using social media. In *IEEE International Conference on Power, Control, Signals and Instrumentation Engineering, ICPCSI 2017.*

Wang, P. S., Aguilar-Gaxiola, S., Alonso, J., et al. (2007). Use of mental health services for anxiety, mood, and substance disorders in 17 countries in the WHO world mental health surveys. *Lancet.* https://doi.org/10.1016/S0140-6736(07)61414-7

Wang, X., Zhang, C., Ji, Y., et al. (2013). A depression detection model based on sentiment analysis in micro-blog social network. In *Lecture Notes in Computer Science (including subseries Lecture Notes in Artificial Intelligence and Lecture Notes in Bioinformatics).*

Woods, W. A. (1978). Semantics and quantification in natural language question answering. *Advances in Computers.* https://doi.org/10.1016/S0065-2458(08)60390-3

Tameem Ahmad, received M.Tech. and B.Tech. Degrees in Computer Science and Engineering in 2013 and 2010 respectively. Currently, he is working as Assistant Professor in department of Computer Engineering, Aligarh Muslim University, Aligarh. He has also worked in Cognizant Technology Solutions. He has published several research papers in journals and conferences of repute. His research areas of interest are Soft Computing, Natural Language Processing, Database Systems and Data Warehousing.

Sayyed Usman Ahmed, received his M.Tech. in Computer Science and Engineering in 2014 from Rajasthan Technical University, Kota and B.Tech. in Computer Engineering in 2007 from Aligarh Muslim University, Aligarh. He was associated with Computer Science Corporation (CSC) as Application Software Engineer and had worked on many enterprise software development projects. He has published several research papers in journals and conferences of repute. His current research interests include Artificial Intelligence, Machine Learning, Natural Language Processing, Software Testing, and Component Based Software Engineering.

Nesar Ahmad, received B.Sc. (Engg) degree in Electronics & Communication Engineering from Bihar College of Engineering, Patna. India (Now NIT, Patna) in 1984. He received M.Sc. (Information Engineering) degree from City University, London, UK, in 1988, and Ph.D. degree from Indian Institute of Technology, Delhi, India in 1993. He is currently a Professor in the Department of Computer Engineering, Aligarh Muslim University, Aligarh, India. He has published many research papers in journals and conferences of repute. His current research interests mainly include Artificial Intelligence, Applied Soft Computing, and Digital Learning.

Index

Printed in the United States
by Baker & Taylor Publisher Services